AFRICA ARRIVES!

The Savvy Entrepreneur's Guide to
The World's Hottest Market

Mark Byron

WITH ROBERT JOSEPH AHOLA

D0813717

PUBLISHED BY FIDELI PUBLISHING, INC.

To my Late Parents:
Emmanuel Olajide Byron & Josephine Olateju Byron

*"Our children may learn about the heroes of the past.
Our task is to make ourselves the architects of the future."*
— Jomo Kenyatta

AFRICA ARRIVES!

The Savvy Entrepreneur's Guide to
The World's Hottest Market

TABLE OF CONTENTS

A Mutable Medium

We feel morally obligated up front to acknowledge a simple truth. Any book about Africa is—by nature—written on shifting sands. At this point and for the determinant future, it is the runaway mobile market in the world—dynamic, youthful and frighteningly subject to change. As such, it is a socio-economic rocket ride whose spirit we can only hope to capture on these pages.

In doing so, we know that the game, the continent and all statistics enclosed herein will risk being outdated by the time the ink dries on the page. But what we are going to do with this book is adapt.

Thanks to a new era of publishing technology this book will do its best to become a living document that will attempt to reflect with current mirrors the exponential energies and dynamic trends of the very subject we are about to cover: Africa and all, in terms of economics, that makes it the Final Frontier.

Africa! The very name inspires awe, a sense of mystery, and virtual volumes of misconception. It is still—after centuries—the undiscovered planet inside of our own. As such it is still a wonder! Capturing and understanding how to negotiate its markets—financial, retail, commodity and international trade—is a challenge even for the most sophisticated entrepreneur. So it is not presumptuous but merely accurate to observe that only those who truly comprehend the vast potential that this continent contains are capable of revealing it. And that takes a professional who not only understands market trends in the worlds of finance and marketing but also someone who is a dedicated student of international trade and the tectonic shifts that occur daily in world markets.

Mark Byron is such an individual. As Co-Founder of Barton-Heyman, Ltd. of London and Lagos, Mark is a business entrepreneur and investment director in the complicated world of finance who has mastered a unique ability to leverage current market trends and meld them into emerging markets such as Africa and Asia.

This book is a work of the heart for Mark, because like so many successful business entrepreneurs, he is a citizen of the world. Having lived in Europe, North America and Africa, Mark leads a group (out of London and Lagos) that has come together to form a financial vanguard in African markets. For that reason he has developed a unique strategy for navigating that wondrous world and helping others to do the same. That is why he has fashioned this unique model—what he hopes will become a living document that will change, adapt and update even as it becomes a constant in our lives.

That is why I got involved—to help Mark make this translation from his mind to the written page. It was my original intention to research and hone the message. But what happened was a kind of epiphany for which I will always be grateful. As this Continent has captured the imagination, hearts and minds of so many, soon enough it infused me as well—with a sense of awe and inspiration I would have never thought possible. This land on the other side of the sun contains that kind of magic. It warms and heals you even as it terrifies you to behold. For all these reasons and more I was determined help bring to this work a very special message, one I hope will lay its imprint on whatever comes next.

This is not a travelogue or a tourist guide or a smart shopper's insight into the "Mysterious Undiscovered Continent." Nor is this a geo-political decoder of the Rubix that is our second largest continent. But it is, in its encyclopedic approach, exactly what the subtitle implies: "*The Savvy Entrepreneur's Guide to the World's Hottest Market.*"

That covers a lot of ground because, as you will soon discover, Africa is not a monolith. Geographically, it is the world's second largest continent, after Asia. In terms of population, it is the world's second most densely inhabited with 1.2 billion people. It contains more than 54 different nations with more than 300 diverse cultures and in excess of 1,000 different languages, ranging from Portuguese to Swahili. It has the most diverse and varied ethnic mix of any other part of the world. And 60% of the demographic is under 25 years of age. Those are the obvious statistics.

Then there is the subtext. In it we find an Africa so dense and so diverse that it is the proverbial sleeping giant … and in every sense of the word "the elephant in the room."

In this book, we examine all African markets in every conceivable category—in finance, in commodity, in heavy industry, in consumer tendencies, demographics, psychographics and trends. In doing so, we come into the world that nobody sees: the different approaches to growth, how nations as well as international consortiums with diametrically opposed points of view have tried to woo the giant, and how visionary entrepreneurs have learned to leverage their peers. Ostensibly, if we were to revert to traditional means of research to cover the African mosaic in all its many facets it would doubtless consume volumes. And few if any publishers could afford to build or market such a tome.

What we offer as an alternative is a way to embrace the new paradigm and apply this *flex model* that addresses the multifarious changes as soon as they occur. That is the applied poetry of electronic publishing—of eBooks and print on demand. Only in this case, we choose not to leave well enough alone. Because as the ground shifts and new trends arrive, we will, as the African paradigm shifts, attempt new editions.

The Greek philosopher Heraclitus once observed correctly that, "The only constant is change."

With that in mind, let us help you discover how *Africa Arrives!* It is a journey in which you will graduate, accelerate and evolve with each new discovery. And your guide will be a son of Africa and an expert in international markets who lives and breathes the journey every single day.

— Robert Joseph Ahola

The Formula

*"If a man will begin with certainties, he is bound to end in doubts;
but if he will be content to begin with doubts, he will end in certainties."*

— Francis Bacon

We are all informed by experience. It determines not only our life choices but also the commitment that goes into pursuing them. We are the Laws of Attraction in small, and all the things upon which we place our focus eventually become us.

My life pursuits as well as my profession have not only been informed but also infused with a passion for Africa and all that it implies. It has crossed my path a dozen times in a thousand ways and I could not be more grateful, for I am a citizen of the world...and a whole new world it is! And yet I am the first to admit that it was not always that way.

Since I was born in London, I am officially a citizen of the United Kingdom. And, because my father was a career diplomat with the Nigerian Consular Service, I also enjoy a Nigerian passport. So somehow I've always had a foot on two continents, a heart in two nations and a mind in two worlds.

Still, when I was very young—about 5 years of age—part of my upbringing entailed a departure from the "Sceptered Isle" back to Nigeria for my early education and upbringing. It was a respectable institution—rather "public school" in its itinerary. And yet I couldn't help but feel like a stranger in a strange land.

Like so many would-be business boot-strappers on the Continent, I believed that my dreams of success were far bigger than the tiny urban African world where I spent the major portion of my childhood and my teenage years. Even though I grew up somewhat in privilege, I always felt the Africa that waited just outside my door was scorched with what can only be described as a "colonial hangover," lost potential and an intractable attachment to the past; one that could not be remedied in my lifetime.

So as soon as I could, I left—for a fortune to call my own, for freedom from corruption, for the West, for the USA and all that it implies, for the UK and the quest for culture in the halls of higher education. I had no plans for coming back. But eventually I learned that plans for a return had me. Within a week of setting my two feet firmly on British soil, I saw I was not alone as I traveled along my expatriate path.

At business school in my university, I found myself surrounded by a circle of fellow travelers. There was George from Mombasa, Abdullah from Nairobi, and Kelechi from Lagos—my Lagos! There I was, a face in the crowd of a diaspora, weary of corruption and greed that could be escaped only by...well...escape.

By definition the term, diaspora, usually implies a mass exodus from one's nation of origin either as a matter of flight from dire circumstances or as the social by-product of leaving a deprived world for a better one. That was my original intention when, at the age of twenty-one, I sought my higher education in several ways—doing a City & Guilds course in application programming.

The biggest challenge was signing onto a job in the first place. Upon completion of the course, my original intention was to learn all I could about the world-embracing technology that it offered. My firm belief was that this was a sure fire way to land a decent white-collar job. My hope was soon to be dashed with a plethora of rejections from IT companies. This was in the mid-1980s when the UK was still going through its share of 'isms.' It was impossible getting a foothold into any kind of position that met my career objectives. I knew the next best thing was to improve on my educational status. So I enrolled in a Bachelor of Science curriculum at South Bank University in London.

Seeking a Bachelor of Science degree at the very least, I soon discovered that this was to be the best move I would ever make. The course not only gave me a well-grounded, thorough knowledge of the world of information technology, it also helped me open the door to go on and work for a number of sophisticated "shiny" financial institutions. Barclay's Capital, Fidelity Investments, Credit Suisse [First Boston] & PLUS Markets Exchange in the United Kingdom—these are some of the tier one institutions in which I earned my spurs. In equal measure, my journey into personal and financial discovery took me to some of the most sophisticated financial markets in the world—with firms in London, Brussels, Amsterdam, Paris, Boston and Chicago.

This job trail of high profile assignments in the corridors of high finance sent me on a high-speed journey and obsessions with success that occasionally came at

"You may find it hard to believe, but these nations of Africa are the final frontier of venture capitalism, corporate investment, and entrepreneurship. These three nations— especially Nigeria—I call the 'Lions of Africa.'"

— Anne-Dias-Griffin

the expense of complete perspective. On the way to discovering all these brave new worlds, somewhere along the way I had abandoned my roots.

I came to be convinced that Nigeria and Africa were merely ghosts from my past—a long, distant past in a far forgotten land—and destined to remain there. London was my home now, my headquarters where I was determined to "make it" in this business.

Intent on getting my professional acumen up to the next level, I even pursued an MBA at the University of Chicago (Booth) in the USA. While, there I came to acknowledge at last that you cannot escape your destiny.

That tipping point came for me in the form of the last modules I was taking at business school when the ex-wife of the Citadel Hedge Fund President Kenneth Griffin—Anne-Dias-Griffin—came to lecture us on the potential of global markets.

Posting up a map of Africa, she suddenly challenged us to think about this market: "You see these nations?" She pointed to a map of that Continent, raking her pointer across the "belt" of what is popularly referred to as the Sub-Sahara, isolating a band of three specific nations— Ethiopia, Kenya, Nigeria—all three, color-coded red. "As an investor, why do you think I've got my eye on them?"

Because all the corruption is a warning to avoid building a business there? I thought to myself, skeptical about hearing anything good about these geographical specters of my childhood. As it turned out, I could not have been more wrong.

"You may find it hard to believe," a wry smile flashed on her face, "but these nations of Africa are the final frontier of venture capitalism, corporate investment, and entrepreneurship. These three nations—especially Nigeria—I call the '*Lions of Africa.*'"

For a moment, I started with a shock. And then the truth of it hit me. Here was the wife of the head of a major international hedge fund worth more then $25 billion in capital investment, not only touting the world I had left behind but also announcing it to be our "last best hope" for exponential growth.

That was the moment when *reality* bit! And I came to the realization—that all my field experience, all my education and training, all my cultivated expertise had taken me full circle. I was being led up to this, and to the very singular place I knew so well. This was also 2008, the height of the "sub-prime debacle," and local financial streams had been tainted with uncertainty and graft—which meant institutional investors looking for alternative markets to invest in would have their eyes fixed on the continent of Africa.

Challenge mastered and met, masters degree in hand, I returned to the United Kingdom, where I continued to study and work. But by that time, the new course was set. And I was forming a game plan to make the biggest change in my life.

I was leaving the safe haven of London and Europe for a place familiar yet strange. I was leaping out of my comfort zone to the place where true progress occurs. I was returning to Africa where my fortune lay all along. I was coming home to a whole new world of adventure.

I had learned a lesson, and yet the greatest one was yet to come. Africa was no longer the world I remembered. It had become that red zone on the map that Anne Dias-Griffin had shown us...and so much more. Africa was "blowing up," and I had arrived just in time.

The rest of the journey I share with you now. So let's take this ride together. I promise you it will be anything but dull.

— Mark Byron

A Few Financial Terms

Theme subtitle of this book is, "The Savvy Entrepreneur's Guide to the World's Hottest Market." And it is used in that context because *Africa Arrives* is at its core a business and financial guide. So we will be taking a business approach to this fascinating, socio-political maze of a continent and grading its 54 Nations from time to time in very familiar "stock market" terms. We do this with the full understanding that a good many of our readers are bottom-line people, and like to cut to the chase. So we offer that option.

For our purposes in this book it is slightly arbitrary and, at times, subjective. World financial markets may see a country in terms of economic viability and risk to Foreign Direct Investment. Our "breakdown" on one of our covered nations, you may anticipate the fact that there will be a "buy/sell/hold" evaluation at the conclusion. It will be listed as a *CMI (Current Market Indicator)*. This is a common term on Wall Street, and is always followed by one of four ratings, which are essentially self-defining.

1) *Buy* — indicates that all the fundamentals are in place for the investor (or in this case the entrepreneur) to consider immediate plans to put stock in this country, including marketing and Foreign Direct Investment (FDI) capital.

2) *Sell* — indicates that this is too high risk to invest in, and if you have holdings in this (country) you should consider getting out as soon as possible. In national terms, it indicates that a nation's fundamentals—political stability, human rights, infrastructure and national debt structure—are very shaky and should be avoided until further evaluations can be made.

3) *Hold* — is the stock market version of an "amber alert." As such, it indicates a company (or country) where you may already have holdings or be considering investment. What it also references to you is that you need to be ready

to move on it quickly when the certain points of critical mass arrive—either sell quickly if you own it, or watch for a rating that moves to a "buy" should the fundamentals start to shift to an upturn. For the purposes of this book, it also refers to a company that bears watching. Accompanying this CMI is also a sub-indicator called *Buy and Hold*. This recommendation is self-limiting in that, though the pundits recommend that you buy an equity, you may need to hold it for a long time in order to achieve the desired results.

4) *Strong Buy (or High Buy)* — not surprisingly is the rating everyone looks for. It means that virtually all the metrics one might apply to new market or a new country are positive and offer a solid long-term horizon. Whether you are an individual investor, an international consortium or a small corporation, this is the Foreign Direct Investment (FDI) cue to move and do so with a good business model going in. That leads us to the other significant acronym that appears regularly throughout the book...

FDI (Foreign Direct Investment) — This indicates investment that comes directly from independent financial institutions, industries, technology companies, retailers and individual investors going into an African country with intentions to achieve B2B (Business-2-Business) or B2C (Business-2-Consumer) transactions, market-making and infrastructure investment. As such it is the vanguard of capital investment and capitalism itself. Not to be confused with foreign aid or foreign loans that might come from altruistic groups such as UNAID and USAID, or longterm lenders such as World Bank or the International Monetary Fund (IMF), FDI is the magic word—the SHAZAM!—that rising economies in Africa want to hear.

AA, A, B, C and Junk Bond Ratings — These ratings exist, and they exist for countries. Yes, "AAA" bond ratings are given to some corporations and a few nations, but countries or companies that rate them seldom request outside investment, nor should they. As for the others, these bond ratings, on the occasions that they appear in this book, are current assessments by major financial institutions, the World Bank, and the IMF.

Fair warning as well, you will be hit with numerous acronyms and abbreviations. They are not inserted in the book to bombard people reading this with nomenclature, but rather to apprise you of the fact—in every imaginable incarnation—that we live in a world of codes, affiliations and umbrella organizations. It is the way of things. And we will try to keep it simple by making sure you understand, every step of the way, what and with whom you are dealing.

AFRICA ARRIVES!

*The Savvy Entrepreneur's Guide to
The World's Hottest Market*

CHAPTER 1

Everything African: Myth vs. Reality

"Truth is like a lion. You don't have to defend it.
Let it loose. It will defend itself."

— Saint Augustine

There is a shiny new video camera technology called the IM 360 (IM for "Image Matrix"). And it does what the name implies: it gives us an image that covers all 360 degrees of its environment, recording virtually everything that goes on 24 hours a day, 7 days a week.

It was revealed in all its glory as part of a global network setup as it kicked-off to US audiences on February 24, 2016 on ABC's *Good Morning America*. This virtual reality segment was a delayed broadcast in the US as a part of the (7 a.m.) morning drive time hour, "to show animals in their natural habitat as never seen before."

It came in the form of a series special being filmed to cover three things: 1) the indigenous wildlife in the southern Serengeti plain and the idyllic Ngorongoro Crater where (you guessed it) the elephants and antelope, zebras and lions cavort; 2) what is referred to as an experience like the "Garden of Eden" (the official title of the show); and 3) as a part of show-host Amy Robach's broader report uncovering the imminent danger that poachers pose to the rapidly vanishing wildlife on the African continent. (And of course, to create the perfect media moment, it had been carefully prearranged for her to hang out with some cute little lion cubs.)

So, in the ultimate well-intended media cliché, there was *Good Morning America's* Amy in her brand new white Range Rover skipping through the savannahs of the

Serengeti while a sky-cam did a chopper fly-by to capture the scope and majesty of the pristine African dusk.

There—in one fell swoop—we got to bear witness to all that is right and wrong, real and unreal, insightful and overgeneralized about the Africa in front of us now. Brought to elevated thought and reduced to the constant cliché, it is both beautiful and simplistic that we, the public-at-large, get to immerse ourselves in this good old "Earth Mother Africa" that everyone sees.

Of course, it's just as we'd hoped it would be. It is. And yet it isn't.

The best thing about this ABC/*GMA* moment is that an entire new 360° imaging format—the very cutting edge of technology—had been conceived and designed in anticipation of just such an event, an infusion of the most futuristic technology almost culture coated specifically to fit into the African vibe.

The most expected thing—that is neither terrible nor wonderful—is that, all in that very same moment, it embraces the false notion that this is everything Africa represents. In that way, it is very much like everyone believing that all Texans wear cowboy hats, ride horses and own oil wells…or that all Mexicans eat tamales, dress like *charros* and play *mariachi* music.

In the first place, the Serengeti Plain inside Tanzania is, in itself, about the size of West Virginia. Rich in natural wonders—golden rolling savannahs and the snow capped peaks of mountains like Kilimanjaro—Tanzania is a lush piece of real estate that approximates the total square area of Texas and Oklahoma combined (or if you're Eurocentric, that of France and Germany combined). It is also, quite surprisingly, one of Africa's poorest countries.

With an annual GDP of $49 Billion it is—by comparison—less than 50% of the gross annual revenues of Apple Computers. And the per capita average income for its 48 million inhabitants sits at just over $1800 a year, or slightly more than half that of the annual average of other African nations. Tanzania has, at present, nearly 40% unemployment, and half of its citizens are under 15 years of age.

Blame Tanzania's slow rise to world prominence on a rather wicked mash-up of Colonialism from, not one but four nations—Portugal, Germany, an Omani Sultanate, British Colonial rule after World War II, and finally (once it gained its independence in 1961) a rather unfortunate experiment with socialism and a predatory trade pact with the Red China of Chairman Mao that lasted for more than 20 years. Even though this all took place over about 500 years, it left Tanzania with a legacy of cultural confusion and bureaucratic hangovers from five different types of government. So in its way it is the poster child for the stunted growth of several African nations.

Finally digging itself out of the morass in the last thirty years to form something of a one party Republic (the ONC), Tanzania still has a rather complicated issue of border disputes and the administration of more than 30 regions including the island territories of Zanzibar, plus North and South Pemba that it very recently plucked away from Omani Arab rule.

As a key member of the East African Community (EAC) along with Kenya, Uganda, Rwanda and Burundi, Tanzania has currently embraced a system of rebuilding its fragile infrastructure in a couple of ways: 1) with the United Nations Development Programme (UNDP), and 2) with an internal anti-poverty program called MKUKUTA. Many pundits believe that most interactions a nation takes with the UN to help in its recovery come at too great a political cost and offer little benefit in return. And in the ultimate irony Tanzania—this rich varied land source, which contains the world's second largest body of natural lakes after the United States—also suffers from a water shortage. (So, if you're someone who believes the glass is indeed half full, imagine what kind of market opportunity this presents.)

Perhaps not surprisingly, two of Tanzania's primary industries are tourism and conservation. In fact, 38% of its entire national landscape is set aside for national parks, natural preserves and safe havens for wildlife. And those two enterprises alone have combined to employ nearly 3 million people...or over 16% of the nation's active workforce. The third

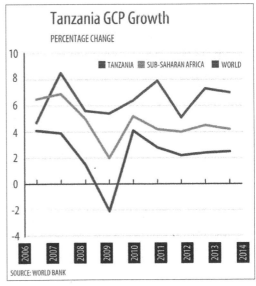

major industry in the Tanzanian trifecta is construction—which now contributes to 22.2% of its GDP.*

Some of Tanzania's other rapidly growing enterprises include electronics and tele-communications because, with more than 72% of the entire population under 30 years of age, there is a rising tide of Millennials…and they will have their apps! So guess what brands of foreign tech companies are jumping into Tanzanian marketplace, locked and loaded and very credit friendly? (And they are doing it in a country where credit is hard to come by.)

In all these ways and more, Tanzania is the classic misconception of what Africa represents to the world. Beautiful, lush and fraught with creatures roaming along the landscape, it is the picture postcard that everyone sees in the Oscar winning film *Out of Africa*—primordial, mysterious and somewhat oversold.

To be sure, this snapshot of Tanzania is the African paradox in a nutshell—because everything we have just told you summarizes everything about this rich, robust phe-nomenal "young" Continent. And yet it does not. Just as it begins to reveal itself, at the same time it tells us nothing…because there are 54 other nations with financial, cultural, environmental, sociological and economic stories of their own—all of them similar and yet every one unique, all of them "blowing up" into a whole new world of opportunities for the savvy entrepreneur.

At the same time, to help everyone better understand this complex mosaic, we need to "get real" about what really goes on in this dynamic hidden universe … and shine the light of understanding on the Myths so that we are able to discover the Reali-ties that lie beneath.

Dateline Africa: A Reality Check…

MYTH **Africa is a Country.** On the surface this seems like a no-brainer. Of course, one would assume that only uneducated, uninformed peo-ple—or clueless Millennials—would have anything resembling such an opinion. (In fact, about 12% of all Millennials questioned in the USA believe this. But America's under 30's are notoriously clueless where the rest of the world is concerned.) There is, however, more to this than meets the eye, because there is this preconceived notion of the African monolith—the belief that Africa is the same cultural continuum with the same ethnic uniformity separated only by borders, natural boundaries and slightly divergent laws and systems of government.

---

* This component also includes mining, manufacturing and infrastructure and is the fastest growing segment of the new Tanzanian economy.

It is an irritating truism to note as well that citizens of Nigeria or South Africa or Botswana are all referred to as "African." As such they are tarred with the same ethnic brush. This brand of cultural bias is also true, to some degree, in Asia. And the "Asian" label is also primarily racial—implying the "yellow" man. References to "Europeans" are more cultural and describe a sensibility that is "sophisticated," urbane and well traveled. Seldom do you hear a reference to North American or South American to describe an entire culture.

Almost without fail, to be called "African" is to imply that one is black, tribal, possibly undereducated and either aristocratic or poor, either "of money" or else definitively on poverty's edge. Blacks in the US and Canada are (politely referred to as) African American, or they prefer to be called that themselves. Expatriate Nigerians or Namibians or Zambians or Ugandans are almost never referred to by their country of origin, but are lumped instead into the "African" melting pot.

In less sensitive times, Africa was often referred to "Black Africa," which used to be the umbrella term for what is now the Sub-Sahara. It also had the unmistakable connotation that this part of the world was untamed, dangerous, dark and troublesome. So, in the apocryphal world-view of virtual generations, the Africa everyone knew was a continent was a country was a race was a tribe was a culture was an economic profile. And, in this case of course, it was also a misnomer.

Having made note of all this, indigenous Africans—especially those native to the lower half of the Continent—must take some responsibility for projecting that image. Acronyms and code words such as "TIA" (This Is Africa) point to a kind of regional pride Sub-Saharan's share that defines the *Paradox*—the *mystery wrapped in a riddle, cloaked in an enigma*. It's their way of saying, "We're not easy. We take some getting to know. Respect us. Be willing to stay and spend the time to find out who we really are."

Kwame Nkrumah, the first President and a founding father of Ghana, once noted: "I am not African because I am in Africa, but because Africa is in me." Therefore, by all means, the mirror has two faces in this regard. But it is one that Africans should be allowed to hold up to themselves…and not have others do it for them. But therein lies the African conundrum—one very much of perception. We must first understand ourselves and not let others do it for us.

REALITY   The 54 nations inside of Africa offer the most diverse multi-cultural mélange of any Continent in the world. Although Sub-Saharan Africa is primarily black, African in a broader context also points to 18% of the population that officially includes Caucasians such as the Hamitic peoples of Egypt, and the Semites of Algeria, Libya, and Morocco, Indo-Europeans of South

Africa (about 7%) and 11% Afro-Asian people, especially around the Horn of Africa, and Malayo-Polynesian peoples of island nations such as Madagascar (Malagasy Republic) at around 2%. Negroid people include virtually hundreds of ethnic origins and subcultures (nations inside of nations) with names too diverse to cover here. The bottom line in all of this is that dealing with Africa intelligently required, and still does require, a certain Renaissance talent for understanding all the nuances of language, race and culture. And the permutations are endless…

MYTH **African Nations, especially in the Sub-Sahara rely on tribal languages as their primary means of communication.** And most of them are essentially the same language with different intonations, sound FX and pronunciations. So the stock perception is that it's either English … or a mishmash of tribal language no one could possibly learn (Swahili notwithstanding).

REALITY **Africa is linguistically rich. And practically everyone "speaks your language."** Although there are more than 2,000 languages and dialects in Africa from Morocco to Mauritius, most nations and their inhabitants are by necessity multilingual. It's true that many of the languages are tribal and that some are interlinked. But a preponderance of cultures—just under 70% in fact—are sufficiently rooted in the "Colonial Connection" to offer an entire Rosetta Stone of traditional international tongues.

Principal languages of several countries include Swahili, Bantu, Berber, Setswana and Zulu…but also include large portions of the population who speak Arabic (Northern Africa), Afrikaans, Portuguese, German and Spanish. In many nations, including the Francophone and Anglophone countries, French and English are the primary languages, and are the second languages in virtually half the nations of the Sub-Sahara. In such countries as Nigeria, Kenya, South Africa, Zimbabwe and Botswana, English is still the language of State. And there are a dozen Francophone nations such as Algeria,

Burundi, Cameroon, Central African Republic, Mali and Burkina Faso where French remains the official national tongue.

Virtually every country in Africa has half-a-dozen lesser languages as well as the official language, many of them tribal. And though it is true that many of these native tongues have clicks in them and sonic affectations that set them apart, about 60% of the citizens of all African countries are fluent in two or more languages, at least one of them recognizable as Arabic, European or (on occasion) Asian.

MYTH In social structure Africa has an undercurrent that is fundamentally tribal. As such, you are either rich or poor, either prosperous or deprived, either upwardly mobile or stagnating in tribal squalor. There is no Middle-Class. It is true to be sure that the "Middle Class" in many African countries is a little late to the party. And the reasons are two: education and economic development. Although more than half the nations of Africa have enjoyed exponential economic growth in the last 30 years, many have not. Robust new economies such as those of Rwanda, Ghana, Namibia and Cote d'Ivoire are helping these nations to join the more stable economies of the Sub-Sahara. But the journey is still a long one. In terms of education, the literacy rate of Africa has jumped considerably in the last 20 years to about 69%. That number is deceptively low because, though many nations such as Zimbabwe, South Africa, Equatorial Guinea, Namibia and Kenya have literacy rates in the 85% range or above. Others such as Ethiopia, Chad and the Ivory Coast are down in the 40% plus range, while Niger is last with an abysmal 19%. So once again, bundling Africa into a single demographic becomes the classic monolithic misnomer.

REALITY With 70% of the population under 30 years of age, many African nations have a burgeoning middle class. We grant you that there are a number of nations that have not yet stepped out of their poverty points enough to qualify for what might be called the "Rise of the Bourgeoisie." But especially in what are called the "Anchor States" of Nigeria, Kenya, Ethiopia, South Africa and Botswana, the middle class is not only rising fast but also competing for lifestyle enhancements, including commodities such as cars and electronics and overall improvements in quality of life. Once thought luxuries, many of these technological advances are now considered necessities by the African Millennials. So the law of supply and demand is rapidly taking hold.

MYTH The majority of the nations of Africa have corrupt, unstable governments. Until recently, the political cliché about government corruption in African nations was fodder for film, fiction and television. The corrupt dictator, the gold for weapons commodity exchanges, the stereotypical "Idi Amin" human rights violators living large while his people starved—all this and more was low-hanging fruit for modern western media. Some of it was accurate. Much of it was not. And we are happy to say that, in today's Africa, a great deal has changed.

REALITY The vast majority of African nations (72%) have been independent from colonial rule for less than 75 years. And most of them, even in times of turmoil, honor their "foreign" contracts. In terms of governance, that is a very short time. Especially in the realm of colonial rule, there existed a level of indentured servitude compounded by tribal custom and illiteracy that such terms as independence and self-determination were abstractions too distant for the tangible mind to comprehend. Then again, Colonialism also brought its benefits—not the least of which were parliamentary forms of government and fixed standards for basics such as health and education. These are the good carryovers, and their influences have been continued.

Still democracy can be difficult to grasp in the abstract. It is a sophisticated form of government started by educated men. So the crossover for some African nations has been arduous and confusing.

(There is the possibly apocryphal anecdote of the liberation of the Congo when it became Zaire in the 1970s. Then President Mobutu Sese Seko told the people they had their freedom from Belgian rule. But the term, "freedom," was such an abstraction to the tribal chiefs that many of them showed up at the first government convention asking for physical evidence of the freedom they were promised. Rather than disappoint them, Mobutu handed them all nicely decorated boxes of dirt. So freedom, at least for some, had gained new meaning.)

One issue that often eludes international awareness is the fact that most nations of Africa—no matter what their political circumstances, states of civil war, *coups d'état* and election challenges—have been almost inordinately fair to foreign investors. In virtually all their international contracts, they have been impeccable in their dealings with foreign industry and corporations housed in their charge. This has been true of nations with complete changes of government such as South Africa, Zimbabwe, Kenya, Angola, and my own native Nigeria, as well as dozens of others. Even Libya, under the rather schizophrenic regime of the late Muammar Gaddafi, honored all its contracts with foreign petroleum giants, including those with the United States.

As a point of contrast, so many countries in Asia and South America did, upon change of government, seize and nationalize all resources and impound the funds and property of foreign corporations. This was true of nations such as China, Vietnam, Cambodia, Cuba, Venezuela and even Mexico in the time of the Lopez Mateos presi-

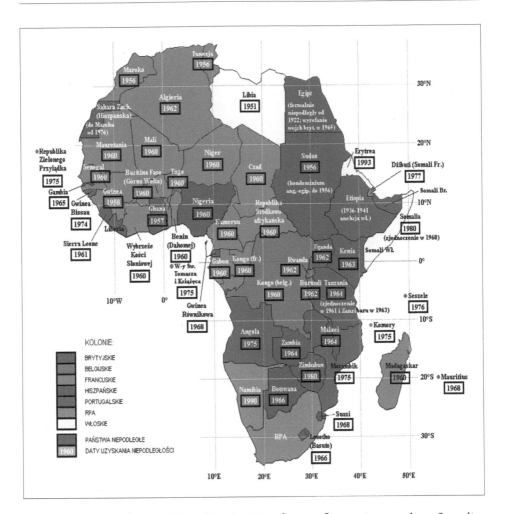

dency. Corporate chaos and confiscation in a few conflict nations such as Somalia, Democratic Republic of the Congo and South Sudan are the exceptions that prove the rule. In fact, the trend of nation-to-business stability has improved so much in the last 20 years that now there are very few parts of the world where corporate contracts have been so honored as they have been in the majority of African nations.

Unfortunately this *integrity pact* has not always been reciprocal. In fact, a number of major international mining conglomerates have been exploitive in the extreme, having depleted the local economy while savaging the region's ecological balance, and then virtually skipping town, paying local officials to look the other way so they could make a hasty exit. As recently as 1999, Shell Oil environmentally looted the Delta State in Nigeria and left with virtually no accountability. (Later, the petroleum giant was sued by local governments in international court and eventually had to pony up considerable restitution. So that is the heavy toll of sophistication in many African Markets. New companies coming in now have a responsibility to the communities they share, and honoring their commitments is part of the contract.)

MYTH **Africa is a major health risk to anyone going there—replete with diseases and dangerous viruses.** It is a panic rumor bordering on superstition. It is inaccurate. And yet the myth persists. A classic example would be the Ebola scare of 2014. Breaking out in the Nation of Liberia in April of that year, the disease spread to travelers from neighboring Guinea and Sierra Leone, until there were about 15,000 confirmed cases and 11,200 plus deaths—mostly in Liberia with significant numbers of deaths in Sierra Leone. Out of a population range of nearly 30 million in the vicinity and another 180 Million in nearby Nigeria, this outbreak—though serious—was not nearly the pandemic it might have been, much credit due to the governments of Mali, Ivory Coast, Nigeria and Chad, all of whom worked with WHO (World Health Organization) to take appropriate counter-measures, locked down their borders and headed off any further spread. The result was a total number of cases in these countries held to a couple of hundred with only 4 deaths coming as a result.

This chain of events received some world media attention but not anywhere near the press and publicity overdose that was to follow … Fast forward to early October 2014 when one traveler from Liberia to Dallas, Texas came down with a case of Ebola and died a couple of weeks later. In this case the man, Thomas Eric Duncan, was a Liberian citizen who had helped an Ebola stricken woman to her bed, and then flew out of Monrovia two days later for the US without declaring the contact. And what followed as a circus of medical miscues.

When Duncan came down with the disease, it wasn't diagnosed correctly until later, and until a number of other people had been exposed. Two healthcare workers thrust into his presence to look after him (without appropriate safety measures) came down with the symptoms, and then a panic ensued.

Not really knowing how to deal with it, the *Center for Disease Control* (CDC) declared a state of national emergency—from one case—locked off air travel to virtually every nation in East Africa, including several that had no signs of contact and then proceeded to dominate the national headlines for better than a month.**

Ramping journalistic sensationalism up to the next level, CNN, MSNBC and other news networks made it sound like Liberia, Sierra Leone and Guinea (who had already successfully stemmed the tide) were coming apart at the seams. And in a classic

---

** West and Central Africa had already been locked down with travel restrictions.

case of good intentions gone entirely over the top, US President Obama not only sent medical teams but also 3000 US Army troops to Liberia and Sierra Leone to construct temporary field hospitals and protect the people from an epidemic that had long since abated. In doing so, of course, they were exposed to further possible hazards and basically left without a single constructive thing to do.

Nothing illustrates the false apocalyptic notion of bacterial plagues coming out of Africa better than this, especially when it was explained by one Nigerian doctor that *Ebola,* now contained, was not the problem—that there were many more deaths (in the millions) each year from such pandemics as *malaria, measles and tuberculosis.* Following this astute pronouncement (an accepted truism in the developing world), a panic article popped up in a US tabloid announcing an epidemic of tuberculosis all over southern Africa.

REALITY **African nations have far fewer health risks than such nations as India, China, Indonesia, Brazil and other countries where population density combined with poor health standards are a constant issue.** Africa's health challenges are very often those of poverty, starvation, deprivation and inadequate government health care primarily for indigenous peoples in rural communities. In this case, it is an issue of economics and advanced medical treatment. As such, the deadly Ebola virus notwithstanding, African nations especially in the Sub-Sahara are not seedbeds for pernicious diseases.

In fact the SARS outbreak in China took down thousands and the Zika virus now coming out of Brazil have presented a dozen nations with health challenges in legion, none of which have been successfully addressed. What's more, in some countries where they sell GMO foodstuffs, processed meats and marginal food-processing threshholds, they are far more likely to have outbreaks of poisons such as salmonella, E-coli, listeria and more recently MRSA (the flesh eating *Staph Aureus* strain). At this point, we also acknowledge the potential for harm: Ebola is deadly and for that reason a scare that must be addressed. Still, we all ignore the deadliest virus of all—world hunger—with millions of fatalities a year, while many nations throw away 30% of their food edible supply. That is excess in which Africa has never indulged.

MYTH **Africa is a dangerous place, replete with rebel groups, fraught with warzones and with terrorists lurking around every corner.** Well...by now we've all seen it on film and TV, on podcasts and video streams. Somewhere, somehow, there is always some tiny African "Republic" in constant state of civil strife, trading drugs or gold for guns and lining entire villages up to be shot. Like *Blood Diamond, Casino Royale,* or *Lord of War,* they're out there in great profusion teaching

10 year-old boys to become killers and murdering women and children. (Of course the revolutionary archetypes are invariably tall and lean and sport "Che Guevara" berets, aviator Ray Bans and paramilitary gear. And they always seem to be toting an AK-47 that rests like a third appendage on their hip.)

Welcome to the African warlord, guerilla leader and counterculture, amoral sociopath; and of course, he (never she) is always black. This is the Africa Hollywood shows us—terrifying and evil, driven to no result except mayhem for its own sake. That's what we're being told Africa holds, and every time the news breaks it is almost entirely negative in ways that reinforce the stereotype.

REALITY **Out of 54 Nations in Africa only 8 are in any state of war, turmoil or civil conflict.** Yes, we have our Somali Pirates. Yes we have Boko Haram in northwestern Nigeria. Yes, Sudan and South Sudan are in a political lock-off that quite often involves an armed exchange or two. The Democratic Republic of the Congo has been engaged in a 20-year internal power struggle that often involves armed conflicts, and Tanzania and Botswana are always in a border dispute. In the main, however, these nations in question are actually striving to achieve a resolution. And in their way, they are less pervasive and less aggressive than your average Chicago street gang.

The drug-lords and cocaine cartels of Mexico and Central America—the ones who hold entire states captive and roam the borders at will—are far more power-ful, pervasive and cruel. The FARC *(Federacion Armados Revolutionario de Colombia)* are far better organized, dangerous and an existential threat to the government of Colombia and Venezuela, as are the *Abu Sayeff* Muslim group in the Philippines. Then of course there's the Middle East. Conflicts on continuous loop, mass-executions, genocide running through Iraq and spilling over into Jordan and even Turkey—now presage a Syrian Civil War that has torn the world of Islam apart. ISIS, Al Qaeda, the Taliban and Hamas (with its non-stop missile strikes against Israel every week) —all conspire to help us understand that Africa, by comparison, is a pretty sane place to be these days.

Of course, as Confucius once observed, "Comparisons are odious." Then again—on occasion—they serve us rather well. With that in mind, let us close on this:

MYTH **"Africa is a treasure trove of natural resources and a masterpiece mining opportunity. But it has very limited industrialization. So it's best to get in and get out, take the money and run."** It is a sad truth of so many countries from Nigeria to South Africa—from Gabon to Mozambique—that Africa is looked upon from an ad hoc industrial perspective. Both in terms of domestic production and foreign investment it is thought of as a finite resource—South Africa for its Diamonds, the Congo for its Gold, Libya for its oil reserves, Niger for its uranium, and Zambia for its copper. So, although initial foreign investment into land lease, manpower and equipment is bullish and bold, every country that comes for that ad hoc assignment, arrives with its own withdrawal kit, complete with a ten to thirty year pull-date and an entire mining and manufacturing matrix with planned obsolescence built-in. So all this influx of industry is a boom-and-bust exploitation. That may not be the evident objective, but it is the end result.

Such "rape and run" mining strategies would never come about, were it not for African governments that enable them to happen. And so the relationship, from the beginning, becomes codependent; and it is ultimately the object nations that pay. They have given up everything and are left with nothing that endures. So what may be good for the local economies in the short run cripples them in the aftermath. Because what do you do with the tent and poles once the circus leaves town?

REALITY **More and more smart nations and smart international corporations are coming to Africa, not only to "play" but also to stay.** One needs only follow the path set by the BRICS nations—Brazil, Russia, India and China (and now South Africa)—and chart their path for investment, building infrastructure and a revolving consumer dynamic—and you begin to catch a glimpse of what so many savvy investors now know: *Africa is young and dynamic, and it's riding on an upward arc that simply will not be denied.*

Anchor nations such as Kenya, Nigeria, South Africa, Botswana, Ethiopia and Rwanda are on a very upward swing. And the Sub-Sahara is rapidly becoming the most robust consumer economy in the world—one that scintillates over the advent of such retail giants as Apple, Ford, Wal-Mart and KFC.

Much of it also has to do with African governments that are negotiating with international megacorporations from a more realistic platform for Foreign Direct Investment—one intent upon reciprocity as the basis for setting down roots.

Summary

There are many more areas where we can dispel the myths of Africa versus the realities. Issues of diet and transportation, urban versus rural, higher education versus tribal lockdown cultures—all these and more conjure a Manual of Misconceptions, all of which need to be put to rest…and will be on the following pages. What we have tried to do is show you the pure potential. The Law of Attraction sets in after that, and how you use it is purely up to you.

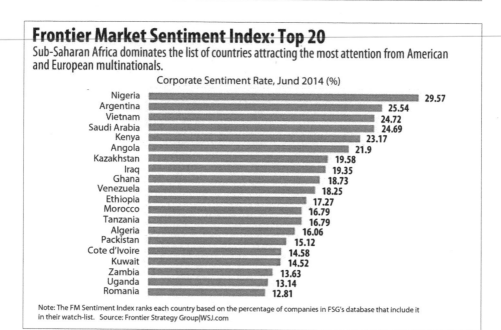

Frontier Market Sentiment Index: Top 20

Sub-Saharan Africa dominates the list of countries attracting the most attention from American and European multinationals.

Corporate Sentiment Rate, Jund 2014 (%)

Country	Rate
Nigeria	29.57
Argentina	25.54
Vietnam	24.72
Saudi Arabia	24.69
Kenya	23.17
Angola	21.9
Kazakhstan	19.58
Iraq	19.35
Ghana	18.73
Venezuela	18.25
Ethiopia	17.27
Morocco	16.79
Tanzania	16.79
Algeria	16.06
Packistan	15.12
Cote d'Ivoire	14.58
Kuwait	14.52
Zambia	13.63
Uganda	13.14
Romania	12.81

Note: The FM Sentiment Index ranks each country based on the percentage of companies in FSG's database that include it in their watch-list. Source: Frontier Strategy Group|WSJ.com

Ultimately we go to the parable of the two shoe salesmen who come to a primitive land. The first one sees everyone running around barefoot and reports back to the home office. "Everyone is barefoot. There's no business for us here."

The second salesman comes to the same place and, observing everyone running around shoeless, calls back to the home office: "Boss!" He cries out. "I've found the perfect place to build a shoe factory."

So, for those of you who would like to join us in building a "shoe factory," read on...

CHAPTER 2

UK. Nigeria:
A Personal Mission

It matters not how strait the gate,
How charged with punishments the scroll,
I am the master of my fate,
I am the captain of my soul.

— William Ernest Henley, *Invictus*

I often point to that quote by William Ernest Henley because I believe it to the core of my being. It is a code by which I live; it's also been something I've embraced over time. It is not something you are taught out of the cradle, but once you come to understand its implied meaning you'll never live any other way. It is, above all else, about taking responsibility for your every thought, word and deed.

To some of you reading a book called *Africa Arrives* this chapter may seem like a sidetrack. It is not, because it drives to a point. The truth for me at least came with the realization that I have, for the entirety of my life, been a dweller on two planets. And in that very singular sense I am a child of this generation.

I now live ex-officio in two worlds. So I get to enjoy the very best of them both. It took some doing—not the least of which was the realization that the only limitation for me was in believing in limits at all.

Because of the fact that my father Emanuel Byron was with the Nigerian Consular Service, I was born in London, England, UK, and—as such—an immediate beneficiary of dual citizenship. At the same time, since we moved back to Nigeria when I was about 5 years old, my memories of jolly old England came in scattered pockets of pleasure.

Later, growing up in Nigeria was a quantum soup of emotion. I knew that somehow this was home, but the dynamics—even for a small child—were different in so many ways.

Even before I was born, Nigeria had gained its independence in 1960 from being a Protectorate in the British Commonwealth to forming an Independent Federation that was a coalition of conservative parties—The Nigerian People's Congress (NPC), the NCNC (National Council of Nigeria and the Cameroons), and later the National Nigerian Democratic Party (NNDP). This triangulated alliance of nations, tribes and political parties finally reconstituted itself in 1966, doubling the size of the country, shifting the locus of power to the South…and then shifting it again later to the North.

Afterwards, from 1967-1970, Nigeria engaged in a bloody civil war over the attempted secession of Biafra in the East.* Initially an ancient tribal dispute, this shook out, after the loss of two million lives, to a stable and unified Nigeria. Finally, after a series of power-struggles, coups and countercoups, Nigeria settled into a kind of *Militocracy* (my term) that included a string of Army Strongmen Dictators who more or less led from behind while permitting career professionals to run the day-to-day operations of the country.

Since, I grew up in Lagos and went to school in a nearby suburb, none of this affected me directly. And although the political pressures were constantly present, we experienced a kind of stability inside the storm.

Credit much of this to the discovery in 1970 of rich oil reserves especially in the Southwest sectors of the country. So in a way, this sudden "mother lode" of the world's most sought after commodity helped the new nation of Nigeria to succeed in spite of ourselves. By the same token, Nigeria soon became a victim of its own success—an economy based on a singular resource at the expense of everything else.

In the 1960s and before, Nigeria had a diverse, if agrarian-based economy. Its principal commodities included cocoa and palm oil from the southern region and cotton and groundnut from the north. During the 1970s, however, the paradigm shifted dramatically and (in fact) perennially. The world was going through its first peacetime energy crisis. It was the game of supply and demand, and OPEC held all the cards. Nigeria had become the oil cartel's newest member and was celebrated as such. We had been thrust upon the global stage, along with some serious leverage.

---

* Biafran secession has been a constant point of agitation since the founding of Nigeria as an independent nation. And it has, as of 2017, reared its ugly head as a point of protest against what it perceives to be pandemic government "corruption."

So, in my own way, I spent my middle childhood and my early young adult years inside the bubble of a dynamic, volatile, popular part of the world. My brothers, sisters and I enjoyed our schooldays free from concern, living an upper middle class life in the eye of a hurricane.

The good news was that, no matter what ad hoc military strongman held the national reins of our country, he always possessed the common sense to let the professional pols press on with sensible governance and all the practical application of doing business as usual. In its way, this summarizes the African paradox—that somehow civilization prevails in the midst of uncertain of times.

Bearing witness to the "politics of energy" and knowing only too well its potential to backfire, convinced me more than ever of the need to seek my higher education elsewhere. When I was growing up and going to school in Nigeria, and later for a year of "prep-school" in nearby Sierra Leone, I never lost sight of that objective. And I knew that someday I would return to England to embrace a path of higher learning in a nation that still honors "the mind."

Personally, it was tough leaving lifelong friends and relocating to the United Kingdom at the age of 20. All my roots, up to that point, were in Nigeria, as were almost all my fondest memories. At that point, what I remembered of England was, for the most part, a fantasy; that and a hopeful resurrection of the ideal.

When I finally got back to the U.K. the last thing I expected was growing to love the life I spent there…and eventually a place I came to call home. What did hit me for quite some time was a massive culture shock, one that I was not prepared to deal with. To my everlasting surprise, adapting to the *change* of environment was an adjustment that would take not just months but years. And it came about in ways that had practically nothing to do with me.

One of the true advantages of living in what are called developing countries, especially those with that crossover connection of Colonial and native cultures, lies in the fact that they tend to be "open societies." Especially with new governments and young countries there is such dynamism of movement that there is little time for digging-in and setting up class barriers.

In retrospect the UK, I remembered as a tike was probably something that never existed in the first place. So what I returned to—that childhood fantasy—turned out to be the ultimate parochial society. Not one of racism (although there was also a back door to that), jolly old England was more of a caste system set by centuries of tradition. Background and breeding, bloodlines and boarding schools, peerages, knighthoods and the "terribly Esquires"—always conspired to make an outsider feel terribly excluded. It wasn't something to take personally; it was just the way things were. Still, I felt as if I had come back to a very strange world indeed. It wasn't racism in the traditional sense, but there existed a hardened kind of classism. And, since I was only 21 at the time and still forming my thoughts, I couldn't help but be daunted by the status quo.

Then I remembered the words of a brilliant American beacon of equality, FDR's first lady Eleanor Roosevelt: "No one can make you feel miserable without your permission."

It is an unfortunate aspect of human nature that 90% of the time we operate from Fear Matrix consciousness. We turn minor obstacles into angry gods and then sacrifice our own dreams without ever really trying to overcome them.

So what I learned quite early on was the importance of reinventing myself. It started during my years at University and it continued during my career. I succeeded at it by applying a law that didn't exist at the time. (In fact, I didn't know it by name, it just occurred to me to do it: Something that has recently come to be known as the *Law of Disruption*. In a way, the term comes off as a contradiction in behavior, but not if we think about it for a moment, because it is always the first step in getting us out of our ruts.)

Put forth by author/researcher Whitney Johnson in his (2015) book, *DISRUPT YOURSELF: Putting the Power of Disruptive Innovation to Work,* the act of disruption goes back to what Neurolinguistic teachers and trainers used to define as *breaking patterns.* According to Johnson, "Disrupting yourself is critical to avoiding stagnation, being overtaken by low-end entrants...and fast-tracking your personal and career growth."

Basically this involves the conscious breaking of limiting behavior. But what you are actually doing is teaching yourself to avoid plateaus and to jump out of merely accepting things as they are. Since that behavioral technology wasn't even known at the time, I applied it more or less without identifying it by name.

Well… spiritual laws, The Laws of Attraction, exist whether named or not. So I was employing *carpe deim* in almost every situation.

Tipping Points …

American Industrialist and master carmaker, Henry Ford once observed that, "The problem with opportunity is that it often comes dressed in overalls and looks like work." He might also have added that opportunities create *tipping points,* and inevitably only those who work hard get the opportunity to find them. Never one to shirk hard work, I came to several major tipping points in my life, and to my everlasting gratitude, I seized upon all of them, turning them into an advantage.

The first point came in my university years when I gravitated toward my own intellectual circle and allowed my scholastic achievements to gain cachet in the world of business. In the midst of what amounted to a personal transformation, I reflected on the power of change to create a better phase of my life. I had to focus on my original purpose: my dream to relocate, to take all the advantages this world had to offer and use them to my benefit. My next step would be my education in both university and business school. And academia always remained a bastion of egalitarian defiance.

In the university culture I knew I'd be rated only on my merit. And it was there that I learned another truth as well: If we focus on the goals ahead—and commit ourselves 100% to the outcome—transitions convert organically into success and gain.

This realization didn't come overnight. It took me up to my second year at University to appreciate the simplicity of life in the U.K. And it developed what would later become the driving force of building a thriving business across Africa. By then I had embraced this *hybrid approach*—a means of using my training there to navigate the "minefields of Africa."

I don't just mean that in the commodity sense, or in the nautical metaphor. I have however come to learn that *survivors* have one set of goals, and *winners* have another. And winners take failure merely as a postponement of success.

We learn from our mistakes. They're not here to repress us. They happen to teach us persistence and how to redefine our purpose.** Failure is a trickster with a keen sense of cunning. It can only defeat us if we view things as impossible and look for the next way out. I never have, even though "pale reason" often dictates that we do. And most of my successes have come with a war cry: *Carpe Diem!*

As a second tipping point, I have a story to share with you. After I graduated from South Bank University with a BS in Computer Sciences, like everyone else, I jumped through the usual hoops of graduate recruitment fairs, applying for every job under the sun with an almost equal number of rejections.

It took two tough years to break into the corporate world. Early in the decade, England was going through the nadir of a major recession, combined with a political tug of war between right wing and left wing political parties. During this time the Tower Hamlet borough where I was living and working was a battleground for the extreme right wing party—The British National Party (BNP)—but rather than be threatened by it, I used it as a course in something called "The University of Life."

** In fact, "mistakes" are considered the new teaching tool for technology. Leaders of major technology companies such as Pete Cashmore CEO of Mashable and Sheryl Sandberg COO of Facebook consider failure to be an essential indicator that you are trying new ideas. Basketball legend Michael Jordan once said: "I have failed a thousand times. That is why I succeed."

And I learned to navigate that most toxic atmosphere and treat the crisis as a means of developing my personal skills.

I continued to press my IT faculties and made myself indispensible, and I got so very good at what I did that I could not be denied. Even when interviewing with five-person panels set in place to turn down "everyone," I had become one with my skillset and even the toughest pro could see it. Suddenly top jobs were opening up, and I was at choice to take the best offer.

Finally two offers from very high profile clients, set me at what can only be por-trayed as *a defining moment.* One offer came from a major Polytechnic and another came with the Cancer Research Institute (for a technical support role).

After consulting with several experts including an ex-girlfriend with British Oxygen, I took the job with the Polytechnic, and started on journey into several prestigious jobs, each one leading to something better just behind it.

...living in the USA imbues one with a constant sense of movement ... mostly upward.

I was highly successful for over a decade but once again decided to invoke the Dynamic Law of Disruption and pursue an MBA—not in the UK but the good old USA. And not just any university, I was admitted to the University of Chicago (Booth). One of the oldest universities in the United States, the University of Chicago is also one of its most highly rated in terms of academic standing. What's more, it became a proving ground that unfolded for me the coming bonanza in world markets—an education from which I would derive a brand new motivation.

As opposed to life in the UK, living in the USA imbues one with a constant sense of movement…mostly upward. Everything is uncertain there, and in a very good way, because even as you contemplate changes they are already taking place. The world is moving at lightning speed, and it's all you can do to hold on. So once I got my MBA, I returned to my London world with a motivation to spread my wings and fly to far corners of the world.

It is one thing to change your circumstances when they have flatlined. (That's where the admonition to "disrupt yourself" is the most constant call to action.) But applying the Law of Disruption when you are really at the top of your game not only takes a sense of adventure, but also the courage of one's convictions: that great Leap of Faith that defines the rest of our lives. *So in a fourth major tipping point,* I interrupted my successful career to regroup and refocus on an entire new area of expertise—sophisticated international markets—and more than that, starting my own consultancy in the burgeoning world of finance.

In July 2011, I gave up my day job as a successful IT consultant to venture into the world of start-ups; becoming an entrepreneur in Africa. I met my expenses by generating multiple streams of income. Business consultancy, public speaker, technology solutions provider and writer—all these professions and more were jobs inside my realm of command.

Was it risky to take all this on? In my opinion, it was never as risky as looking to just one company to be in charge of my future. Nothing is ever accomplished in a void. Yes, I was going in business for myself. I would be an entrepreneur. And I was only doing so after establishing some strategic alliances.

For me, the consummate entrepreneur is also the constant learner. Learning, improving, then applying those lessons in the daily conduct of my business is everything that separates the amateur from the apprentice. Success in the Circus Maximus of today's global marketplace involves having a Renaissance command of every single aspect of one's operation—finance, sales, accounting, technology, and markets...in this case international markets. Knowing about these things will help synergize your success, while also enabling you to keep your overheads low.

We all live in virtual worlds that offer both safety and danger. The safety comes with point and click, with text orders, iMaps and online market building that can lift a company or sink a currency in the matter of a few hours. The danger comes with complacency—with believing you never have to be there with your feet on the ground and your heart in the jungle in every sense of the word.

Nothing defines that more than Africa. It now sits at the soul of this planet. In the next twenty years it will be all that this world has to offer—in growth, in life, in prosperity, and whether we, as a species, will rise or fall.

I know it sounds melodramatic, but I've been training for this my whole life. It is a treasure, and I am holding the map that I'd like to share with you. In doing so, I refer you to the beginning of this chapter, and challenge you to the words: to become *the master of your fate.* Start by turning the page. ☺

CHAPTER 3

Critical Mass:
Four Strategies. One End Game

*"When written in Chinese, the word 'crisis' is composed of two characters.
One represents danger and the other opportunity."*

—John F. Kennedy

By definition, *Critical Mass* is the point at which change occurs. In physics, it is determined by the number of materials introduced into a formula to create a chain reaction. In every other sense of the word, it emphasizes a point that—once reached—will never be the same again.

In a socio-political sense, especially in this New Millennium that is exactly the point at which Africa has arrived. Having that grasp of global awareness dictates a strategy, a game plan if you will. And every nation, corporation, consortium, cartel, conglomerate and savvy entrepreneur is striving to come up with the right series of strategies—in just the right combinations—to enter this very new market replete with young countries that are both vibrant and volatile in the extreme.

With that in mind, this chapter is a tale of convergence—of four different strategies to arrive at a single result: doing smart, prescient, profitable business on The Continent.

One is *bearish*.

One is *opportunist*.

Another is *bullish*.

And the final one is something called *Gestalt*. Its etymological origin is German, and it essentially refers to something—a whole—made of many parts that are somehow different from, and often greater than what they appear to be. In business, finance, war and art, it implies an ability to see the whole picture.

Gestalt thinking is the code of the visionary. It supports resolution and cancels fear. Those who lack it tend to follow trends. Those who have embraced Gestalt are those who create them…and those who embrace the three other approaches and incorporate them into a long-term strategy.

So let's take a look at all aspects of each strategy.

The "Bear Scare" has a Honey Pot! To say the least, South Africa from late 2014 through early 2018 has finally been shaken to its roots ending in a change of government. Under pressure for charges of corruption and relentless investigations of his misappropriation of funds, President Jacob Zuma was finally forced by his own ANC party to resign. He was replaced by Cyril Ramaphosa sworn in as South Africa's 5th Elected President since its inception as a new democracy. Known for having gone through several finance ministers and en masse cabinet resignations, Zuma finally retired from office in February 2018, "for the good of the nation." Unfortunately, "the nation" of South Africa currently faces a 36% jobless rate, even for college students once they graduate.

This shaky approach to the South African job market wasn't helped in the least by some of the cross-cultural animus that recently came under scrutiny and condemnation. With a dubious # 1 Ranking for crimes against women, not only is South Africa now the acknowledged "Rape Capital" of the world, in 2015 it also gained a reputation for violent xenophobia with assaults and attacks against foreign nationals from Nigeria, Zimbabwe, Somalia, Ethiopia and Malawi.*

Triggered in April of 2015 when a Somali shopkeeper killed a South African teenager he claimed was trying to rob him, there were outpourings in the streets from Johannesburg to Durban that saw thousands of protestors wielding knives, hurling petrol bombs and, in turn, being met with fire hoses and teargas from local police.

---

* Some nations, notably India and Indonesia, do not report statistics such as sex crimes and are suspected to have much higher per-capita instances than anywhere else in the world. But at least for the moment, South Africa has been willing to own up to it…and to try and fix it.

Three died and several were injured. And though it was not nearly as violent as the 2008 outbreaks (where 60 were killed and dozens injured), it still managed to add fuel to the raging perception of South African instability.

Soon enough, the Pretoria government managed to quell the riot and offer safe-haven to any foreign nationals under duress, and in short order it managed to calm the savaged nerves of newcomers coming in. Still, it was symptom rather than cure, and further indication that this nation has infrastructure problems that are dysfunctional at several levels.

To add to the negative resumé, South Africa is now the runaway number one nation for "economic theft" at the corporate and institutional level. With a 68% hijack ratio and billions of dollars in losses, it nearly doubles that of any other nation. (The global average is about 39%.) The South African Rand, once the continent's flagship currency, has gone through a steep devaluation. And it looks as though the nation's recent economic instability is going to have world financial markets downgrading its Bond Rating from investment grade to "junk!"

By every aspect of evaluation, the current calamity in South Africa looks like a horror show on steroids and all the more reason to bail. But wait a minute! There is a "by the same token" to all of this that screams out to any smart investor as a *buying opportunity.*

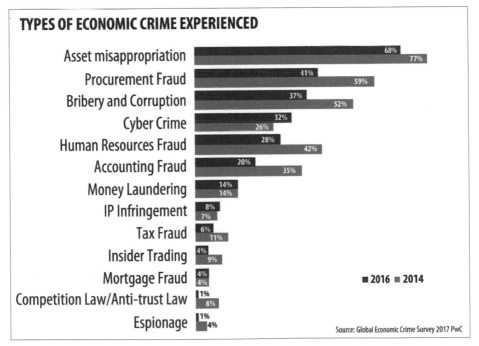

TYPES OF ECONOMIC CRIME EXPERIENCED

	2016	2014
Asset misappropriation	68%	77%
Procurement Fraud	41%	59%
Bribery and Corruption	37%	52%
Cyber Crime	32%	26%
Human Resources Fraud	28%	42%
Accounting Fraud	20%	35%
Money Laundering	14%	14%
IP Infringement	8%	7%
Tax Fraud	6%	11%
Insider Trading	4%	9%
Mortgage Fraud	4%	4%
Competition Law/Anti-trust Law	1%	8%
Espionage	1%	4%

Source: Global Economic Crime Survey 2017 PwC

Despite accusations of rampant corruption, as recently as May of 2017, the FDI Index still rated South Africa as the number one African market for investment in new business, finance, construction and dynamic growth. And it remains by far, China's largest trading partner in the Sub-Sahara with no indication of cutting back its considerable holdings. Real estate booms in cities like Durban and Cape Town have seen property values triple virtually overnight. Many electronic giants such as GE are heavily invested in becoming a part of South Africa's utility infrastructure, and recently Teracon (one of Africa's home-grown tech giants) announced that it would build its most extensive technology center in Johannesburg.

South Africa has, in the last five years, become a major exporter of goods to other African nations (exporting technology & retail brands in volume such as MTN, Shoprite, DSTV and many others). And it has also become home to a score of brand new OEMs (Original Equipment Manufacturers) and has become a major investor in the rest of the Sub-Sahara, as well as the fifth largest exporter of goods ($20 Billion) to other nations in Africa.

South Africa's mineral rich landscape still contains the African mining mother lode—with 11% of the world's gold, 23% of the world's diamonds, and 71% of its platinum. Add-in its vast reserves of chromium, copper and aluminum, and you have what has to be one of the most solid foundations for a strong economy not only for any African nation but also for any nation anywhere.

What begs the question is this: Why would any investor, business entity or government want to run to the nearest exit over what amounts to short-term volatility? Still it happens. It is the way of the (investment) mob. And it is the same mob and mob psychology that the true visionaries in global finance (such as Warren Buffet) anticipate and use to counter-invest. Savvy entrepreneurs know how to "hedge," and they know how to *buy and hold.*

Right now, South Africa requires a bit of both. Still, patience has its own rewards, and one must stay the course. Only fools rush in, and then rush back out.

The Opportunist: "The Starship Enterprise" comes to Somalia. "To boldly go where no one has gone before!" Back in the day, that was always the opening epigram that challenged the *Star Trek* fan. This, in virtually every sense of the word, is the way the smart investor should approach the African mosaic.

In keeping with the Star Trek metaphor, going into Somalia would be like spearheading a reckless foray onto the planet Kronos and trying to establish a working relationship with Klingons. An incessant civil war topped of by an ideological schism that has seen the entire Southeast portion of the nation under the control of the Muslim extremist group Al Shabaab, would be enough to discourage any company, manufacturer, nation or private equity firm from investing much of anything. Certainly all FDI venture capitalists have been advised to stay away, and most have listened. A nation of about 11 million inhabitants, Somalia's annual average income is $225 per capita (75¢ a day), and its national GDP is about $5.8 billion…which puts it just slightly below the personal net worth of Virgin's Richard Branson.

The country has been locked in a nonstop series of conflicts—on and off for no more than a few days at a time—for about 25 years. It has ripped through five changes of government since 2009. Its population has been decimated in the last 15 years. Its banking system has been in a state of perpetual chaos for at least two decades. And, from Bosaso to Mogadishu, there probably isn't a single citizen who hasn't been robbed or mugged on the street, threatened or extorted in some way.

Often referred to as the "sick man of Africa's Sub-Sahara," Somalia wouldn't seem to offer anything resembling an investment opportunity much less a high-tech service such as phone apps and mobile money. Ah, but therein lies difference…between the smart *Opportunist* and the financially faint of heart.

Hormuud Telecommunications, a Somali corporation set up in 2002, has carefully built itself into a "mobile money" game changer inside that otherwise troubled economy. Merging the best of cost-effective mobile phone technology with the most modern financial apps anywhere in the hemisphere, this phone-app, mobile money technology is now the banking method of choice for 40% of the Somali people (51% of whom now have cell-phones and the available technology to use it).

For a longtime Kenya, with 60% of its population under 25 years of age, was the runaway leader in this kind of mobile money technology. But now Somalia—out of pure urgent necessity—has caught up with Kenyan based companies like Safaricom (parent company of M-PESA, Africa's leading mode of virtual currency).

In recent years, the lack of retail banking in Somalia and fears of continued al-Shabaab attacks throughout the country have basically frozen and made invalid financial transactions by traditional means. This is a crisis instantly converted into an opportunity by the market-smart techies at Hormuud. Rather than subject depositors to the dangers of bricks-and-mortar banks, Hormuud holds the cash in a "bitcoin-like" manifestation, acting in essence like a bank.

This is a step up in technology according to Hormuud since it seems to have designed the software for EVC-Plus with the help of Kenya's Safaricom. EVC-Plus works like Safaricom's mobile money transfer service M-PESA, which has brought banking services to millions since its introduction in 2007.

Even though the Somali shilling is still in circulation, Hormuud's money transfer system uses US dollars, which is now the country's preferred currency of trade. Users can transfer up to $3,000 a day throughout southern and central Somalia. And that gives it not only a leg up on the competition but also a constant flow of traffic to the world's money standard.

With mobile money and a broad range of banking services at their fingertips, virtually all the Millennials of this troubled nation have found a whole new network—one that includes the ability to shop at any time or order a wide range of services simply by inserting a code. The pride of the Somali Economic Forum (SEF), this mobile money is the bane of Muslim militants and street thugs alike. In fact, it has been so effective, that radical jihadists have issued a fatwa against it. But, for the time being at least, technology is winning out. Al Shabaab is losing leverage. And so it appears that hope has arrived in a smart-phone—another example of how technology trumps ignorance every time.

Diamond's in Our Own Back Yard. (And he's a Bull on African Banks!) Bob Diamond is a name that strikes strong chords in the edgy music of international asset management and investment. As former CEO of Barclays Bank, he has more than a journeyman's knowledge of global finance. In fact, he is inarguably acknowledged as one of the world's foremost experts.

During Bob Diamond's stewardship at what was then Barclays Capital, the company grew over the next 15 years in seeming direct proportion to what people saw as his ambition and reputed lack of humility.

Bob Diamond

Since I was there during some of Barclays most bullish years, Bob's ambition and management style are aspects of the man that I happen to know fully well. When Diamond took charge of Barclays Capital in 1997, it was the unloved rump of the BZW investment bank group, most of which had just been sold-off at bargain prices.

With Bob Diamond as the CEO, Barclays Capital soon became "the golden child" of the parent company Barclays Bank. Over the next decade, Bob Diamond transformed BC into one of Europe's leading trading houses. He completed the transformation in September 2008 by picking up the U.S. arm of failed Lehman Brothers, and at that point his star was rising at meteoric levels. In the first half of 2010, Barclays Capital accounted for more than 85% of the bank's pre-tax profit. At roughly $22 of Barclays $28 billion that literally became the tail wagging the dog.

So, when Barclays eventually got hit with the "leverage lending" scandal, rumours were widely spread throughout the industry that Bob Diamond had been set up as the fall guy. (No one will ever know for sure. But he definitely got a platinum parachute for a settlement; some say, out of guilt.)

Officially forced to resign from Barclays in 2012 for allegedly trying to leverage lending standards called LIBOR (London Interbank Offered Rates), Diamond was never prosecuted and was, by all reports, only nominally involved. Still, with a name like his to add celebrity power to ambitious investigation, the rate scandal accelerated into £ billions in leveraged funds that cost Barclays £320 million to settle and rather precipitously cost Bob Diamond his job.

Out of work for about five days in real time, Diamond almost immediately rallied by allying with Dubai-based super-financier Ashish Thakkar in 2013 to form Atlas Mara, an Africa-focused financial services investment group with special concentration on buying up banks in several African nations. Originally, Atlas Mara placed

"We still believe in the (African) story, and the entry points in terms of prices are lower. ..."

— Bob Diamond/Atlas Mara

emphasis on the ones in ECOWAS (The Economic Community Of West African States)...but soon they expanded to include the whole of Africa.

Meanwhile over the next three years, Barclays' new CEO, Jes Staley, started unloading the firm's stake in Barclays Africa Group in 2015; claiming that "double taxation" at the home country level was savaging Barclays profits.

Never one to waste a good crisis, Bob Diamond and Atlas Mara have already snapped up banking operations in Botswana, Zimbabwe, Zambia, Tanzania, Mozambique, Rwanda and Nigeria...with acquisitions of Africa Bank, Union Bank of Nigeria, and others. The fact that these very nations have been hit hard by the recent downturn in Africa's commodity based economy, has caused Atlas Mara to drop its share price by over half its 2013 IPO valuation. Undaunted, Diamond, Thakkar and company press on with bullish optimism.

In fact, they clearly seem to be doubling down on their Africa presence, and Atlas Mara recently announced their intention to expand its interests into "10 to 15 more key countries" in the next two years.

Included among this bold new move in the midst of a bear market for Sub-Saharan financial institutions may be the purchase of Barclays Africa division. Once one of Barclays four financial pillars, the Africa connection and its surface volatility has caused some jitters at the venerable London-based institution. In fact, they look to be selling...and guess who's on the front row to make a bid? None other than Bob Diamond and Atlas Mara.

In February 2016, Diamond spoke at a Bloomberg Africa Business and Economic Summit in Cape Town, South Africa and announced that, despite slowing growth in markets such as South Africa, his risk appetite to invest in African banks was even greater than before.

"We still believe in the (African) story, and the entry points in terms of prices are lower. The competition for acquisitions is lower. The currencies are cheaper compared to international currencies. So frankly we see this as an improving environment."

Part of that improving environment may be the acquisition of Barclays South African affiliate, an entity in which Diamond has expressed a keen, if not ironic, interest. (And after all, as someone once said, "Success is the best revenge.")

What Diamond and Atlas Mara see is that the fundamentals are sound. That defines the "bull" philosophy: Look at the bloodlines first. Then be willing to stay the course when others fall away.

Enter the Dragon: "The China Connection." The Law of Supply and Demand.
China's commitment to Africa began in two stages. Stage One in 1999. And Stage Two—one of exponential involvement— in 2011. And it has amplified every year since. It epitomizes *The Gestalt* approach to the African market because it is all in. No strings, no political leverage, no death by good intentions, no caveats, no manipulation or exploitation of resource—it is just a simple business rapport and a commitment to the future.

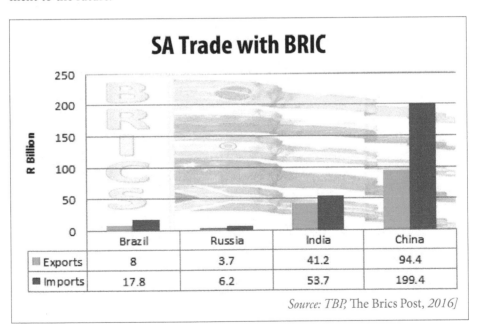

SA Trade with BRIC

	Brazil	Russia	India	China
Exports	8	3.7	41.2	94.4
Imports	17.8	6.2	53.7	199.4

Source: TBP, The Brics Post, 2016]

Purely in terms of investment and long-term financial capital commitment, China has embraced Africa as its own kind of Index Fund. In every good sense of the word, it has bought the whole market, aka *The SPDR ("Spider")*. That is the Gestalt approach. That is the entrepreneur's version of "unconditional love." So, in a very real sense it has embraced a partnership at all levels, and has instilled a great deal of goodwill in the process.

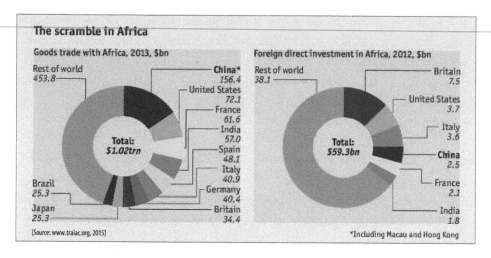

The scramble in Africa

Goods trade with Africa, 2013, $bn

Rest of world 453.8

Total: $1.02trn

China* 156.4
United States 72.1
France 61.6
India 57.0
Spain 48.1
Italy 40.9
Germany 40.4
Britain 34.4
Brazil 25.3
Japan 25.3

[Source: www.tralac.org, 2015]

Foreign direct investment in Africa, 2012, $bn

Rest of world 38.1

Total: $59.3bn

Britain 7.5
United States 3.7
Italy 3.6
China 2.5
France 2.1
India 1.8

*Including Macau and Hong Kong

Not surprising then that it leads all other BRICS nations in the Sub-Sahara. And yet there is an almost pandemic misunderstanding of China's involvement. In the first place it is not a "government" commitment. Granted the Beijing treasury has, since 2012, provided large multi-billion dollar loans to resource-rich nations such as the Democratic Republic of the Congo, Angola, Botswana and Ghana. These are what are known as concessionary loans, and come with no expectation of political leverage… but with access to plush resource contracts that are largely open-ended.

Not that China isn't aware of some of the demographic challenges. Owing to weaknesses in capacity, healthcare systems plus limited education and lowered skill levels especially in East Africa, the general population of Sub-Sahara Africa still has a long way to go. But it is a socio-economic challenge with which the Chinese are familiar…since they went through much of the same thing before the 1980s.

Rapid growth in the urban populations at about 7% a year has placed enormous strains on weak municipal infrastructure and led to the growth of urban ghettos where living conditions are poor.

Africa's youth bulge, especially in the ECOWAS group has exerted external pressure on already stretched education systems, and shortages of a skilled labor force are still a problem. Still, the overall growth and stability is very much on the uptick, especially compared to 20 years ago. And the Chinese have, for a long time, been on the front line to take advantage of it.

What needs to be recognized is the fact that, despite its self-described communist/socialist government, China has—since 1991—been one of the most aggressively capitalistic economic forces in the world. It has the fifth largest cadre of billionaires of any nation in the world, and its *Africa Deal* includes a national government indemnification policy that has encouraged Chinese businesses to open operations there.

At present, China has approximately $108.5 billion in Foreign Direct Investment (FDI) in African nations coming from more than 2,000 independent corporations and businesses in every range of operation—from consumer products and aviation, to agriculture, finance and even tourism.

No question, a large portion of China's African courtship is motivated toward commodity, especially oil and natural gas. And its government operated National Petroleum Corporation has gone into nations often where "angels fear to tread" to invest in Sudan's oil sector as well as cutting sweetheart deals with Algeria and Nigeria. Its major utility China Power has invested $6 billion in Guinean bauxite. And, since 2011, the nation of Ethiopia has seen nearly 600 Chinese registered companies set up shop there.

China's strategy for Africa has been simple and direct. In 2012, during a period of turmoil and flux, China moved into Africa just as many nations of the EU and the US were getting cold feet and pulling out.

Originally, China and its broad-spectrum of companies were concentrating their fiduciary commitments in a handful of African nations. Now the number has doubled, and some of its more sophisticated tech giants such as (publicly traded) ZTE have become one of the principal telecommunications providers for the entire continent.

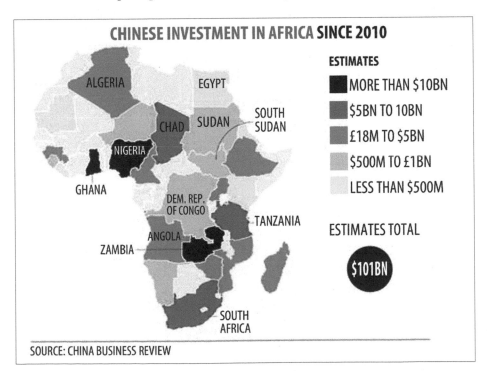

CHINESE INVESTMENT IN AFRICA SINCE 2010

ESTIMATES

MORE THAN $10BN
$5BN TO 10BN
£18M TO $5BN
$500M TO £1BN
LESS THAN $500M

ESTIMATES TOTAL

$101BN

SOURCE: CHINA BUSINESS REVIEW

So what does China offer to Africa that other nations and corporations do not? Very simply, they're all in. They come with funding, friendly companies, manpower and cross-cultural mindscapes.

That epitomizes the *Gestalt Strategy* in all its manifestations. They see the big picture, and they have no problem supporting (and in some cases subsidizing) the businesses that want to share the adventure with them. Recently, as world markets grow shaky and Chinese financial institutions that hold about 38% of the debt paper in the west feel the impact, the China strategy might well be called into question. In that regard, they seem more than ready to field the criticism. And it might best be summarized with the words of (Indian born) English author Rudyard Kipling:

> *"And as for rivals, in this I trust:*
> *I pay them nary a mind.*
> *I just leave them eatin' my dust*
> *A year-and-a-half behind."*

Summary...

Invariably all investment strategies tend to overlap. China's commodity starved economy is a natural fit for Africa's rich resources. So the Gestalt Strategy is not only sensible, but also bullish. Bob Diamond's brave new "buy now" investment strategy in financial institutions throughout the Sub-Sahara is certainly bullish. But is it not also opportunistic? And only a bear on the dare, like Hormuud, would seize the day in "sick man" Somalia by turning the need for security on its head, and using the world's most modern mobile money innovations as a consumer service breakthrough.

In truth, in today's global markets, everything is a hybrid. What we have offered here are ways to approach the Continent—the youngest, most resource rich continent on planet Earth—the final frontier where everything worth happening will come to pass in the next two decades.

CHAPTER 4

Home Grown:
Building Africa From the Inside Out

In a way, Africa has always been in a struggle for its soul. That is a broad, sweeping statement when you are referring to 54 different nations, each with its own individual set of tribal divisions, history of colonialism, cultural traditions, and extrinsic geopolitical and financial influences. But it all boils down to an argument that divides the "Continental Consciousness" into two camps: Exploitation versus self-determination…or the *corporate raider* versus the *compassionate capitalist.*

Nothing reflects this ongoing dilemma more than some of the players in the Africa's modern economic tapestry. Africa still has vestigial traces of "dictator drainage" such as that which exists in Zimbabwe, or billionaire *kleptocracies* whose poster child is Angola's Isabel dos Santos—Africa's richest woman at $3.3 billion—who happens to be the daughter of longtime Angolan president, Jose Eduardo dos Santos. (Rumor has it that Isabel dos Santos is the basic beneficiary of every bit of baksheesh that comes into the country. But there is more to this than meets the eye. In a rather complicated Rubix involving the "politics of enhancement" much of Isabel's activity is helping create a kind of reverse diaspora that is profoundly benefitting Angola…to be covered later.)

In fact, we have found it much easier in this New Millennium to stress the rising tide of *philanthrocapitalists and billionaire African visionaries* who have come to number in legion throughout the Continent. We cite a few of them here, along with some of Africa's largest and most innovative home grown corporations—specialists in everything from food to advanced technology that is the prize of Africa's under twenty-fives who now represent 64% of the entire Sub-Sahara.

The Forerunner...

"The young lions of today want to be like me, but they want to do it overnight. It's not going to work. To succeed in business you must start small and dream big. In the journey of entrepreneurship, tenacity of purpose is supreme."

—Aliko Dangote

Nigerian billionaire Aliko Dangote could easily qualify as the recruitment poster Marine for an entire continent. It is common knowledge that he is the richest man in Africa and arguably one of the 100 wealthiest people in the world. Due to tanking oil commodity prices and recent manic mood swings of the Nigerian naira, Dangote's net worth has taken a major hit since 2014—and is now estimated somewhere between $12.2 billion and $26 billion (USD) in any given month. As such, he belongs to that small group of earthshakers who can point and click or make a phone call and change the fate of nations. And

PHOTO CREDIT: BELLANAIJA.COM

Aliko Dangote

yet he wields his power deliberately and with a complete comprehension of the impact it makes, because he knows he must.

To gain some perspective, the market cap on his holding company, The Dangote Group, is currently around $14.5 billion (USD)…roughly more than the annual GDP of 31 of Africa's 54 nations.

One Dangote Group acquisition (such as a recent Moroccan phosphate acquisition and another potash purchase from Congo-Brazzaville) can move the needle for an entire stock exchange for a day or a week. In this case, The Dangote Group is moving into these markets to restock a Nigeria-based fertilizer plant that will enable its home nation to grow up to 2 million tons of rice. Right now, the rice cooperatives in Nigeria are anemic and something of a commodity cripple in terms of leverage. The newly fortified rice crop with the proper healthy growth medium will go far toward making it more agriculturally independent.

At present, Nigeria imports 2.8 million tons of rice a year, most of it on the black market. It is therefore priced at a premium with no guarantee of either quality or consistency. To counteract this rampant commodity fraud, the Dangote group is offering a safe-haven and stability to traders and buyers by guaranteeing product reliability.

Aliko Dangote's other major project is raising $3.3 billion for a $14 billion refinery near Nigeria's commercial capital, Lagos…and a $1.5 billion natural gas pipeline nearby. The thrust of this run of investment(s) is one that pours directly into the Nigerian economy and contributes mightily toward shoring up his home country's economic infrastructure so that it becomes more self-sufficient. (This is also good news for Dangote, especially since Nigeria's Minister of Petroleum Ibe Kachikwu recently announced that as of 2019 his nation will no longer import oil products.)

If it did not sound disingenuous, one could point to the fact that Aliko Dangote is in fact a "patriotic investor." That applies in every sense of the word, because easily 90% of his (estimated) $20 billion in personal net worth has come through manufacturing, industrialization of assets and virtually plowing every cent back into the companies he started.

This of course flies directly into the face of the "vulture capitalist" notion of cut-and-run investing that has so often laced the oil-rich Mediterranean regions of Africa—Libya, Algeria, Egypt and Sudan—or the inherited resource Eurocentric family corporations that jot the tip of the Sub-Sahara in places such as South Africa, Botswana and Mozambique.

In fact, Aliko Dangote defines the Horatio Alger notion of the self-made billionaire. And he did it the hard way. With a $3000 loan from an uncle in 1977, he set up what was originally a food brokerage company called The Dangote Group. And wading his way through half a dozen "militocracies" in the 1980s, Aliko built DG into a soft commodities trading empire, specializing in sugar, salt, flour and grains that served all of West Africa. Later, he expanded into processed foods, telecommunications and cement (the latter literally forming the building block for much of western Sub-Sahara).

Today, the Dangote Group is a multitrillion-naira conglomerate (worth about $35 billion USD or 6% of the total Nigerian GDP). With many of its operations in Benin, Ghana, Nigeria, and Togo, Dangote has expanded to cover food processing, cement manufacturing, and freight. The Dangote Group also dominates the sugar market in Nigeria and has recently emerged from its origins as a trading company to being the largest industrial group in West Africa. The Dangote Sugar Refinery, Dangote Flour, and Dangote Foods—all these and more are familiar household names. And more recently, the DG has expanded into real estate, banking, textiles, oil and gas. It also exports several raw commodities such as cotton, cocoa, cashews and sesame seeds and oil to other countries. When you consider the fact that Dangote Group provides Nigeria with 70% of all its sugar (for soft-drinks, cereals, distilleries and confectioners) and supplies West Africa with 80% of its cement, you don't have a company or a stock or bond as much as you have a diverse, eclectic mutual fund… with unlimited upside potential.

The richest African on the Forbes 2016 List of 1841 billionaires, Aliko Dangote is also occasionally referred to as, "the world's richest black man." Forbes listed him as its *Africa Person of the Year,* which isn't as patronizing as it sounds, since Forbes lists its main businessperson for every continent (except Antarctica) and many nations.

The most salient aspect of the Aliko Dangote's entrepreneurial strategy is his very single-mindedness. When it comes to applying his business acumen to build his native land and his home continent from the inside out—he is always right on point. It stops short of a "Nigeria first" kind of xenophobia. Quite the contrary: it is a mandate toward expansion.

Nowadays, Aliko Dangote is famously quoted for having expressed the following sentiment:

> *"Let me tell you this and I want to really emphasize it...nothing is going to help Nigeria like Nigerians bringing back their money. If you give me $5 billion today, I will invest everything here in Nigeria. Let us put our heads together and work."*

Although he is only 59, Dangote is looked upon as the Patron Saint of Nigerian business and industry. He is certainly the Paragon for a new breed of Afro-centric entrepreneurs—those who give back extensively to the nations that bred them and the ones they call home. Generous beyond measure to several charities, Aliko Dangote has a broader perspective in mind. It is the Law of Attraction in a very African sense.

ROOTS:
Bethlehem Thinks Globally and Acts Locally!

Bethlehem Tilahun Alemu has more in common with Nigerian billionaire Aliko Dangote than you could possibly imagine. They're not from the same country. They're not close to being the same age (he is 22 years older). They're not even the same gender. (She is a woman with movie-star good looks.) But they share the same patriotic passion and sense of social justice combined with the conviction that you grow your business by turning to your own roots—from the inside-out, from what you know best, from your heart and from an innate sense that character, dedication and a good game plan will ultimately drive one to a great result.

PHOTO CREDIT: DAILYWORTH.COM

Tilahun Alemu

Bethlehem Alemu is 36 years old. Start there. She is Ethiopian. She built a business from $10,000 in seed money to anticipated revenues in 2016 of more than $12 million USD. She is one of Africa's top rated women entrepreneurs...and she accomplished all this without ever leaving her local "underprivileged" suburb of Zenebe-work, just outside Addis Ababa.

Alemu started passionately on her path over 12 years ago with an idea she had apparently had since childhood. Very aware of Ethiopia's lamentable 41% literacy rate and its even more distressing $2 a day average per capita income, Bethlehem was determined to become a "home-grown" entrepreneur who could make a difference.

Fresh out of college in 2004, this honors graduate immediately set about to challenge the absurd shibboleth that Africans in general—and Ethiopians in particular—lacked the ability to innovate their way out of poverty and into prosperity without outside "good intentions" or foreign investment.

> ## *"Certain nations, people and elites always seem to have a vested interest in positioning Ethiopia as 'needing*

Determined to help her native country shed the yoke of codependency that seemed to be holding it back, the miracle of Bethlehem Tilahun Alemu is that she created her business model for SoleRebels, Ltd. by designing and test-manufacturing a line of casual footwear made out of purely indigenous plants and recycled materials native to the shanties, suburbs and small farms outside of Addis Ababa. And she started with one or two simple "shoe designs" that have more recently blossomed into dozens of styles and presentations.

At the moment, SoleRebels makes sport shoes, sandals, slip-ons, and lace-up shoes (including some very sleek sexy athletic shoes) from such materials as recycled tires, hoses, jute fiber, and the roots and leaves of the ancient Koba plant (native to Ethiopian soil and used as a fabric and plant-base plastic for over 10,000 years). Working with this eco-friendly, innovative material base SoleRebels has kicked out some "hip shoe designs" with a strong western influence and with a broad base of appeal.

What's more, the SoleRebels product applies Ethiopian craft practices, locally resourced, hand-woven and hand-spun in a way that virtually generates a zero-carbon footprint fashion statement that is also very cost-effective. Emphasizing the fact that she always works with local "artisans," Bethlehem and SoleRebels currently employ over 100 people in their "hometown," with plans to expand production facilities to other nations in Africa as well.

With what started out as a local brand, SoleRebels are now sold on the Internet and in brick and mortar empire builders such as Whole Foods Markets and Urban Outfitters in 30 nations all over the world. Prices range anywhere from $20 to $99.

Recently, SoleRebels as a company was one of the finalists for the Legatum Africa Awards for Entrepreneurship in 2012. And in 2014, Bethlehem Tilahun Alemu was awarded the Most Outstanding Businesswoman" by *African Business Magazine.*

With a retail outlet now in Taiwan, SoleRebels is also opening in Austria, Switzerland, the US and the UK, with franchise proposals for Italy, Australia, Spain, Japan and Canada.

In view of the exponential growth anticipated for SoleRebels in the next five years, Bethlehem also announced her expansion into a new venture—a sibling entity called "The Republic of Leather." In starting up, she is applying the same principles and business model that have worked for companies like the GAP and other visionary world retailers. Working with some "iconic designers" she is applying the option of customer choice for…design, artisan producer, variation of local natural materials and other options that appeal to the modern Millennial obsession with freedom of choice.

Very community conscious, Bethlehem Amelu also includes her customary built-in tithing from the store-side of the purchase. (5% of all proceeds from sales go to designated local charities in Ethiopia.) So the customer always knows they have a partnership with a company that cares for the world around them—price, empowerment and eco-sensitivity. As such, SoleRebels lives up to its name: a revolution in consciousness rooted in traditional values.

Native Son. A Quantum Leap of Faith…

Multimillionaire Patrick Awuah is a new generation of African entrepreneur who has reversed the "African diaspora" back to his native land and, as such, has disproved author Thomas Wolfe's adage that *You Can't Go Home Again.* Awuah has, in fact, done so and has flourished in the process. So has the university he came back to fund, found and accredit in his native Ghana—Ashesi University in Accra.

PHOTO CREDIT: RISINGAFRICA.ORG

Patrick Awauah

In 2002, after living in the USA for almost two decades, Patrick Awuah returned to Ghana, leaving his job at global tech giant Microsoft, where he earned millions as program manager to set up Ashesi, to educate young Africans into the best possible educational mélange of science and liberal arts.

When he made this major paradigm shift in his life, it came as a surprise to everyone, not the least of whom was Patrick Awuah himself. By every lifestyle metric,

Awuah had all the reason in the world to stay right where he was. In 1997, he was already 15 years into a longstanding lucrative job with Microsoft where he'd made millions working as a program manager. When he decided to take this leap of faith, the most supportive person of all was his wife who saw in Patrick the burning desire to return to his African homeland.

Originally, Patrick left his native Ghana in the early 1980s as a part of the traditional cultural diaspora to Europe and the US, where college-age African students come to their supra-society of choice, attain a degree from a highly regarded university and stay on with a path to citizenship and a lucrative career. His job at Microsoft, especially during the exponential growth years of the 1990s paid huge dividends, and it would have been very easy for him to stay right where he was and amass an even larger fortune.

But Patrick Awuah had always nurtured the idea of a private university in Ghana, because he recognized the need for institutions of higher learning especially in his homeland as something of paramount importance. To shore up his own academic credentials, Patrick even went so far as going back to get his Masters Degree at the University of California at Berkeley. But even after he had gone that far into the pursuit of his dream, he would wake up on more than one occasion, wondering if he'd done the right thing.

"And then I read the words of Goethe," Patrick remembers: *" Whatever you can do or dream you can, begin it. Boldness has genius, power and magic in it — begin it now.'"*

Begin he did, and in so doing, he found the gap—the critical path—that created the opportunity. On his return to Ghana to begin his university curriculum in 2002, Patrick Awuah found out that for every problem three things kept coming up; corruption, weak institutions, and the people in power who run them – the leaders. Patrick asked two very important questions: where were these leaders coming from? What was it about Ghana that produces leaders that are unethical or unable to solve problems?

In search of answers, he scanned the country's educational system and realized that nothing had changed during his time away.

"It was the same learning by rote, from primary school through graduate school. Very little emphasis on ethics…and the typical graduate from a university in Ghana has a stronger sense of entitlement than a sense of responsibility. And that's just wrong."

Patrick's resolve to address this problem resulted in the conception and birth of Ashesi University, an institution launched specifically to help develop young African leaders. Its very name, Ashesi, translates into the term, "Beginnings." And it was to that standard that Patrick Awuah wanted this unique collection of colleges to aspire.

As a part of its charter, the University has in place an Honor Code, where the students pledge to be honest, attend their classes and operate their course of study with

> *"While the Honor Code may constitute a reach for a perfect society, which is unachievable, we cannot*

the utmost integrity... and to hold each other accountable. The students of Ashesi University take ownership of their ethical posture on campus. Originally this was a radical departure from the norm in most African universities where corrupt practices are often the order of the day. And even many American Universities, in today's atmosphere of entitlement, have dropped their honor code stipulations and have paid the price in lowered student performance and expedient academic standards. Not so at Ashesi.

"While the Honor Code may constitute a reach for a perfect society, which is unachievable, we cannot achieve perfection," Patrick observes. *"But if we reach for it, we can achieve excellence."'* (Awuah acknowledges that the quote is actually a paraphrase from Hall of Fame Football Coach, Vince Lombardi, but he doesn't mind crediting others if it creates the desired result. And in this case the result is a refurbished more academically sound educated Ghanaian.)

"Every society must be very intentional about educating its leaders...so this is what I'm doing now."

When Awuah chartered Ashesi in 2002, it began with two small buildings and 30 students. Today the university campus is set on a bucolic 100-acre plot of land in a town called Berekuso, about a 1-hour drive from Accra itself.

As of 2016, the Berekuso campus has become something of a small college showcase, with over 500 students partaking in a curriculum that is said to be the perfect mélange of Liberal Arts and Sciences.

Along with a strict academic curriculum, Ashesi also features a varied program of awards, athletic programs (the APL, Ashesi Premier League Soccer) and a special ASC event in the spring—now a 10-year tradition—dedicating a week to building esprit de corps by helping students to celebrate their own role in co-creating the synergy of Ashesi.

What Patrick Awuah wanted to initiate was an academically sound, internationally accredited university in his native Ghana that would help educate the country's next generation of leaders...and to make it "affordable."

Originally, that took some doing, and it often required some healthy investment and subsidy, not only from Patrick Awuah and his various funds, but also from donors, investors and independent foundations—any outside support that could come in without "strings" so often attached to traditional funding.

"In our last freshman class, 50% of that class paid full tuition, 25% were on full scholarships and 25% on partial scholarships," Patrick notes. *"The reason why diversity is so important is that the most important conversation on campus is a conversation about… the good society we would like to see in Africa?' That conversation is a lot more interesting if you have diversity in the classroom."*

Looking ahead, Awuah says he hopes Africa's universities will cultivate a new generation of bold and innovative leaders, helping the continent to transform itself.

"If you come back in 30 years, universities will be competing for the best and brightest students…I hope that universities will also be competing on things such as whose students are the most ethical, the most principled and the most visionary…If that happens, it will change the continent."

Averaging at about 71%, Ghana has only a fair literacy rate, right in the middle of the 39 nations in the Sub-Sahara. In view of that, or perhaps because of it, it also has an underperforming track record at higher levels of education. This is underscored by consistently disappointing performance levels during advanced vocational courses called TVET (Technical and Vocational Education and Training) that have been considered something of a flop by the country's 28% unemployed graduates. In truth, *higher education* in Ghana—one that includes liberal arts—at the college level is considered something of a rarity enjoyed by only the few who can afford it. As Patrick Awuah observes:

> *"In this country, only 5% of college-age kids go to college…And that same 5% will invariably end up running the country…So when I look at universities I see Africa fast-forward 30 years. When this 20-year-old is now in his or her fifties, that person is going to be a leader. And so I felt that engaging how that future leadership core is educated could be catalytic."*

Honored numerous times, and one of the most famous men in Ghana after former UN Secretary General Kofi Annan, Patrick Awuah recently received the MacArthur Foundation Fellowship Award for Education.

A Story of Survival ...

Kenyan businesswoman and industrialist Tabitha Karanja is one tough lady, and she has had to be. Originally, the Founder and CEO of Keroche Breweries Ltd, Tabitha and her husband Joseph were the proud proprietors of the first fully owned Kenyan brewery and distillery in 1997. An extremely good student with honors at her university, Tabitha had always had an entrepreneurial disposition but wasn't quite sure where to put her effort.

Tabitha Karanja

Then in 1997, liberalization of the alcohol industry (which also removed government controlled price ceilings) exposed a critical market imbalance...and through that "crisis point," an opportunity.

Keroche's marketing research on drinking patterns within middle and low-income earners immediately showed them that the established liquor manufacturers were totally off base with their price points. (They were just too expensive.)

"One day I felt that we really wanted to go into full manufacturing, but I didn't know which sector exactly," Tabitha remembers. *"But soon enough, after doing a bit of market research, we found out that there was a big gap in the liquor market and it was in the "price effective market" with good quality but low cost beverages where customers were virtually being ignored. So we thought, 'Why don't we come with a product that is hygienically produced, that meets international standards and was affordable?'"*

With the locally available raw materials and with a start-up capital of 500,000 Kenyan shillings (KSh), Joe and Tabitha decided to venture into *fortified wines*. And due to the low cost of production they were able to bottle and bring to market a high quality product at an affordable price that resonated with the low-to-medium income drinker.

It proved to be an inspired venture...because within six years the new company at last had given an additional option of four bottled and quality drinks to persons reeling from the high cost of spirits traditionally purveyed by multi-national brewers. Originally a pride and joy of Kenyan free-enterprise, Karanja and Keroche were awarded 'Moran of Burning Spear' by former President Mwai Kibaki in recognition of her efforts to liberalize the beer manufacturing industry in the country.

And for a decade, Keroche Breweries was the largest competitor to East African Breweries, which had previously monopolized the Kenyan beer manufacturing industry for decades.

In 2007, with a regime change in Nairobi, the government enacted heavy taxes on locally made wines, Keroche's products were priced out of the market. Ordered to pay 1.2 billion KSh in back taxes in 14 days, Keroche took the Kenyan government to court and won the case. Not one to be accused of a failure to innovate, Karanja retooled Keroche's manufacturing capacity to make ready-to-drink gin and vodka, which her state-of-the-art factory still makes today.

In 2008, Tabitha Karanja added beers—Summit Ale and Summit Malt—to Keroche's repertoire of alcoholic drinks, putting a dent in East African Breweries lock on the industry, and creating something of an affordable and highly popular "microbrewery" that Kenyans latched onto as a pop classic. In 2012, the factory began expansion plans to increase beer production from 60,000 bottles per day to 600,000 bottles per day by launching a state-of-the-art brewing plant, the first of its kind in East Africa.

Then in 2013, the door dropped down when the Kenyan government, through the Kenya Bureau of Standards, tried to clamp down on an epidemic of "illicit brews and distilleries" throughout the country. (This had long been a problem in east Africa, and it needed enforcement. But in this case the methods the Kenyan government used were both draconian and heavy-handed.)

One day, to Karanja's surprise, in what seemed a pro-forma move, the KBS actually sent an MP to "inspect" Keroche's new state-of-the-art brewery.

By that time, Keroche was an 18-year-old company that had invested in global brands, won international awards, created thousands of jobs, paid billions of shillings to the Kenyan Revenue Authority (KRA) and been touted on five different occasions as "Africa's new entrepreneurial model." But to their surprise, Keroche was suddenly lumped into a large category of "unsafe" brewing and distilling facilities. The main reason for this judgment: some of Keroche's traditional brewing and bottling practices were determined to be inconsistent with newly established standards. (In other words, they needed "tweaking.")

Politically motivated and considered by many a cynical government move prompted by "big brewery" lobbies, the summons to cease and desist levied against Keroche shook the multibillion-shilling business to its foundations.

Anyone who has ever opened a marketing or retail business anywhere can tell you that it takes intense commitment and enormous investment to establish an international brand. And yet, on the whim of revisionist government "health-standards," it can all be brought down overnight.

In this case, the Keroche story is also the story of a young Africa, of new African governments and burgeoning businesses coming into conflict. In this case, it was also a testament to the balance of powers in a presidential republic. Upon appeal from Karanja and Keroche Breweries, the Kenyan High Court ruled that The Kenyan Bureau of Standards had acted precipitously in declaring an 18-year-old (venerated)

> *"The only person who fails is one who forgets that there are people behind him or her. In fact, I am going to do a special lunch for my dear husband. As an African woman, being supported by your husband is something very special."*

home grown company "illicit and unsafe," and came down in favor of Keroche. Case closed.

In the ultimate irony, in the same year (2014) the Kenyan High Court ruled in Keroche's favor, Tabitha Karanja was awarded "The Business Woman of the Year for 2014" at the CNBC *All Africa Business Leaders Awards.* And it is seldom mentioned but known to a few that, though husband Joe funded the original operation, Tabitha has been the guiding force behind Keroche and the de facto CEO—something she acknowledges with gratitude and humility.

"The only person who fails is one who forgets that there are people behind him or her. In fact, I am going to do a special lunch for my dear husband. As an African woman, being supported by your husband is something very special."

As part of the New Africa, husband and wife business teams, though not yet commonplace, are a growing phenomenon. It is doubtless a generational issue. It is also a modern generational synergism that everyone seems to welcome.

African Corporations: Life Among the Lions...

In today's global business climate it's a given: If you're going to be an elite level, multibillion dollar African corporation these days, you had better have four common qualities: 1) An excellent business model; 2) solid financial underpinnings; 3) a young energetic core group that not only has phenomenal work ethic, but also knows how to think outside the box; 4) an original product or service that everyone wants but nobody has.

Those are four qualities important to any new business. In Africa, they are survival essentials. And so we're using this space to introduce three Africa based corporations that have more than met the criteria...

Based in Nairobi, Safaricom™ is East Africa's largest mobile telecommunications provider and easily ranks as one of the most innovative companies in Sub-Saharan Africa. What sets it apart and a cut above the competition is a financial app called M-PESA™ *(M* for "Mobile" and *Pesa*—a Swahili word for "money"). Although there have been several imitators since it originally came out, M-PESA is Africa's first SMS-based money transfer service.

HOME NATION: Kenya

INDUSTRY:

As a unique feature, M-PESA is a highly flexible monetary app that lets users deposit, transfer and withdraw funds via text message. A subscriber who wants to send money across simply visits a registered M-PESA agent with the money and the phone number of the recipient.

For a fee of 100 KSh (a little over $1 USD), the agent sets up a virtual account for the Safaricom subscriber, credits the account with the money, and then sends the specified amount to the recipient's account. A subscriber can send money even to a recipient on a different mobile network, who can cash it at any M-PESA agent simply by presenting an ID and entering a secret code. Safaricom has also pioneered a service that offers subscribers airtime on credit that has introduced the payment of utility bills through the M-PESA platform and also runs a robust customer loyalty award program that offers perks, travel points and bonuses.

Adding to its appeal as being very ahead-of-the curve, Safaricom recently contracted with leading international technology companies such as Samsung. In the contract, Samsung agreed to provide all its "high-end" smart-phone and electronic tablet technologies to Safaricom as its own brand of iSurf and Smart Tab electronic tablets at affordable prices.

At present, Safaricom's strength is also its greatest weakness—in that it offers accessibility while it has yet to master the burdensome African subtext of affordability. Even though it offers easy credit terms to East Africa's under 30's, it is constantly challenged to work out terms to finance this ravenous new millennial market.

They are very involved in helping local economies and empowering low to middle income users. Through its M-PESA and Safaricom Foundations, the company has partnered with Action Aid International Kenya (AAIK) to address issues of drought, starvation, and labor empowerment for East Africa's underprivileged.

HOME NATION: Nigeria

INDUSTRY: Media &

If it is true that *Nollywood* (Nigeria's phenomenally popular movie industry) is rapidly becoming the Hollywood of Africa, it might well be said that IROKOtv helped to glamorize it. IROKOtv —often referred to as the "'Netflix of Africa"— is currently the world's largest digital distributor of African movies with an immense and growing following both in Africa and Asia.

Leveraging on an on-demand TV platform, Nollywood lovers around the world can watch the latest Nigerian movies by paying a fee of only $5 a month (about half compared to Netflix rates). And though perhaps expensive in terms of African median incomes, it is still a player with a virtual lock on the market up to now.

IROKOtv typically buys the digital rights to the movies from producers and film distributors and currently has a catalogue of over 5,000 films that goes out to more than 600,000 registered users. At present, IROKOtv is the world's largest online catalogue of Nollywood movies, with over 10,000 hours of original film and TV content that is streamed on-demand. It has also pioneered video-on-demand (VOD) in Africa and delivers the easiest, safest and most affordable means of watching the very best of Nollywood content.

IROKOtv stakes its future on patterning itself after the successful solid technology shifts and updates offered by its role model companies Netflix and Amazon.com…powering from streaming in different bandwidths to providing downloads in Africa, including 24/7 customer service and advanced tech support. And though hints of its going into its own purchase of intellectual property and content production are considered unfounded and premature, rumors nonetheless persist. And coop monies from African film commissions are readily available.

Nando's™ is not just an African food chain. It is now a global brand in more than 30 countries. (So the food has got to be good…and unique. In fact, it is both) Its secret is simple—and yet similar to other rapidly rising restaurant chains— delicious food with proprietary seasoning and very affordable prices.

HOME NATION: South Africa

INDUSTRY: Food & Beverages

Nando's likes to start with a legend about the "mythical flavor" of its tasty cuisine by making reference to Portuguese explorers discovering its unique foods and flavors centuries ago. According to the tale, the explorers (Vasco da Gama *et al.)* were lured by "the muse" to sail and under the warm sun, sample the redoubtable African Birds-Eye Chili or what is referred to as PERi-PERi (the Swahili—'Pili Pili', alluded to mean "fire in the mouth.")

But the real story emerged over 30 years ago with some rather innovative marketing and a great deal of local energy. Founded by Fernando Duarte and friend and business partner Robbie Brozin, Nando's began as a modest Portuguese eatery in the heart of Rosettenville, South Africa. And its reputation for great food that was a little out of the "norm" grew gradually into something of a phenomenon.

Since opening its first restaurant in 1987, Nando's has expanded to over a thousand locations on five continents. The secrets of its success may well lie in its exceptional media savvy and its "outside-the-box" creative. In fact, Nando's numerous provocative yet witty commercials, such as an ad featuring a dimwitted busty blonde and another depicting Zimbabwe "president for life" Robert Mugabe reflecting on the good times he enjoyed with fallen dictators such as Colonel Muammar Gaddafi and Saddam Hussein have made Nando's' flagship flame-grilled *Peri-Peri* chicken a hit among Africa's young and hip… if politically incorrect!

Nando's food formulations are "master chef concoctions" based on traditional Mozambiquan-Portuguese home-style meals and spices such as *Peri-Peri and* other signature dishes. The company also manufactures a range of sauces that are sold in Nando's restaurants and in supermarkets.

In 2010, *Advertising Age* magazine named Nando's as "One of the World's Top 30 Hottest Marketing Brands." Nando's also promises to allow anyone to eat free for life if they can prove they have been to all of Nando's 1000 restaurants.

Summary...

The portraits we have just given you are triumphs of substance over style in that they may appear on the surface to be glamorous and "high-profile." In truth, they represent a determination to succeed while playing "inside the lines" of their respective economies. They have a common cause and a set of goals consistent with most successful African businesses in that they are in it for the long term.

To nations and to a continent beset by centuries of "outside-in" economics and international corporate raiders, these are not only the faces of fierce national pride but also represent the wave of the future.

CHAPTER 5

Lions and Lunch:
Winning Africa Wins

It may seem categorical these days to observe that Africa is currently creating a larger rising class of empire builders than any other part of the world. Young African entrepreneurs are leading the way—it's not even close. There are a couple of theories being put forth about it, and both make sense. One is what career Africa journalist and author Dayo Olopade refers to as *Kanju*.

Kanju is a word in the Yoruba language that means, "to move quickly," or "respond rapidly," usually as a means of getting out of difficult circumstances. By Olopade's interpretation, it means *creativity that comes out of struggle*—African struggle in this case. We say it a bit more directly by simply observing that *Opportunity rises out of Difficulty.* Either way, they are two tracks to the same destination.

The other theory, the rapid rise of the new African entrepreneur, is one that tends to be both pragmatic and circumstantial. And it is this: *when you come from nothing, everything is an opportunity.* Of course, it takes a positive state of mind and a cultivated sense of self to make it happen.

Many have made their millions/billions by filling in the missing gaps in a nation's infrastructure—building, rebooting and providing basics that governments have ignored. Others have done so by recognizing the need and creating an immediate vehicle for the solution. A final group has capitalized on the fact that technology takes quantum leaps. Rather than follow the careful step-by-step advantages in calculator-computer-internet-iPhone-Cloud apps, chain of progress so characteristic of developed nations in the West, Africa has done it differently.

Africa has—by virtue of its primitive, technology-deprived and underprivileged population—been thrust from "stop" to "hyperdrive" by the situational demands of a

New Millennium. In many cases, especially in nations where the challenges to infra-structure are the greatest and 68% of the population is under 30, African Millennials, *Afrillennials,* have made the leap of faith from utter deprivation to the eFarm, Bitcoin-virtual networks and eUniversities of the world.

In a way this only seems logical, because—as the universe abhors a void—at last the black hole represented by the disenfranchisement of Africa's youth is finally being filled with a new bright light. The light comes by way of discovery, by that magic bullet of economic empowerment called *Choice.* When provided with choice, the right kind of choice, we like to believe as Jean Jacques Rousseau did that this species called *homo sapiens*—the human being—will do the right thing, the good thing, the sound constructive thing that builds a society. What it takes is a little thinking outside the restrictive frameworks that have been set for most of Africa's young, something born out of creative capitalism that we call *guerilla marketing.*

Guerilla Marketing vs. the Warlord

Perhaps we should use another metaphor, because the common cliché of Africa's younger generations has been one of a kind of monolithic militancy. The women are predominantly depicted as tribal, barefoot, gaunt, starving, sexually mutilated and lacking any formal education. Often their only way out of dire poverty is either through sweatshop labor or sexual slavery…or for the rare few (just over 12%), some kind of community outreach.

The men, little better off, are commonly portrayed as lean to the point of mal-nourishment, athletic, militant, dressed in paramilitary camouflage, combat boots and beret, wearing sunglasses, potentially violent and little more than teenage; in other words, warlords in the making.

Horrible depictions, and antiquated…or are they? When one thinks about it for a moment, terrorism in a social sense is born out of two issues—power and community. Young men—otherwise sub-literate, disenfranchised, jobless and lacking any viable group affiliation—are set upon by their counterparts, all of whom have food, shoes, clothing, membership in a group or gang…and the ultimate tool of social negotiation, an AK-47 (or something like it).

This doesn't' apply just to Africa. The same "male tribal matrix" can be superim-posed on Afghanistan, Syria or Iraq (or a dozen other nations from the Philippines to Mexico). And the profile is precise: average age 21.5; jobless; little or no education; limited prospects for the future. In the case of the African model, many of them have never had shoes before or a new shirt or a pair of pants that weren't hand-me-downs. Suddenly along comes something larger than themselves—an organization, an army, a gang, a counter-culture collective, a cult—something (anything!) that promises power and involvement, a cause, a sense of meaning…a franchise.

They're given a polo shirt, a new pair of Dockers, some Nikes and an ideology to embrace. They're promised food and a roof over their heads and something even more important: change! Some of them are pre-teen—9, 10, 11, 12—and their families can no longer afford to feed them. So, these otherwise powerless male children (impressionable and not yet formed) sign up and get radicalized later, programmed and educated because their own governments have chosen to deny them any chance at a future beyond the dull, deprived repetition of all that has gone before them.

It appears extreme. It is, by its very expression of that extremism, shameful. It represents less than 1% of the male population. But it is there—and very much a *sinister career option* in developing countries. And unless it is replaced with something of value, it is always that very dark alternative that some of our best and brightest embrace if for no other reason than a lack of any other viable options.

This summarizes the *Warlord* profile in a nutshell. It is the "employment pool" for Boko Haram, Al Shabaab, the Taliban, Al Qaeda, Abu Sayeff, ISIS, the FARC and a few dozen other terrorist groups around the globe—many Muslim, but some other fanatical religious and political ideologies as well. And these deadly socio-political pathologies thrive entirely too often because there is absolutely no infrastructure to offer an alternative. Power grids, transportation, basic utilities, public sanitation, food, water, health, welfare and especially education—all these and more are either difficult to come by or go missing entirely from their lives because the states fail their own citizens.

Smart nations with improved governance—such as Ghana, Botswana, Rwanda, Mauritius, the Seychelles and even South Africa—have grasped the importance of all this and have adjusted their infrastructures accordingly, each one with vastly improved secondary and tertiary educational programs, and career training in the process. Others—Kenya, Tanzania, Nigeria, Cote d'Ivoire, Ethiopia and many more—have encouraged the long strong arm of something called *Africapitalism* to come in and embrace their Millennials.* And they are doing it through a solid entrepreneurial strategy that perfectly fits the African model—what we now refer to as *Guerilla Marketing.*

By definition Guerilla Marketing is innovative, unconventional, and low-cost marketing techniques aimed at obtaining maximum exposure for a product. In a way it describes the way a product, service or new innovation may build its franchise with the consumer by creating immediate engagement, usually by non-traditional means.

---

* *Africapitalism* is a very appropriate term coined by Nigerian billionaire philanthropist, Tony O. Elumelu, and set into a very effective course of action. (See Chapter 12.)

In terms of the Sub-Sahara, traditional means—through media, television, radio and print advertising—are harder to come by. But due to Africa's maelstrom of youth, non-traditional means—the Internet and telecommunications—have become the norm. It is a norm that wasn't there before, the norm that successfully interweaves its way into our lives by being imaginative, accessible and ultimately affordable.

Good guerilla marketers always identify the need and then bring in the STICKS factor to set it up as quickly as possible.** But to apply STICKS, one first must undertake a little forensic research and get to the root of the need. Once they do, they are able to apply those basics as rules for survival. And since we are so enamored of acronyms, perhaps we can ring in with a set of investment strategies we call JOB-1.

1. *Just Do Your Homework (The Force of Forensic Marketing.)*

2. *One Size seldom fits all.*

3. *Be Ready to adapt, recover, and "disrupt" to accomplish your goals.*

4. *1% Rules. Understand it. Celebrate it. Apply it.*

Let us elaborate beginning with *Strategy 1: Just Do Your Homework.* It may come as a surprise to everyone reading this but… Most businesses or capital enterprises fail in the Sub-Sahara in particular because they come into it with a G 8 mindset that either assumes Africa has no modernity at all or that it is ready to take on every new technology. And they are wrong almost every time because, like the doctor who listens to a patient for 2 minutes and then throws them a bottle of pills, they haven't truly tried to understand the intrinsic challenges set down in front of them. They don't do any *forensic marketing,* and no one is immune to it.

By definition forensic marketing is the willingness to go into any demographic, nation, state or economic group and analyze the potentials—not only the risk/reward, but also what is missing, what is needed and what is oversold. But that takes work. It requires a willingness to be disappointed. And more important, it demands decision-making that goes to our *Strategy 3*—the readiness to adapt, recover and disrupt.

A recent example: MTN the exponentially successful South African tech giant went into war-ravaged, economically depleted South Sudan with a bold new $120 million IDIOS phone program and complementary apps and, inside of 18 months, found itself having to write the whole thing off because it could grow no sustainable customer base. The war-torn younger market just didn't have the discretionary income

---

** STICKS. Stability, Technology, Infrastructure, Credit, Kinetic resource, Strategic alliances

to buy into the projected growth, and more: the troubled government felt threatened by the influx of unregistered SIM cards, and subsequently blocked MTN from further expansion. Inside the same approximate time frame, China (able to do its homework) was able to come into Sudan, South Sudan and other East African nations with a cheap, battery-powered, tabletop egg and food cooker, and the locals scrambled [sic] to buy up every one.

In another example, we know by now that Safaricom is one of the most successful Internet, virtual retail shopping, and professional networking financial access apps in Africa. And its M-PESA program had practically taken over as virtual banking app of choice throughout East Africa. So it made all the sense in the world that M-PESA—the mobile money transfer superstar—would immediately catch on once it was introduced into South Africa at the end of 2014. Right?

Apparently no such thing occurred, except the stinging realization that the success of virtual money rises in inverse proportion to the accessibility of traditional sources such as ATM machines and easy access to branch banking. How could they anticipate such a shocking lack of market response? All Safaricom and M-PESA had to do was look in their own back yard and realize that the success of mobile money was related to its ability to provide freedom of movement where none existed before—that and the adaptive communications habits of Millennials. In conflict nations such as Somalia, Ethiopia, Tanzania and even Kenya where mobile money is successful, personal freedom of movement is often restricted and occasionally dangerous. In Rwanda, Botswana and Zambia where U-30 Millennials comprise 76% of the population, mobile money has become a way of life.

Strategy 2: One Size Seldom Fits All. It is the most common conundrum of Africa that we lump all the countries of the Sub-Sahara together in terms of demographic, infrastructure needs and basic market profiles. In truth, each nation of the 54 has arrived at its own state of political progress, social evolution and demographic mobility. FDI fund managers, investment bankers, and product to market specialists have their own personal checklist that enables them to see market gaps, which nations have them, and how to fill them in. More often than not they differ in what nation has openings in which industry. The following is something of a consensus and all of them differ dramatically in range of opportunity, need and potential.

Mozambique: As recently as 2015, *The African Retail Development Index* ranked Mozambique among the top 15 most bullish new retail markets in Sub-Sahara Africa. Despite a bumpy ratings slide between 2014 and 2015, an increased PPP (Purchasing Power Parity) among middle class Millennials has created a vibrant retail bubble that runs from health foods to fashion. A massive reverse diaspora prompted by newfound wells of natural gas along the coast have sent expatriates flooding the shopping malls in the Capital of Maputo. And rapid urbanization has hit secondary cities such as Pemba, Nacala, Nampula, Beira and Tete. This has caused a real-estate boom in major metropolitan areas. So retail property developers are experiencing a bonanza.

The question remains, are they doing it right? New homes and properties have to come with infrastructure—utilities, sanitation, plus access to roads and government facilities. In the past Mozambique has been notoriously slow to do this. So this recent "hot market" tag also gives those who run the country the opportunity to be responsible to its citizens.

AFRICAN RETAIL DEVELOPMENT INDEX (ARDI) TOP 15 COUNTRIES

2015 RANK	2014 RANK	COUNTRY	MARKET ATTRACTIVENESS	COUNTRY RISK	MARKET SATURATION	TIME PRESSURES
1	5	Gabon	20.2	13.0	20.7	12.1
2	8	Botswana	22.3	25.0	0.2	15.9
3	12	Angola	16.6	3.5	22.0	15.8
4	2	Nigeria	13.0	4.1	18.4	22.4
5	4	Tanzania	4.9	7.9	19.8	25.0
6	7	South Africa	25.0	22.7	0.0	9.6
7	1	Rwanda	5.7	11.2	21.6	18.4
8	3	Namibia	18.2	21.9	0.0	14.0
9	6	Ghana	10.9	11.3	21.6	8.5
10	14	Senegal	8.9	7.6	21.1	14.6
11	NR	Gambia	7.8	4.4	23.7	13.3
12	13	Zambia	8.8	8.4	13.5	18.2
13	NR	Côte d'Ivoire	4.7	2.9	25.0	14.5
14	10	Ethiopia	4.7	2.9	25.0	14.5
15	9	Mozambique	4.3	6.3	18.2	18.1

NOTE: RANKINGS FOR 2014 INCLUDE ONLY THE TOP 15.   SOURCE: A.T. KEARNEY ANALYSIS

Liberia: Since nearly 90% of Liberia's population of 4.5 million have no access to reliable power grids—and therefore no electric power— *Hydroelectricity* has become the flavor of the day. Not only does Liberia have a rather prolific coastline, it is also an estuary for six major rivers—the Mano, Saint Paul, Lofa, Saint John, Cestos and Cavalla—that send through over 60% of the country's water. This gives outgoing President Ellen Johnson Sirleaf an opportunity to actually earn her Nobel Peace Prize by leaving a legacy of real electric power for the rest of Liberia outside Monrovia, something her successor should appreciate, and the rest of the nation as well. Unfortunately, although its primary GDP output of less than $2 billion USD lies in shipping and as a seaport for major cruises, the country is notoriously poor. So the funding for hydroelectric power in this cash strapped nation is going to have to come either from foreign aid, or as an excellent FDI opportunity for the right company.

Guinea: In almost direct contradiction to the politics of exploitation that have plagued other nations in the Sub-Sahara, many of Guinea's resources remain virtually "underexplored." Attribute at least some of that to the fact that some of them were only recently discovered. Now, a great deal of FDI capital is flooding in to win the "hearts and mines" [sic] of this new mineral rich nation. Included in this run of recent discoveries have been large veins of bauxite, diamonds and gold. And in 2012 Guinea's Simandou mountain range was found to hold the world's largest untapped iron ore deposits worth billions of dollars—an actual mother lode. Of course, this kind of boom economy requires accelerated modernization, including transportation, communication and banking. A proposed $20 billion project to mine these mountains also includes the construction of a new 650 kilometer railway (about 400 miles) and a proper port of call to be built south of the capital at Conakry. This provides a stellar opportunity for Foreign Direct Investment that is actually willing to come in and help shore up the infrastructure and stay for the long term.

Gabon: It would just seem logical, if someone were willing to look past its oil and gas production for five minutes; but no one has… yet. Apparently, this deceptively cash-rich country is notoriously poor when it comes to looking after the basics—like feeding its own people. About 73% of Gabon's 1.6 million population is involved in agriculture, but output is scandalously inadequate. According to the government, the same agriculture that involves 73% of the workforce accounts for just 5% of GDP. That means, despite its highly arable land, 90% of Gabon's finished food products are imported. Gabon spends $500 million importing food and reselling it at "import prices" to consumers too poor to pay for it. The government is seeking partnerships with private investors not only for its agriculture but also its related agro-industries to boost its contribution to the GDP to at least 20% by 2025.

Four different African countries, four areas of massive potential for Foreign Direct Investment—if you are willing to look. What too often happens is a complete disconnect between traditional channels of foreign aid and foreign direct investment. Groups such as World Bank, IMF and UNAID look at a nation's challenges with sloppy oversight and either fund them into notorious kleptocracies or deny them altogether if certain (MCC) criteria aren't met. FDI conglomerates and financial institutions, even though they watch the trends, are too timid to do their own marketing forensics. So once again we encourage you to return to the JOB at hand: if you are an investment group or an industry that is willing to examine the demographic, make the right decisions and remember that challenge creates opportunity, you can thrive in these markets when no one else is willing to do so.

Strategy 3: Be ready to adapt, recover and disrupt to accomplish your goals. It is a truism to note that some concepts, innovations and technologies—even when they seem like a perfect fit for the need—often encounter resistance and a constant need to retool.

Since the number one issue in the Sub-Sahara remains one of power generation just to support the basics of life, it would seem logical that you could never overshoot the market by offering inexpensive localized power grids that poor rural (and even urban) families and businesses can afford.*** This defines capitalism at the Bottom of the Pyramid. And his well-structured eponymous book, *The Fortune at the Bottom of the Pyramid* (Eradicating Poverty Through Profits), C.K. Prahalad put forth a viable capitalist strategy called BOP investing, so there would seem to be many ways that you could apply this model and have it be accepted everywhere.†

*** Renewable energy sources are the obvious answer. Wind, solar, thermal and hydroelectric are technically unlimited and utterly self-generating. But the vehicles by which we may utilize them are underdeveloped or non-existent. So, until we remove the politics of energy from our social conversation, we will be held hostage by energy companies that keep power just cheap enough to allow the corporation or government to survive, while the forgotten masses on the fringes of every nation continue to struggle.

† BOP game plans are simple and yet effective. What they simply tell us is that the best way to build so-called challenged markets is from the bottom up. And that is accomplished by treating Africa's poor as customers—extending them credit, purchasing power, exposure to variety of life and (for the first time ever) offering them choices. It is the psychology of fulfillment that goes beyond mere support in the traditional sense. It is providing them a sense of self—something few if any have ever had before.

Embracing that strategy, when a company came along like US-based E+CO in 1994 that offered low cost, block energy contracts to pilot markets in select developing nations, it would have logically seemed like a match made in heaven. It is conservatively estimated that in Africa in 2016, nearly 500 million people still live without any electric power (nearly 80 million in Nigeria alone).

In 1994, when E + CO was funded for a pilot project by The Rockefeller Foundation that number was more like 700 million, about 50% of the entire "utility-deprived" portion of the world population. So bringing power grids in small blocks to rural African areas, villages and neighborhoods would seem to be something that would experience a welcome mat everywhere it was presented and that the needs would be uniform. What they quickly discovered was that there were no absolutes where rural energy needs were concerned and that energy demands in small farm communities, especially in developing nations did not have "a one-size-fits-all solution," to the problem. So there were many issues they had to deal with.

First, in parts of rural Africa, people could not even pay electric power because even $5 or $10 a month would represent as much as one third of their annual per capita income. Second, in cases where small local governments were willing, they could not necessarily subsidize the "modest" block services. Third, in areas where E + CO could afford to set up the power grids, there were few if any assurances that they would be maintained or operated with any degree of consistency. Fourth, some kinds of energy sources were more plentiful in some areas than others; so one had to adapt between finite, basic energy grids and those that might be considered renewable. Finally, giving the small power grids away would quickly bankrupt the project.

What E + CO finally realized is that it would be able to function best by supporting companies committed to renewable energy sources (solar, wind, hydroelectric and thermal), and through loans to small businesses and "energy entrepreneurs" in various areas throughout the world, especially those energy challenged pockets of developing countries. By 2012, their *adaptation business model* had funded, financed or otherwise provided structure for 250 different energy enterprises all over the world—mostly those committed to renewable energy sources—activating more than 300,000 people and reaching into two-dozen countries. By that time, they had established active field offices in San Jose, Costa Rica, Bangkok (Thailand), Dar es Salaam (Tanzania), Accra (Ghana) and Johannesburg (South Africa).

Now, having reinvented themselves into a new incarnation—Persistent Energy Partners (PEP)—the group continues to support energy entrepreneurs with loans, equity investments, business development services, and technical assistance

Of course the bottom line, is that E + CO went in with one business model or paradigm in mind and quickly realized that it wouldn't work. So yes, they applied our *Item 2* as part of their philosophy. (Further evidence that our JOB-1 overlaps as a market-measuring tool.) They also applied the *Law of Disruption* that I made note of in Chapter 2. And it applies in today's global marketplace more than ever before. Simply stated, upon review, it means the need to make changes. Even when you think you have a lock on a market, a demographic, or a business model, you have to take complacency out of the equation.

Strategy 4: The 1% Rule. This rule is simple but often overlooked. The 1% are the difference makers; they run everything. The 1% are the disrupters. They're the ones who refuse to accept things as they are, and they're the ones who make changes. 1% of the population controls 99% of the wealth because they're the only ones who decided to find out how things really work. In America, the 1% that failed Democrat presidential candidate Bernie Sanders denounced as the over-privileged wealthy are notably those who earn an average of $325,000 a year. Many are e small family businesses who very often work from 60 to 100 hours a week to achieve that level of income. And they pay 22% of all the taxes in the United States of America.

In developing nations, the 1% are often those young men who countervail their circumstances by joining rebel armies or terrorist groups if for no other reason than their refusal to accept things as they are. The 1% are also those who put themselves through schools, work three jobs, and get degrees, leave their nations in a program of educational diaspora only to return later and form a business that makes a difference. The 1% fight for political causes, make protests, serve in the military, and are willing to give up their lives for what they believe in, and will do what it takes to make a difference.

In business it is the 1% who find new ways to innovate—who rise in down markets and act upon opportunities rather than wait for help, aid and subsidies— and work to make a difference in their societies.

What FDI funders and financiers need to do—rather than look solely at general market indicators—is to embrace the principal of forensic marketing and examine the inner workings in countries, in the companies that are making a difference or those that have new ideas and that intangible called passion. They need to dig deep, and they need to embrace them. In Africa, these people are everywhere. For those investors willing to undertake due diligence, they stand out like flowers in a storm. That is what savvy entrepreneurs have learned that others have not. The Question remains, which one are you? And what is your course of action?

New Markets. Young Lions

A $31 Billion Passion for Fashion. African fashion never ceases to make a major splash wherever it is shown. One of its signature statements has always been its daring use of color—from tamarind oranges to effervescent blues. They were given an unimpeachable international advocate in 2013 through the (former) First Lady of the United States when Michelle Obama, during her Africa tour, wore a top by Nigerian designer Maki Oh.

Maki Oh (full name Maki Osakawa) is a thirty-something designer who is more or less the unofficial spokeswoman for the Lagos school of design—a style she embraces readily. According to Maki, Nigerians are born with true grit and a competitive spirit. And she spoke about it in an interview recently: "It's

A Jewel in the 'Town'

Rule No. 1 of starting a business: "Name it after yourself," Henry Ford once advised. "That way, no one can confuse your intention."

When she started her jewelry design company in 2012, Cape Town-based artist Katherine-Mary Pichulik did just that with her brand—PICHULIK(see www.Pichulik.com). And applying a great deal of talent and innovation, it didn't take her long to capture the imagination of a strong rising and affordable line of bespoke jewelry and accessories handcrafted in "The Mother City." Katherine Mary's strategy is simple: creating bold accessories by tapping into the intimate relationships so many women have with their jewelry, including their personal experience, family traditions, and heirlooms.

Trained artist and Patissier Katherine-Mary Pichulik, started PICHULIK in Sept 2012 after a trip around India.

Along the way, Pichulik believes that, "Being an entrepreneur in my twenties in South Africa is exciting because it gives me agency to cultivate a new conscious way of doing business, based on sharing and kindness." Being young with no dependents or high personal expenses, she is enjoying all the flexibility and discretionary revenues of a young single African entrepreneur, free to use her capital and energy to be creative, innovative, break new markets and empower others. She feels South Africa has room for growth and endless possibilities for young people. "There is a 'Phoenix rising' feeling of hustling, bootlegging and a community of young courageous creative Millennials forging a new South African identity in the global marketplace.

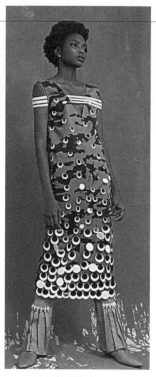

Maki Oh design.

in our DNA to want to be the best at everything we do. I guess it's our time for fashion *now*."

Maki's new line, *Man Repeller,* is an irony of feminine self-expression centered, for a change, entirely on the woman and how she feels about herself. One might even define it as introspective fashion that celebrates not only ones femininity but also an embrace of native fabrics. Maki Oh believes that the woman wearing her fashions digs deeper than the mere physical, because she is a woman who projects her whole being into everything she does. And that extends to the styles she wears.

Another major fashion line is KISUA, a Ghana based fashion group that not only funds designer collaborations through the KISUA Designer Fund, but also provides financial support to African designers by paying a portion of every sale from collaborative collections directly to the designer. A full-blown conglomerate KISUA has established large scale manufacturing capabilities set up to assure "the seamless delivery of African fashion to the world." KISUA prides itself in working hard to create economic opportunities for women—from women designers, to fabric suppliers and a large staff of employees, CEO Sam Mensah Jr. declares that we are inspired by the strength and spirit of African women.

In South Africa, Tanzanian-born Anisa Mpungwe is the locus of power behind a hot new women's wear label called Loin Cloth & Ashes. Perhaps "hotter than new," LC&A has been around for nearly a decade by now, evidenced by the fact that in 2008, Anisa became the first black woman to win the New Talent Award from *Elle* Magazine. "My views, conflicts and triumphs affect how I conceptualize my clothes." says Mpungwe. Noted for an unapologetic attitude Anisa Mpungwe believes the continent is not, nor should it ever be, afraid of patterns and colors. "That's the one thing that we do in our sleep, so we use it to be louder amongst our foreign friends."

All these new trends and more have been captured along with a dozen other fashion lines in a hot new book called *Fashion Cities Africa*, that features everything from the elegant eveningwear to and street styles of four major fashion hubs—Johannesburg, Lagos, Nairobi and Casablanca (in Morocco).

The book's editor, Hannah Azieb Pool announced recently that the book will be the first major exhibition of contemporary African fashion to be showcased in the UK as well as other major fashion centers in the world. And she goes all the way from featuring African links to LVMH to giving tailoring tips and fabric choices that help the new entrepreneur navigate the gold mines and minefields of African fashion.[††]

The Bottom Line on Fashion in Africa...

The African fashion industry, already $31.5 billion, is blowing up. There are more than 300 vibrant, bullish, imaginative fashion boutiques, fabric manufacturers and very creative SME's all over the Sub-Sahara. They're networking, interacting and growing exponentially. Especially noteworthy is the fact that this business empowers women. More than any other business on the continent—for women—this is the next big thing!

Meanwhile, down on the farm...
a battle for the soul of African Agriculture

Of course farming is not a new market; and yet it is. Agriculture is the second oldest industry in the world. And yet nothing needs new technology and sensible distribution more desperately than this oft ignored African stepchild. Because up to now the more things change, the more they stay the same.

Despite all the innovation and new technology in the Sub-Sahara, 61% of the population still spend most of their lives in agriculture—about two-thirds of those small subsistence farms of 2.5 hectares or less. Actually, were it not for South Africa ruining the curve, the real number would be much closer to 70%.

Then there are the economic realities of production: Farming contributes less than 24% of the GDP in most countries (and only 5% in nations like Gabon, Chad and Namibia [the latter due to the Kalahari desert]). That means we're talking primarily about subsistence farming at less than $1.25 a day. The good news is that there

---

†† LVMH is the acronym for Paris based fashion and lifestyle powerhouse inspired by industry icons Louis Vuitton, Moet and Hennessy. Included in this high-end lifestyle conglomerate are 70 different quality houses devoted to fashion and clothing, watches and jewelry, wine and spirits, perfume and cosmetics and selected retail. LVMH has become the new symbol of excellence and social responsibility especially in the EU, and any affiliation with it is a market maker for new enterprises.

are all kinds of power brokers working to better the plight of the African farmer. The bad news is that they can't quite seem to agree on how to go about it. And people of influence with the best of intentions are divided into two schools of thought about how to accomplish it.

James Mwangi

School One. The Big Gun GMO Connection. By any standard of measurement Equity Group Holdings Limited, CEO James Mwangi is an African hero. The Kenyan heads the banking group with the largest customer base in the Sub-Sahara—Equity Bank—and it has become that way for a reason. It empowers its customers, especially those who need credit. And Mwangi's visionary thinking put into practice prompted his well-deserved Ernst & Young Entrepreneur of the Year Award for Africa in 2012.

Based in the Great Lakes region of East Africa, EGHL and Mwangi have recently turned their investment power to help fund, empower and subsidize East African farmers.

According to Mwangi, empowering small African farmers goes beyond just extending credit (although it certainly starts there). That has to be immediately followed by showing small famers how to build capacity so they can learn to use credit appropriately. Then Mwangi and EGHL have put together a plan to show farmers how to build linkages—teaching them how to hook up with the chains of distribution all the way to post-harvest produce managers, occasionally all the way to finished product. One of the secrets according to Mwangi is networking them to warehouses with a "chit" system, so farmers are not forced to sell all their produce at the time of harvest—usually at rock bottom prices. With a "chit system" farmers can go to a produce manager and get a warehouse receipt that they can cash in as a credit once the final sale is made.

Over the last six years, Mwangi's Equity Group Holdings has been able to use its credit leverage to empower over 460,000 small African farmers to advance from subsistence farming to full agribusinesses. It is the Mwangi Group's belief that, if agriculture in Africa is going to move to the next level it will have to be an across-the-board buildup of *1) productivity, 2) quality,* and *3) value addition.*

It is an excellent marketing and distribution plan that EGHL has been putting into motion by working with groups like AGRA (Alliance for the Green Revolution in Africa). It is directly tied to, and funded by the Bill and Melinda Gates Foundation, and it comes with something of a hitch. That "hitch" (and there always seems to be one) lies in the fact that the AGRA initiatives have been completely coopted by subsidies underwritten through Monsanto and Gargill—the number one and number two progenitors of GMO laced foods in the world. Environmental groups like "Voices From Africa" have denounced the hookup for myriad reasons. But so far the caravan moves on.

The debate over GMO foods may rage on for decades. But in terms of empowering African farmers, they translate into robust production, great variety and an ability to mass-market. The negatives are the Faustian pact that is often made with large seed, fertilizer and pesticide manufacturers and the addictive cycle it creates—both in terms of dependency on one group and possible exploitation of food chains on a global scale that (some believe) may throw carcinogens into the food chain.

Ultimately, there is no definitive answer, but there are healthy alternatives—organic farming being among them.

School Two. Organic Farming—the Uganda Model.[†††] Uganda has occasionally been referred to as "The Pearl of Africa" due at least in part to its reputedly lush farmland. Innately, it has a larger successful agricultural base than most other countries in the Sub-Sahara. And at present, Uganda has arguably the fastest growing organic certified plots of farmland in Africa.

Due to Uganda's exceptional topography and soil variations, a wide range of organic products can be grown in the country. Ugandan crops currently grown and sourced organically include cotton, coffee, sesame (simsim), dried fruit (pineapples, apple bananas, mangoes, jack-fruit), fresh fruits (pineapple, apple bananas, passion fruits, avocadoes, papaya (pawpaw), ginger, vanilla, cocoa, shea nuts, bird eyed chilies, dried hibiscus, honey and bark cloth. These products are exported to Europe, USA, Asia and other parts of Africa among others. The numbers of organic exporters in Uganda has been growing and are fully certified or in conversion, from internationally accredited certifying bodies operating in Uganda. That's a large crop base under "conventional" growing practices. In terms of organic foodstuffs—and especially in terms of Africa—it is nothing short of remarkable.

This didn't just happen overnight. Over the last decade especially, Uganda has made "all the right moves" when it comes to transforming conventional agricultural production into an organic farming system. And it's not something that is easily done because "Certified Organic" is not a label that is easy to come by.

[†††] Organic Agriculture is officially determined by the *Codex Alimentarius Commission*. The CAC is a holistic production management system that promotes agro-ecosystem health and biodiversity while it specifically prohibits the use of synthetic drugs, fertilizers and pesticides.

What has turned out to be most exceptional feature of Uganda's organic agriculture has been a uniformity of commitment. As is often a contradiction in some sectors, all the stakeholders in the organic farm model saw the value of the program and committed to it up front. From the Ministries of Trade and Agriculture to the Uganda National Bureau of Standards, from private institutions (all under the umbrella of NOGAMU) everyone caught the vision and stayed the course. These groups also include farmers associations, export companies, NGOs and even agricultural schools inside private universities—all buying into this unique public/private partnership.

Currently, Uganda has over 400,000 internationally certified organic farmers, including the first and second largest certified farms both globally and in Africa. Uganda has the world's 13th-largest land area under organic agriculture production and the most in Africa. By 2013, Uganda had around 350,000 hectares of land under organic farming, covering more than 2 percent of agricultural land. And there are 44 certified export companies that do international business with them. Member organizations are over 500 inside Uganda as well as many outside the country. The value of trade at the source, less organic turnover, is currently coming in at a modest $37 million USD per annum, while increased demand for organic products from Uganda has now pushed it up toward $700 million.

As a significant producer of organic products, Uganda benefits from an important source of export earnings and revenue for farmers, farm conglomerates and farm cooperatives, as well as the farm-to-market networks they support.

The lovely irony in all this comes with the fact that the government of Uganda, flawed in so many other ways, has managed to get it very right where its "organic" agro-business is concerned. The question that remains is this: Can they spread the seed of this impeccable way to approach the healthiest possible farm-to-market connection—one that seems a win-win for everyone?

Agri-business in Africa: The Bottom Line

No one denies the fact that agriculture and agribusinesses in Africa could benefit from some major innovations in growing and cultivation, credit, modernization, networking and marketing logistics—not to mention some highly improved farm-to-market techniques.

Starting with the newfound empowerment given to small farms, improvements seem to be in the works. But there are two highly divided schools of thought driving each. Given the legacy of impoverishment that has gone before us in Africa, it would appear that either would be welcome. And at present in the Sub-Sahara, there seems to be room for both.

Welcome to Africa 2.0:
The Business of Disruptive Diaspora

If there is one term that sends out a double meaning to most young African entrepreneurs it is this: Diaspora.

Diaspora has a system of etymological origins. Currently, in common usage, it has the following meanings: *a) the movement, migration or scattering of a people away from their established ancestral homeland; b) the people actually settled from their homelands into new countries; c) the place where these people have settled.*

The word gets tossed about a lot these days, especially as regards its implications in Africa over the last 60 years or so. As it stands, diaspora can signify a very good thing, or a very bad thing. And your attitude will determine the outcome: Is the glass half-empty? Or is it half-full?

In modern African terms it signified flight from a nation such as Nigeria, South Africa, Angola or Rwanda, often in a context of refugees from political or civil conflict. Later, it came to mean African flight from deprived circumstances to seek a better life in Europe or North America, and eventually the return from those worlds empowered and ready to contribute to African society. Finally, in the nuance of rapprochement, it signifies a new kind of attraction from outside sources.

Apparently if you are South African Mamadou Toure, capitalizing on diaspora is a new kind of industry, because it means bringing back our best and brightest to combine global knowledge, expertise and direct investment into the African culture.

Toure is the founder of Africa 2.0—a pan-African organization that brings together young African business leaders who share a common vision of the continent's future. And they do it by implementing sustainable solutions to accelerate Africa's development. Toure calls Africa 2.0 a social

Mamadou Toure

contract between the private sector, civil society and governments. In effect it is a businesses think tank that 2.0 likes to refer to as a "D-ink Tank," meaning they not only come up with great new entrepreneurial ideas but also apply active game plans to fund them and put them into motion.

They do this by developing relationships with those who share a collective vision for Africa. That shared vision includes a commitment to finding and implementing sustainable solutions that will advance the development of the continent in geometric progressions. At present Africa 2.0 has 600+ member businesses and "visionary entrepreneurs." And the momentum is growing steadily.

Africa 2.0 was created to promote the idea of a free trade area that would span 26 of the 44 countries officially in the Sub-Sahara. Working as a connecting rod between governments and business, Africa 2.0's strategy is based on four core elements: *inclusive growth, the upgrading of infrastructure, an enabling environment, and the "uplifting" of Africans.*

One of the ways in which Toure and Africa 2.0 do this is by working with the IFC (International Finance Corporation) to gain funding and start up capital for deserving new business entities. An investment-funding group that has spun itself out of the World Bank, the IFC has managed over the years to reincarnate as a mobilizer of scarce capital especially in places that experience critical constraints in finance, infrastructure, employee skills, and the regulatory environment. This, as it happens, perfectly fits the pan-African profile. So, in this case, the prospect of the two bodies working together is a match well made.

In addition to its occasional partnerships with the IFC, Africa 2.0 also works to empower Africa's youth through entrepreneurship with its Start Up Africa and mentorship programs. And they are rebranding Africa through sponsorship of a number of events, including Africa 2.0's Annual Leadership Symposium. And since 2012, the Annual Symposium has successfully brought Africa's movers and shakers together for 3 days of celebration, co-creation and community building.

Summary

One of the difficulties in trying to put ones arms around the temblor that is the African economy comes with the realization that it's easy to become simply overwhelmed by the potential of it. By now you're probably drowning in acronyms, each seemingly more meaningful than the next. We have AGRA and the IFC. We have EGHL and BOP strategies.

Well…rather than being daunted by them (we have a Glossary for that), it's best to streamline and simplify. Just remember the JOB-1 mandate, and you can apply it to every single business we have mentioned. Africa is replete with possibilities. It is also fraught with pitfalls. Knowing how to recognize them, to distinguish between them and then apply the proper strategies makes all the difference between success and failure, between vision and stagnation, between staying stuck in old paradigms or disrupting your way into new ones.

Stay the course…

CHAPTER 6

The Two Africas:
The North-South Dichotomy

On the surface the world impression of an Africa divided into two separate sub-continents has real logic in it.

First there is the natural land barrier called the Sahara Desert. At 9,400,000 square kilometers (3,600,000 square miles), it is roughly the size of China. Through its various patches and fingers of land, the world's largest desert runs from the Red Sea in the East to the Atlantic Ocean in the West. It cuts across 10 nations and makes up the majority of the real estate in six of them, including Egypt, Libya, Algeria, Niger, Mali, Mauritania and (the contested) Western Sahara. More than 25% of this "desert of deserts" is comprised of sand dunes, many as high as the average football field is long (about 120 m) and sporting surface temperatures during the day that are close to 140° Fahrenheit.

Since more than 88% of this broad apron of sand is unfit for human habitation, what economic benefit it might possess remains virtually untapped. And basically it is very much like separating two continents by a broad expanse of ocean that is simply unnavigable.

On the surface, the Sahara—or very small portions of it—offers the single benefit to outsiders of massive energy production. And yes! It does kick out its fair share of petroleum and natural gas production, which make up more than 70% of the industrial output of nations like Libya and Algeria. Additionally, potential reserves in the protectorate of Western Sahara are crippled by civil strife that has been going on for decades—as well as the persistent politics of energy. That leads us to the elephant in the room—Solar Power, or the lack of it.

To anyone with two entrepreneurial brain cells to rub together, the Sahara Desert is one big solar panel, so much so, it was recently determined that the right channeling of Solar Power from the Sahara would be enough to provide electrical power for parts of North Africa and a great deal of Western Europe.

Needless to say, such a venture was considered and set in motion back in 2009 under the aegis of a German-based conglomerate called Desertec. For a projected budget of €400 billion ($560 billion), the venture was to pipe clean solar power from the Sahara Desert through a Mediterranean super-grid to energy-hungry European countries, including Spain, Portugal, Italy, France and Germany. Supported by the German Energy Ministry and key underwriters such as Siemens and Bosch, the venture appeared to be the next big thing in modern alternative energy breakthroughs. Other major industrial backers seemed to line up on the runway, and big corporations and major governments were salivating over the notion of a "green energy" Europe.

Then some nasty realities set in. North African governments, seeing their principal sources of income (in Oil and Gas) threatened, blocked construction of panel positions and energy centers, tied them up in red tape and unnecessary restrictions. (As the core of this, Spain, due to its constant feuds with Morocco, refused to be the energy pipeline to the rest of Europe. So a lack of cooperation became the stigma for the entire fragile "co-venture.") Without a way to route energy to Europe, logistics became a nightmare, as did a shortage of skilled laborers. And after 3 years, not one energy generator had been successfully set up. By 2011 there were still none operational.

Then came the "Arab Spring" and the overthrow of not one but three major governments in four months—Tunisia, Libya and (especially) Egypt, while a fourth (Algeria) barely survived intact. Engineered by the Muslim Brotherhood, it shook both Northern Africa and Europe to their foundations where renewable energy was concerned. And even the German Economic Ministry and several key investors withdrew their support.

Falsely labeled as impractical, Solar Energy once again goes begging for sponsors. And as long as new fields of fossil fuels continue to be discovered and prices are conspicuously kept down, cheap, the world's largest energy anvil will remain untapped—because there is apparently not enough "profit" in harnessing the Sun.

In its way, "The Sahara Solar Metaphor" defines the paradox of Northern Africa. First, it is primarily a one-industry economy—oil and natural gas. Second, it is ethnically weighted more strongly toward Caucasian (Semitic and Hamitic), Berber and Maghreb peoples—about 80%.

Historically, the seafaring civilizations of the Phoenicians, Greeks, Romans, Muslims and others migrated across the Mediterranean Sea onto the Northern Coasts of the modern nations of Libya, Tunisia and Morocco. So the cultures of North Africa became much more closely tied to Southwestern Asia and Europe than Sub-Saharan Africa. Due to the influx primarily of British and French Colonialism (and to some extent Spain and Italy), it is highly focused on European and Mediterranean influences. Six of its seven nations are heavily rooted in Islam and, to be sure, Northern Africa is a major part of the Islamic world. The root language of Northern Africa is Arabic. And for the most part either French or English are the second languages of the home countries. Mind you, none of these characteristics are self-condemning in and of themselves.

For us to make these observations implies a kind of bias that Northern Africa lacks diversity, that it is some kind of socio-economic monolith. And nothing could be further from the truth. So at this point it is important to make a quick sketch of each of the major North African Nations by taking them in descending order—with the largest and most strategically significant first.

Egypt
(Arab Republic of Egypt)

Since some of its logs and records go back more than 10,000 years, Egypt is arguably the oldest recorded civilization in the Eastern Hemisphere. With roots that deep, it is certainly North Africa's most stable point of reference. Bridging the legendary fertility of the Nile basin and the Sinai Peninsula making the Suez Canal the only viable port of transit between the Mediterranean and Red Sea, it is the only nation of Africa that is literally a dweller on two continents—the other (technically) being Asia (once referred to as Asia Minor).

In its way, Egypt is also Africa's most balanced nation above and below the Sahara. The fertile Nile Valley takes it deep into the African psyche. And it has the broadest racial and religious diversity of any North African nation. Although Islam is the official religion of Egypt, the nation also honors the beliefs of Coptic Christians who comprise nearly 22%, or 18 million of its 94 million people.

Egypt is the third most populous nation in Africa (after Nigeria and Ethiopia), and recently nudged South Africa out of its spot as the second highest GDP of any African nation with $330.7 billion. Its average income is around $5,955 a year, ranking it #12 on the Continent in terms of quality of life. About 75% of Egypt's 90 million inhabitants live on or near the fertile Nile Valley, and half dwell in urban areas such as Cairo, Alexandria and Port Said.

Egypt has fairly well-balanced economy with its principal exports being natural gas, and non-petroleum products such as ready-made clothes, cotton textiles, medical and petrochemical products, citrus fruits, rice and dried onion, and more recently cement, steel, and ceramics. Egypt's cotton is still considered some of the finest in the world, and its strategic position as a seaport and traffic corridor between the Mediterranean Sea through the Red Sea, and around the Horn of Africa to the Indian Ocean provide it with a great deal of political leverage and economic pressure.

In recent years, the Egyptian government has invested in communications and physical infrastructure. Still somewhat reliant on foreign subsidies, Egypt still receives nearly $3 billion in aid annually from the United States, and it continues to be one of the largest beneficiaries of foreign aid on the Continent. (Most consider this something of a bad habit that has created too many codependent relationships between African nations and foreign interests. Still, the prospect of "free money" is often too tempting to resist.) Apart from that, Egypt's economy mainly relies on three sources of income: tourism, remittances from Egyptians working abroad and revenues from the Suez Canal.

The birthplace of the politically aggressive Muslim Brotherhood (in 1928), Egypt had nonetheless maintained a solid secular republican "autocracy" that grew to great prominence under Gamal Abdul Nasser from 1952 to the early 1970s.

Egypt has taken a hit lately in terms of its Index Economic Freedom ranking, mainly due to the military coup in 2014, overthrowing "popularly elected" President Mohammed Moursi by head of the Egyptian Armed forces, Abdel Fattah el-Sisi, who later ran unopposed for President.

That was overturned somewhat in 2016 due to the infusion of foreign capital. And once again it's China to the rescue. Looking upon Egypt as a "buy" and encouraged by the new political regime (draconian but stable), the China Fortune

Land Company announced a $20 billion investment in Egypt—22% of China's "Africa Budget" for all of that fiscal year.

The de facto overthrow appears much worse than it was, since Moursi had virtually corrupted all Egyptian government, allowing open public oppression of Coptic Christians and all other non-Muslim religions, setting virtual storm troops of Muslim Brotherhood activists loose on the streets of Cairo and other Egyptian cities. He had, for the first time in 60 years, made access to the Suez a political bone-of-contention. Moursi had further openly allied with radical Islamic groups such as Hamas, and had used Sharia Law as a court of first resort in a blatant attempt to hijack the Egyptian constitution and establish a virtual Caliphate. The Moursi regime was threatening to throw the delicate balance of the Middle East into chaos when the rational wing of the national assembly encouraged el-Sisi to step in.

Not surprisingly, Egypt's human rights rankings have fallen precipitously due to President el-Sisi's repression of militant Muslim groups and all political dissenters. And his secret privatization of government-controlled industries is neither very secretive nor very popular. It is a short-term fix for the government's cash-flow problems but a long-term nightmare for the Egyptian employment horizons. Since the Government in Egypt is the nation's number one employer, the ranks of those going on the dole will soon swell in near geometric progressions.

Bottom Line

Now somewhat back in political balance—despite some pretty savage coverage by the Western press—Egypt is able to work its true influence on the rest of Africa as well as the Middle East in terms of that all too often lightly regarded intangible called *Civilization*. In fact the ancient culture has for so long been a source of political and economic stability that it was only until the years of 2012-2016 that the dwellers on two continents came to realize just how much they relied upon it and how they had—somewhat mistakenly—taken it for granted. China may be its saving grace; only time will tell. And like Egypt itself, the economy remains on shifting sands.

Current Market Indicator: Hold!

Egypt is often as mysterious as the Sphinx. And although its political future might be more stabilized, economically at least, it seems to be heading South and looking to the Sub-Sahara and its Arab neighbors to shore up its commercial markets.

ALGERIA

(People's Democratic Republic of Algeria)

Algeria has traditionally been a regional rival to Egypt but without any of Egypt's political consistency or cultural bloodlines. Richer than any other North African nation in natural resources, especially valuable minerals, it is known to have considerable reserves of iron ore, copper, zinc, mercury, antimony, lignite (coal) and phosphate—all these and more being manned and mined out of a nation whose topography is 90% desert wasteland.

At about three times the size of Alaska, Algeria is Africa's largest nation in terms of area, and (due to its reserves of oil and natural gas) is its fourth richest economy. Algeria has the second largest oil reserves on the continent (after Libya) and the 17th most lucrative oil fields in the world. It supplies large amounts of natural gas reserves to Europe, and energy exports are the backbone of its economy. With an annual Gross Domestic Production (GDP) of $214 billion USD, Algeria has a per capita income of just over $7,000. And Sonatrach, Algeria's government-owned oil company is the largest single corporation in Africa.

All this points to the illusion of stability, when in fact Algeria has historically been anything but that. Even now, Algeria maintains the largest defense budget in Africa and arguably the largest and most well equipped military. Going back to the USSR's logistical and political support of Algeria's move toward independence against French Colonialism in 1961, Russia remains Algeria's longest standing political ally, and that "alliance" may have helped it survive the Arab Spring of 2012 more or less intact.

After Algeria won its independence from France in 1962, the fledgling nation adopted a "socialist" regime loosely fashioned after the Soviet model of government. Eventually that proved to be an abysmal failure of corruption, mismanagement and a repressive series of governments that have somehow stumbled into the 21st century almost purely on the basis of the nation's rich natural resources.

Due to broad political corruption and a highly inconsistent judicial system, the rule of law in Algeria remains fragile at best. Decades of political uncertainty do not seem to have abated. And Algeria's perpetually "statist" regime has perennially blocked full integration into the world economy.

After a generation of civil strife and constant agitation from fractionated splinter groups inside Islamist parties, Algeria finally appeared to have stabilized in 1999 and seemed to level out what had been one of the most troubled political histories of any nation in the world. President Abdelaziz Bouteflika, sworn into office in 2000 (in what was a token political race) has survived through four election cycles and still appears to have a steady hand on a government that has at least flattened out in terms of what had previously been 40 years of chaotic socialism. By 2004, Bouteflika won another, more ecumenical run for office, and shortly thereafter instituted The Charter for Peace and Economic Reconciliation. Granting an amnesty to all Islamic and socialist splinter groups, the referendum did little to ease the ongoing restrictions on either civil disobedience or human rights.

Having safely withstood the violent influences of the Arab Spring that had spilled over from Tunisia and Libya and finally putting an end to two decades of "emergency" restrictions on civil liberties, President Bouteflika stood for a fourth term despite apparently having survived a stroke. Then in 2015 the government, feeling the pressure from additional Islamic agitation slammed the lid back down on dissent of any kind. So, any stability that Algeria enjoys today has come at the expense of its reputation for political equanimity.

Due to serious ISIL and radical jihadist incursions in the south of the country and travel warnings to foreign visitors in effect since 2016, Algeria is undergoing its fair share of heavy-handed governance and explicit instability. Consistently inconsistent as a force in Northwest Africa, it has taken a pretty severe hit according to The Index of Economic Freedom. In just the last year, the IEF has dropped Algeria from a 154th to 172nd out of 185 nations in terms of personal freedom and human rights. At the same time, it ranks it as very high in terms of fiscal stability and "economic independence," and yet in terms of being business friendly, it is rather begrudging of foreign investment. Stopping short of being downright protectionist, Algeria is an active member of OPEC, the United Nations, the African Union and the Arab Union. But it has never joined the WTO (World Trade Organization), or any of the other African trade treaty cooperatives. So, by reputation, it remains reputedly grouchy when it comes to outside economic influences.

Bottom Line

Despite an embarrassment of riches in natural resources, most major industries in Algeria are government owned or feel the heavy hand of government influence and economic revenue sharing. Currently, the Bouteflika government seems to have successfully loosened the leash, especially in its attempts to encourage foreign investment and provide businesses with more economic flexibility. This has recently been reflected by the fact that in 2016 it finally moved into the Top 10 African countries in terms of Foreign Direct Investment, recording a 42% increase across 12 different sectors. What's more, hangover socialist bureaucracies still clumsily intact, seem to be relenting in their perennial ideological paranoia. And the judicial system, opaque at best, is doing a little better to clean things up. For now, Algeria bears watching. It has stabilized quite a bit. Still government rigidity and a lack of fiscal imagination are notable for their ability to reverse themselves. So caution, in market terms, is a byword.

Current Market Indicator: Buy and Hold

Cautiously take a taste for now. After that, wait and see if Algeria keeps on its course for intended reforms and stays true to those intentions. For now, it seems to have made a bumpy but successful run in the right direction.

MOROCCO

(Kingdom of Morocco)

Morocco might easily be described as the flipside free state face of Africa that stands in direct contrast to Algeria and neighboring Libya.

With a GDP of $105 billion USD, Morocco enjoys the 6th highest total Gross Domestic Product of any nation in Africa and ranks it solidly in at Number 3 in North Africa. Credit much of that to a stable financial structure and excellent trade and commerce policies known for encouraging foreign investment and fostering local industries. Although it may appear to look diminutive on the vast landscape of the map of Africa, it covers about 274,000 square miles or roughly half again larger than the state of California (or the island nation of Japan).

Morocco is a Constitutional Monarchy with a fully elected parliament. Not at all a figurehead monarch, the King of Morocco—Mohammed VI—wields extensive executive leverage over the military, foreign policy and religious affairs. And while the King works with the two chambers of Parliament—the Assembly of Representatives and the Assembly of Councilors—most of the powers of execution still remain with the Crown. As such, the king can issue decrees (called *dahirs)* that carry the force of law. He can also dissolve the parliament after consulting with the Prime Minister as well as the President of the Constitutional Court. And yes (to answer the unasked question)! Mohammed is an autocrat. He is also living testimony to the fact that—given the proper moral core—an autocracy can be effective.

Mohammed VI has been the King of Morocco since the death of his father in 1999, and recently issued a mandate in 2011 to extend even greater powers to his duly elected Prime Minister, providing improved legislative powers to the Assemblies and increased civil liberties to all Moroccan citizens.

At present, the current coalition government led by the (moderate) Islamist Justice and Development Party leads the way among most African nations in helping to pursue macroeconomic stability and social reforms. Morocco rivals and, in terms of actual volume, excels its Northern neighbor Egypt in terms of vibrant tourism and a growing manufacturing sector that includes aeronautics, technology and electronics. It is also super facilitative to developing new business inside the country and attracting new Foreign Direct Investment from Europe and Asia.

Additionally, in terms of healthy economic adventurism Moroccan businesses and individual investment has, more than any other North African nation, sought strategic alliances in the Sub-Sahara. Over the past 15 years, Moroccan Companies have been investing in gaining market share in a number of West African economies and by doing so they are rapidly becoming leading players across Sub-Saharan Africa.

In this first episode of a 3-part series titled 'Morocco Rising", Baldwin Berges spoke prophetically with Youssef Lahlou—Senior Portfolio Manager at Silk Invest and based in Casablanca—about the expansion of Morocco's leading companies in key industries across the African continent and how they are becoming a gateway to Africa: As recently as early 2016, Moroccan companies had been heavily invested in banking, telecom and construction. Major financial institutions, including BMCE

Bank, Bank Populaire and Attijarawafa Bank are all planting flags and building new business relationship with nations in the Sub-Sahara from Rwanda to the Democratic Republic of the Congo. These key financial institutions are extracting as much as 25% of their total new revenues of more than $8 billion USD, and they have been exporting technologies such as affordable housing, building supplies and construction to nations such as Kenya, Cote d'Ivoire and Nigeria.

Morocco's major telecommunications player—Moroc Telecom—has also expanded to a host of African nations that include Mali, Mauritania, Burkina Faso, Gabon and Niger, and is expected to expand to another dozen nations in West Africa by 2020. Its national airline, Royal Air Maroc, flies to 48 cities in the African Sub-Sahara.

Above all else, and to the nation's considerable cachet throughout the Sub-Sahara, this ancient bedrock of the Moor has been able to see its own king Mohammed VI perform as the face of the franchise for the Moroccan "chamber of commerce." Reeling from its close ties to Europe and the shaky status of the EU, and determined to shore up the investment of Morocco's largest bank, Attijarawafa (with 312 branches in the Sub-Sahara alone), King Mohammed is often seen making goodwill tours to Abidjan (Cote d'Ivoire) and other cities on the burgeoning West Coast of the Sub-Sahara.

Casablanca, Marrakech, Tangier—all are glamorous cities that have actually been movie titles. Those along with ocean side tourist magnets such as Rabat and Essaouiria now form what amounts to the North African Riviera. And each offers a luxury lifestyle that includes an idyllic seaside climate shouldered by the Atlas Mountains to the South and East.

Tax incentives and growth credits for new businesses add to the allure of the Moroccan business climate. And of course, all is not entirely rosy there. Lack of judicial transparency and government double-dipping into the corporate economy is typical if not desirable aspect of doing business in Morocco.

The Bottom Line

Morocco is strong and keeps getting stronger. Recent findings according to Africa investment reports rate Morocco a solid number 5 in FDI investment, and number 2 in most FDI total development projects behind South Africa. When one observes Morocco on balance, it remains an African showcase, and the best place on the Northern Coast to put down your financial roots. Such an island of stability, especially in the volatile North, points to a brighter future and the power of positive commerce. What's more, Morocco's ties to the EU help to form just the kind of intercontinental connective tissue that—in every political sense—is needed more often between Africa and Europe.

Current Market Indicator:
Morocco is rated a Strong Buy

Now is the best possible time to engage this progressive aggressive economic *force majeure*.

LIBYA

(The Libyan Republic)

I f you have read the headlines just since the beginning of 2016, Libya is on the rocks in every socio-political sense that underscores the madness of what was once heralded as that "great moment of liberation" called The Arab Spring. ISIS has now put down deep roots in the Northeast region of the country and now enjoys its strongest toehold in the Middle East to replace its loss of franchise due to losses in Iraq.

There are still three rival governments vying for control of Libya. There are two governments in Tripoli. One of them is the UN backed Government of National Accord (GNA), which has struggled to exert authority following the elusive 2015 Peace Deal. This is mainly due to the refusal of authorities controlling eastern Libya to recognize the GNA as Libya's official government.

Recently, in 2017 the situation in Libya has stabilized a bit, but not enough. An oil hungry world markets and an IMF bridge loan have sent GDP growth in Libya soaring to a roaring 53%. But this has to be looked upon as a false positive, since the embattled nation had nowhere to go but up after bottoming out in 2016.

Massive diaspora to Europe, including fleeing boatloads of the desperate and disenfranchised, has become weekly fodder for the media. And now a "Prime Minister-Designate" (a scary title if there ever was one) has been introduced by UN resolution to bring stability to the government. (The fact that new interim PM Fayez al-Sarraj arrived by sea because the fly-zones were too unsafe says a great deal about a situation that will change by the time we publish this book. And the sad thing about all of this is that it was all probably unnecessary.)

In purely geopolitical terms, since 2011, Libya has become the classic case of "The Devil you know," being better than the devil you don't know. And even the most cynical observer now has to admit that, despite the corruption of the Muammar

Western Sahara
(The Territorial Paradox)

Occupied by Spain since the late 19th century, the resource-rich Western Sahara has been on the United Nation's list of non-governing territories virtually since 1963. In 1965 the UN General Assembly adopted its first resolution on Western Sahara, asking Spain to decolonize the territory, although Spain—still a dictatorship under Francisco Franco—somewhat characteristically dragged its heels.

Led by Morocco, that had laid claims to the territory since 1957, the Assembly requested that a referendum be held by Spain on self-determination. In its infinite Wisdom, the UN issued a joint administration of the territory by Morocco (which had both territorial and cultural ties to the people) and Mauritania to its immediate South...with the worst human rights record on the African Continent. Not surprisingly, war broke out when these two nations, unable to workout their differences, fell into a protracted civil war with the Sarawhi International movement, a Polisairo front group, which proclaimed the (SADR) Sarawhi Arab Democratic Republic while enjoying a government funded exile in Algeria.

Since a United Nations-sponsored ceasefire agreement in 1991, two thirds of the territory, including most of the Atlantic coastline, came under de facto control by Morocco and the remainder by the SADR, strongly backed by Algeria,

After a number of resolutions, including the failed Baker Resolution (named after US Secretary of State James Baker), Western Sahara has ex-officially become a Moroccan protectorate. And the Morocco-controlled parts of Western Sahara are divided into several provinces that are treated as integral parts of the kingdom. The Moroccan government offers considerable economic, political and military support to the Saharan provinces under its control with cut-rate fuel and related subsidies, to appease nationalist dissent and attract immigrants from Sahrawis and other communities in Morocco proper.

Until recently this territory was considered a bit of a White Elephant, but in 1998 discoveries of vast oil and natural gas reserves have made it the focus of considerable political and economic leveraging. So now it is something of an economic gem, left primarily in the care of the Moroccan monarchy. At this point, the fit seems to be a symbiotic one and the one preferred by the protectorate's indigenous tribes.

As a counterpoint and one that poses a positive contradiction, Morocco's military has an entire commando brigade devoted to troubleshooting expeditions to counteract the terrorism of Al Qaeda, Al Shabaab, Boko Haram and other branches of radical jihad when they pop up in the Sub-Sahara. (Part of this is practical: to protect its economic interests. Still, it is a very pragmatic move on Morocco's part—this from a nation that is 54% Muslim and from a king who traces his lineage back to the prophet Mohammad himself.)

Gaddafi regime, things were far better then than the chaos that has followed on the heels of the Arab Spring.

Rich in petroleum and natural gas, Libya is 93% desert and 90% a single commodity economy. As it is, 80% of all national revenues come from one industry—oil and natural gas. And 97% of its exports are oil and gas and unfinished petroleum by-products. The International Monetary Fund (IMF) noted exponential growth in Libya from 16.7% in 2013 and 14.5% in 2014 after tanking (to -60% in 2011) due to the government upheaval and subsequent civil war. 2015, however, was marked by steeply declining oil prices. And for a single resource economy, that has since become a major cause for concern.

Unfortunately, although Libya still holds the largest number of oil reserves in Africa and the 9th largest measurable resources in the world, it has lost most of its leverage in the African economy. Since the nation only has about 6.5 million inhabitants, most of them living on or near the longest coastline in Africa and a majority of those in three cities—Tripoli, Benghazi and Misrata—Libya is in a position of having much of its population affected by the constant conflicts throughout the nation, and civilian casualties have spiked to the thousands just since the beginning of 2017, causing it to become a number one "no-fly zone," rivaled only by Syria and South Sudan.

Oil production has rallied from its zero production lows of 2012. But at 700,000 barrels a day it is still less than half of its (1.6 million bbl.) production under the regime of Muammar Gaddafi.

There is no question that Libya is still carrying the scars from the 51-year dictatorship of Gaddafi and his overthrow in 2012. Strongman regimes can only become mirror images of the dictator who leads them and as such are only as moral (or immoral) as the man in charge. Popular and apparently visionary at the assumption of his power in 1961 there was little question that the General had, over the decades leading up to 2011, fallen victim to drug addiction, personal perversion, a bizarre expression of religious fanaticism and an obsession with the exportation of Islamic terrorism to the West.

During that five-decade span of time, Muammar Gaddafi's behavior toward the West became contradictory to say the least. Although he was a notorious exporter of state-sponsored terrorism, US and European citizens on assignment in Libya as well as major corporations, including several oil companies, were always allowed to live, operate and conduct commerce with the complete cooperation of the Libyan government. In 1980, Libya boasted one of the richest economies in the world, with a per-capita income that was higher than most European nations. However, due to its open complicity in numerous acts of international terrorism during the 1970s and

1980s, Libya incurred a laundry list of political and economic sanctions by the UN that condemned Gaddafi and essentially turned his country into the definitive "rogue nation" for more than 20 years.

These sanctions were precipitated in 1988 by the infamous mid-air bombing of Pan American Airlines Flight 103 over Lockerbie, Scotland. With all 246 passengers and 16 crew-members listed as fatalities, Libyan extremists claimed credit for this act of international sabotage and the Gaddafi regime openly refused to denounce it. The ultimate indignity in a series of state sponsored terrorist acts, the event served to drop the curtain down on Gaddafi and Libya. Since the passenger list included citizens of 14 different countries, including the US and UK, the UN had little trouble instituting economic boycotts against Libya that lasted for 15 years and were not lifted until the Supreme Leader's open contrition and renunciation of terrorism in 2003.

Apparently influenced by the US led invasion of Iraq, Muammar Gaddafi went on television in Tripoli, renounced all WMDs and petitioned the West for better relations. Finally, early in 2004, the UN lifted sanctions, OPEC returned its blessings and Libya petitioned for membership in the World Trade Organization—a petition that was ultimately granted on a trial basis. More than 100 government businesses were privatized, including a number of foreign companies returned to status. Oil giants Shell and Exxon-Mobil resumed their capital investment and operations, and all seemed back in balance. Unfortunately, Gaddafi's personal depredations and physical decline took the country down with him…so much so that the Muslim Brotherhood engineered coup that took place in 2011, seemed to be a kind of well-timed regime change, and overall mercy-killing.

Starting with the overthrow and assassination of Gaddafi in October of 2011, the Arab Spring has turned out to be Libya's Winter of Discontent. Islamic factions and tribal conflicts continue to flare up four years later and have as yet failed to be resolved. In September 2012 Libya's international credibility hit an all time low when an Al Qaeda terrorist group invaded the US Embassy in Benghazi and killed four Americans including Ambassador Christopher Stevens. Rather than try to diffuse the incident Libyan Prime Minister Mustafa Aubshagur went on ABC television and defied the US Government to take action, threatening repercussions. (Somewhat characteristically the US Administration did nothing, and even lied about the real cause.)

Abushagur's ouster one month later flung the nation into even more violent tribal conflicts. And even National Council elections in 2014 did nothing to diffuse the factional struggles. In June 2014, Libya held a second parliamentary election ruled "illegitimate" by the Libyan Supreme Constitutional Court. Since that time pro-Islamist militias allied with the Muslim Brotherhood have established parallel institutions. What's more, violent agitation, peppered by pocket skirmishes and new challenges from Libyan followers of Islamic State (ISIS) remain a constant threat to stability, evidenced by the disastrous events in the spring of 2016.

Bottom Line

It's a funny thing about Africa. Just when you write a country off as a loss, it bounces back. And Libya seems to be headed back toward some semblance of stability (much like a drunken uncle who decides to go "on the wagon.") Still, proceed carefully anytime where Libya is concerned. Things could change overnight and do. Even with the best intentions and promises of reform, the current Libyan government is facing an uphill battle. And local Bureaus of Statistics, now notorious for falsifying information, are so inconsistent that the nation cannot even get a ranking with the Index of Economic Freedom. Try though it may to attract new infusions of capital into its economy—even with a zero tariff rate on imported goods and elaborate enticements to foreign corporations—FDI interest in the country remains at an all time low. As of this writing, the Libya of today faces serious threats from Islamic extremists and

LIA and the Goldman Sachs Debacle

In its way, nothing underscored the corruption and ineptitude of the Muammar Gaddafi regime more than the LIA (Libyan Investment Authority) and its attempts to gain new footholds in the West by establishing relationships with major European and US financial institutions. Buying into several specialty funds in 2007 from investment groups at Societé Generale, HSBC and JP Morgan, the LIA eventually sank $1.3 billion of its sovereign wealth fund into a bonding group from Goldman Sachs just prior to the Wall Street meltdown of 2008.

After pulling a classic bait-and-switch with an initial $350 million in Libyan investment, the boys from Goldman set up high-risk, high-yield investment options with groups like Citibank, Italy's UniCredit and Spain's Banco Santander (both financially troubled groups in two very unstable economies). By 2010, the "too big to fail boys from Goldman-Sachs" had lost all but $25.1 Million of Libya Investment Authority's $1.3 billion—a 97% paper loss, and a write off by any measure.

This massive trashing of the LIA's principal investment caused such reverberations through the world financial community that it was widely (and rather cynically) rumored that, "If someone had truly wanted to take down the notorious Libyan dictator, they should have gone to Goldman-Sachs a long time ago."

tribal dissentions from a dozen splinter groups, all eyeing its rich petroleum reserves as a multi-billion dollar cash-cow for their international ambitions.

▶ Current Market Indicator: Sell

At the moment this commodity rich but politically fractured nation is in a shambles. Sell Libya until the fundamentals re-stabilize and the nation once again regains a sense of itself.

Tunis. Capital of Tunisia.

TUNISIA

(Republic of Tunisia)

Tunisia is credited as the birthplace of the Arab Spring. It was. And yet it wasn't. Yes, it was (more or less) given impetus by the Muslim Brotherhood. But no! They were not the instigators. And unlike the Arab Spring in Libya that resulted in chaos or the one in Egypt that came close to destabilizing the entire Middle East, the people's revolution in Tunisia was apparently overdue.

Triggered by a personal martyrdom and weeks of street protests, followed by some armed conflicts, it (by all available evidence) appeared justified and ended, at least at this point, in a positive result—one hallmarked by civil and political reforms, the unseating of a very unpopular government and what is now ranked by many as the only true Constitutional Democracy in North Africa. Still, opinions vary. So it's a good idea for the outsider and anyone with an FDI virtual bankbook they might want open up to pull back the layers and take a look at where we really stand.

Historically, Tunisia is something of a blueblood as ancient societies go. Rivaled only by Egypt for its illustrious and storied past, Tunis as a nation was settled by the Phoenician migrations who culturally merged with the indigenous Berber inhabitants in the 4th Century BC to form a new Mediterranean civilization in the formidable nation of Carthage. By 202 BC Carthage was the archrival to a nascent but rapidly rising Republic of Rome, and their rivalry for dominance of the region triggered the infamous Punic wars that lasted the better part of a century.

Led by their legendary general Hannibal (the African Caesar), Carthage had its way with Rome for nearly 20 years, even occupying Southern Spain and the Northern part of Italy. Hannibal, superb tactician that he was, continued to work his way with the Romans until his forces were repelled by Roman general Scipio Africanus in 201 BC. Forty years later, Carthage was finally razed to the ground, never to exist as an empire again. Had Scipio been less brilliant in his military tactics, Carthage might have prevailed, and the entire complexion of European history would have been altered in ways we cannot even conceive.

Later, after occupation by the Ottoman Turks for 300 years, Tunis was liberated as a French Protectorate in 1881—only to become something of a colonial satellite, albeit a civilized one, as a part of the notorious "African Scramble of 1885. Sixty years later, Tunisia became a flashpoint in the Axis Powers battle with the allies in WWII and finally gained its complete independence in 1956.

Although it is Islamic by tradition and a member of the Francophone nations of Africa and North Africa, Tunisia began its national identity in the late 1950s with a unique Constitution called the Code of Personal Status. Exceptional in any society of Africa and the Middle East, the code (among other things) granted women full status of citizenship, including the following: the right to higher education; the right to have a national identity (with passports!); the right to own their own business; further laws granting full rights to *all religions* and the elimination of polygamy as a state institution.

As it is, in 2009, the World Economic Forum ranked Tunisia as the most competitive economy in Africa and the 40th in the world. Tunisia was the first Mediterranean country to sign an Association Agreement with the European Union, in July

1995. And seemingly proactive on all economic decisions, the government of long-time President Zine Al Abadine Ben Ali (1987-2011) started dismantling tariffs on bilateral EU trade. Tunisia finalized lowering all trade barriers for industrial products in 2008 and subsequently became the first Mediterranean country to enter into free trade with the EU.

Creative, innovative and ahead of the curve on most things, the Ben Ali regime had also become a classic case of Lord Acton's dictum that "Absolute power corrupts absolutely." Over the years, the government had grown repressive and started receiving very low marks for government corruption, draconian police practices, skyrocketing unemployment and human rights violations, including limitations on freedom of speech and freedom of the press.

The death and martyrdom of a street vendor in Tunis set off weeks of riots and street demonstrations, finally forcing President Ben Ali to step down in March of 2011. In a constitutional election the following October, new human rights activist Monzak Marzouki was made president and managed to hold on to a secular democracy despite a serious attempt by Islamic fundamentalists to make Sharia the law of the land.

Even after a regime change in 2011, Tunisia remains a major democratic force in North African politics and has managed to attract many international companies such as aviation giant Airbus, IBM, Ford and Hewlett Packard. Today, the EU (European Union) still stands as Tunisia's first trading partner, presently accounting for 72.5% of Tunisian imports. Tunisia exports virtually 80% of all its goods, services, products and intellectual property to the EU, Eastern Europe and the Middle East.

Until recently, with its personal freedoms seemingly back in place, and with a continued rise in government accountability, Tunisia stays bullish in terms of its Euro-centric economy and modern marketing vision. In 2014, they commenced construction on Tunis Sports City, an elaborate Athletic complex—one very driven to attract Tunisia's rising population of Millennials (about 68% under 30). "Tunis Sports City" consists of apartment buildings, sports facilities and nightclubs at a cost of $5 billion USD. Additionally the Tunis Financial Harbor (in Tunis Bay) has been set up to deliver North Africa's first offshore monetary center at $ 8 billion and nearby an IT center called Tunis Telecom for another $3 billion (all funded by the Bakitahr Group).

Tunisia Economic City, being constructed in nearby Enfidha, is due to be completed in 2018. And the new complex is projected to consist of residential, medical, financial, industrial, entertainment and touristic buildings as well as a port zone for a total cost of $80 billion (US) (project to be financed by Tunisian and foreign enterprises). With a population of about 11 million inhabitants and a GDP of $46 billion, Tunisia has a respectable median PPI of $11.5 K per anum.

All this newfound consumer confidence was rocked to the foundations in June, 2015 by several Radical Jihadist attacks against tourist hotels across the Northern Tunisian Coast, most notably in the resort city of Sousse. Killing 38 mostly British Tourists, the carefully coordinated mass-murder followed an earlier assault at the Bardo Museum in Tunis that killed 22. The attacks set in motion by an ISIS splinter group were a deliberate attempt to destabilize the government and shake FDI confidence.

In the short term this spate of terrorist attacks seems to have worked. Government clampdowns over the last year have had a demoralizing effect on the population and some European investors have put their real-estate acquisitions on hold. Heavy military retaliation has done little to stem the tide and restore the order necessary to pacify the resistance.

As recently as March, 2016, a large ISIS inspired attack flared up in the Eastern part of the country but was successfully repelled by Tunisian military forces. And despite more than 60 fatalities, by all appearances, the jihadists have successfully been driven East toward Libya (where, by all reports, they are now headquartered).

Bottom Line

Despite the illusion of being more stable than it is, Tunisia seems to be headed in the right direction. Its main drawback as a potential partner for the Sub-Sahara seems to be its continued love affair with the EU and its Eurocentric Mediterranean tradition. Still there is an inevitable awakening. And when it occurs, Tunisia could prove to be an enterprising partner and a reliable ally. At present, Tunisia is still working to stabilize external threats and constant pressure from the radical wing of Islam. If it holds center, and it appears that it will, this will be a very good place to do business for the next two decades. Granted the risk is there. But so is the reward. And on balance this is getting high ratings on the FDI play list.

 Current Market Indicator on Tunisia: Buy and Hold

Summary

North Africa is very much a mixed bag of isolation, religious and political turmoil and phenomenal growth in some nations. Although still suffering a hangover from the Arab Spring and agitation from Islamic fundamentalism to overthrow secular governments, nations like Egypt and Morocco continue to provide progressive governments and economic leadership, much of which is starting to flood in terms of money, leverage and economic influence into the Sub-Sahara.

Separated by the natural barrier of the world's largest desert, by Maghreb and Arab cultural influences as well as Eurocentric trading traditions, the North is on the right trajectory. It is one that sees it working toward a "One Africa" solution in many areas that are economically beneficial to both sectors of this very diverse continent. Once it does a bit of more political house cleaning, economic engagement from the North is only a matter of time.

CHAPTER 7

The Four Africas:
The Sub-Sahara Anchor Nations

I t is a results-driven world we live in, like it or not. And the rules are simple, occasionally ruthless, but invariably bottom-line. Whenever international financial institutions or global marketing giants look to invest their capital, manpower and technology in a new market, they invariably ask one question: Are the fundamentals sound? If the answer is "yes," they continue. They set down roots. And they often use that nation as a base-point to expand their franchise to neighboring countries.

In the Africa of the Sub-Sahara, there are four countries that the EU, the US and the BRICS nations have been looking to for solid partnerships. And after a quick scan of their political, economic and demographic profiles one can arguably arrive at three out of the four choices: Nigeria, South Africa and Kenya—due to their industrial dynamism, business friendly profile and youthful demographic—are logical linchpins for lower half of the continent. Ethiopia may seem to be a contradiction to some. But its case for inclusion has recently grown to be both consistent and (ultimately) logical to explain.

Collectively these four "anchor states" account for $1.2 Trillion of Africa's estimated total $2.5 Trillion GDP (or approximately 47% of its wealth). They represent roughly 376 million (or 35%) of Africa's 1.1 billion inhabitants. And yet they take up less than 5% of the continent's total land mass.

Nigeria leads the way with an annual GDP of $594 Billion, a population of 180 million people, and one of Africa's most economically varied revenue streams from a dozen different industries. Although it is erroneously looked upon as a "one industry economy (oil and natural gas)," Nigeria has done more to diversify in the last 10 years than any other African nation. And with all its flaws and growing pains it is currently viewed as the economic engine that drives the Sub-Sahara. Despite the tanking, Naira (tied to falling oil prices that have already doubled since the November nadir of 2015), Nigeria leads the way in terms of telecommunications technology, internet retailing, heavy industry, agricultural production, fashion, entertainment and lifestyle appeals to its under 30 Millennials who now represent 73% of the population. In the last 10 years, it has seen the influx of more FDI capital and international partnerships than the next three closest nations combined.

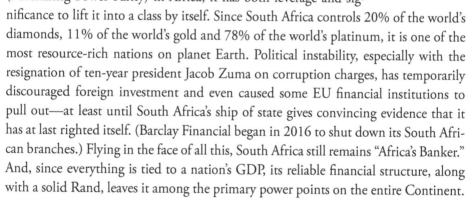

South Africa is next with an annual GDP of $295 billion. It has slipped recently (much of it due to alleged "financial theft") to become Africa's third largest Gross Domestic Producer. And yet with a population of 54 million and the third highest real PPP (Purchasing Power Parity) in Africa, it has both leverage and significance to lift it into a class by itself. Since South Africa controls 20% of the world's diamonds, 11% of the world's gold and 78% of the world's platinum, it is one of the most resource-rich nations on planet Earth. Political instability, especially with the resignation of ten-year president Jacob Zuma on corruption charges, has temporarily discouraged foreign investment and even caused some EU financial institutions to pull out—at least until South Africa's ship of state gives convincing evidence that it has at last righted itself. (Barclay Financial began in 2016 to shut down its South African branches.) Flying in the face of all this, South Africa still remains "Africa's Banker." And, since everything is tied to a nation's GDP, its reliable financial structure, along with a solid Rand, leaves it among the primary power points on the entire Continent.

Kenya is often referred to as the surprise player in the Sub-Sahara, but in reality it is anything but a surprise. With approximately $61 billion in GDP, it is now Africa's 11th largest economy. And though Sudan at # 7 ranks above it in Gross Domestic Production, the political turmoil of Sudan and the secession of South Sudan combine to render that nation chaotic in terms of development, economic freedom and Foreign Direct Investment. Besides a stable population, a large rise in working Millennials and a strong connection with BRICS nations like China and India, Kenya has done a great deal to modernize its technology and is one of the leaders in telecommunications, internet technology and virtual money. Tourism is still one of Kenya's leading industries, as are its natural resources, its national parks and the rapidly growing lakes area. The Two Rivers Mall in Nairobi is the largest shopping mall in the

Sub-Sahara, and the Great Lakes Area shared with Tanzania is rapidly becoming one of East Africa's most desirable places to live, work and build a new community.

On the surface Ethiopia is a living contradiction. It has less than a 42% literacy rate (one of the five lowest in Africa). And its per capita income is only $1,505, making it one of the poorest nations in terms of individual quality of life. The Index of Economic Freedom gives it a relatively low rating in terms of economic freedom and mobility. And yet, it has a dynamically growing base of educated 25 and under Millennials. With 90 million people, it has the third largest population in Africa (after Nigeria and Egypt). And it ranks 9th in GDP with $73 billion (USD). So where is the disparity? And how is it stepping out of a very low rating on most international indexes into becoming a progressive "player" in the world economy? Well, as British Prime Minister Benjamin Disraeli once said: "There are lies, damn lies...and statistics!"

Caveats and Clip Notes

At this point, it is very important to make some mental notes on the fact that, for now, we are examining some of these nations in terms of economic vibrancy, dynamic demographics (especially among Millennials) and rapid rises in national prosperity. Other world measurements such as indexes of economic freedom, human rights, and personal development are often factored in based on changes of government and turn-arounds inside an individual country. Governments that have recently reformed from totalitarian autocracies to new democracies or have held new "free" elections make a careful point of representing their new policies in the best possible light. Some of them are set in such ways to obtain national grant monies, economic aid from the World Bank, the IMF and other funding groups. As such, statistics are often nascent, overly optimistic, and generally unreliable.

Our criteria here are primarily those that make the nations in question desirable in terms of GDP, economic viability and financial leverage. In these cases, positive long-term track-records along with a sense of economic vision are essential.

Lagos, Nigeria.

Nigeria: Despite the fluctuations, it's 'Too Big to Fail'

With a population of 180 million people, a current annual GDP of $572 billion and one of Africa's most economically varied revenue streams from a dozen different industries, Nigeria as a nation is now "simply too big to fail."

Sometimes, it worries us all... a lot! And yet it progresses with a kind of deliberate madness in the right direction. Despite the tanking Naira (tied to falling oil prices which have already doubled since the November nadir of 2015), Nigeria has done more to diversify in the last decade than any other African nation.

Even when struggling with an antiquated infrastructure and pathetic travel routes to outlying areas, Nigeria still manages to lead the way in at least half a dozen burgeoning industries. Telecommunications technology, internet retailing, heavy industry, agricultural production, fashion, entertainment and lifestyle appeals to its under 30 Millennials who now represent 73% of the population—other African nations know this, and so do serious FDI players. In the last 10 years, Nigeria has seen the influx of more FDI capital and international partnerships than the next three closest nations combined.

Nigeria is often referred to as "the soul-train" that drives the Sub-Sahara. This is something of a hyperbole, and yet it's closer to being accurate than not. In a way the numbers speak for themselves. 180 million people representing approximately one-fourth of the entire economic output of the world's second largest continent make it a force to be reckoned with. And at this point it cannot be otherwise. The national debt to GDP ratio is 11%, one of the best in both Africa and Asia. And recently the IMF designated Nigeria as one of the Top Five Emerging Global Economic Powers.

All this comes as something of a contradiction, especially since the beginning of 2015 when new President Muhammadu Buhari took office. Coming in with great promise and all the aspects of integrity Buhari has, in the last 24 months alone, had to cope with the following 9 Major Issues: 1) An infrastructure and electronic grid originally constructed for a nation with the population of Poland (about 40 million people) forced to serve a population of 180 million, rolling blackouts and not enough energy to run heavy industry: 2) $45 Billion in unaccounted for funds that have just disappeared either from the national treasury or through massive corporate theft; 3) finding that the nation's previous Minister of Finance has been indicted for malfeasance and illegal extraction of government funds and his predecessor Goodluck Jonathan is being investigated for fraud; 4) discovering that his administrative staff contains one or more "moles" from Boko Haram; 5) the tanking of the national currency, the Naira, to its lowest level in 15 years and runaway inflation as a result; 6) a precipitous drop in oil production to 30% of previous years; 7) the first predicted recession since 1987; 8) a flight of FDI investment due to fears over terrorism and financial instability at all levels; 9) such a spike for food basics at retail levels (as much as 8 times as much) that shoppers now have a new term for it—*Buhariya!*

Not a very good resume for the first two years. And this cascade of bad news has been compounded by the fact that Nigeria's chief of state is spending most of his time in London clinics for a number of undisclosed systemic illnesses—brought on no doubt as side-effects of the sickening decline of his nation's credibility and reputation. In fact, the man inherited a mess that would take anyone some time to fix. And another inescapable truth is that Buhari has shown little ability to address the problems as they arise. The only thing the beleaguered PON has going for him is that that Nigeria—for its Pandora's Box of problems—has grown into one of those rare economic Leviathans that is "too big to fail."

In every way imaginable that presents a paradox that will take some time and space to explain. So let us begin…

The First Revolution

Nigeria at the inception of its formal independence showed much promise of success (it was on the right path of economic growth and development.) An appreciable percentage of the population had acquired at least some level of political sophistication. The civil servants were efficient. Hopes were high.

It is both ironic and yet a peculiarity of African history that very often military commanders are some of the most progressive and pragmatic leaders to evolve outof the morass of new nations. So it was with Nigeria. After freeing itself from British Colonial rule in 1960, Nigeria went through a series of *ad hoc* governments equally divided between the Christian led coalition in the South and the Muslim led leadership in the North. Religiously driven with tribal underpinnings, this new nation survived a rather violent and aborted Biafra secession in the late 1960s to become internationally recognized as a progressive economic power.

As early as the 1970s, Nigeria had visionary leaders interested in the welfare of the nation. Endowed with remarkable natural resources, Nigeria's economy had the potential early-on to become self-sufficient at several levels. Before their departure, the British had helped Nigeria develop several cash crops. And by the early 1970s, it was successfully producing cocoa, cotton, oil palm, rubber and several varieties of rooibos black tea. The Northern Region—replete with soybean, peanut, rice and cotton production—was long considered the Nation's grain belt. So through the end of what was commonly considered its "First Republic," Nigeria's economy was largely sustained by the agricultural sector with gradual explorations into mining and minerals. This was especially true in the western part of Nigeria, where my family originally hails from. Even today, it is regarded as the most economically well-developed area of the country.

The economy blossomed during this early 10-year period. The Nigerian economy was looked upon in the same vein as the popular BRICS countries of the 21st century. The country with a group of visionary "founding fathers" (Obafemi Awolowo, Nnamdi Azikiwe, Tafawa Belewa and Ahmadu Bello principal among them) had developed a blueprint for the future of Nigeria. And everything seemed destined for a solid, unshakable foundation—at least in those early days:

Early Economic and Educational Success Stories

1. In the North we had the 'Groundnut and Cotton Pyramid' generating vast revenue and foreign exchange for Nigeria. In the Western region, we had Cocoa and Palm Oil in abundance.

2. Our Universities were first class institutions with R&D facilities considered among the best in Africa. Many nations sent their college-age students to our Nations universities to conduct their research.

3. Then in 1974, the discovery of the third largest oil reserves in Africa and the 9th largest in the world proved to be a real game changer and not in a very good way. Although Nigeria became one of the most commodity-rich

nations in the history of the continent, it developed overnight into a *boom-bust mentality* that always seems to "barrel in" with the mining of natural resources. American, British and Dutch oil companies converged on us with rapacious one-way exploration drilling, and the inevitable scenario set in of "short-term economic spikes" followed 20 years later by ghosts of abandoned boomtowns.

The Second Revolution and the Demise of Diversification

The military intervention, civil war and the crude oil discovery radically altered the course of Nigeria's economic development. The military discarded the solid fiscal underpinnings of the original federation of states and instead made them answerable to a large centralized federal government that was both indifferent to the people and irresponsible to their needs.

The discovery and development of vast fields of crude oil led to complacency and lack of future planning. They forgot that "crude was an extractive commodity with a limited life span." As the military leaders were sleepwalking their way through the euphoria of petrodollar earnings, Nigeria was growing in geometric progressions with the highest birthrate in the Sub-Sahara. Meanwhile its nascent energy infrastructure was too underdeveloped to meet the needs of a population that seemed to double overnight. In the ultimate point of irony one of the most energy abundant nations in the world lacked the utilities necessary to provide for its own people.

Management expert, market developer and author Peter Drucker recently wrote in his bestseller *The Practice of Management* that, "Innovation is the specific instrument of entrepreneurship. It is the act that endows resources with a new capacity to create wealth." For more than two decades Nigeria's military leaders chose to disregard that economic axiom. Instead, they used their positions of political power to "feed the greed," raking the top off Nigeria's boom-bust Big Oil economy while leaving little in return.

During this oil boom period from the mid-1970s to around 1999—with its single revenue focus—there was no dedicated investment in power, technology, broad based construction and the other fundamentals of infrastructure. So the original foundations of a well-set economy were ultimately left to ROT! And so one of the most clearly cash rich economies of Africa paid ultimate the price.

Ultimately government—any government—can only justify its existence by the economic prosperity it produces. It invariably falls short if it does not improve or at least maintain the wealth-producing capacity of the resources entrusted to it. The populations end up in lack. And poverty trumps all governments. The "militocracies" of the 1980s failed to learn this lesson. And Nigeria suffered because of it. The only good news is that the human spirit yearns for resolution. And there would be a reckoning, sooner rather than later.

The Third Revolution and a Part to Play in 'Making Nigeria Great Again!'

As Mark Twain once observed, "Rumors of my death have been greatly exaggerated," the same applied to Nigeria about ten years ago. Nigeria is a nation of both immense opportunity and unlimited potential. In a world evolving at light speed where nations and governments are constantly flipping the script—where weak nations (with good potential) have become economic giants and the strong nations (due to government instability, corruption and "foreign influences") suddenly transform into economic weaklings, Nigeria remains the locus of power when it comes to making a difference. And as we have come to learn, especially where the Sub-Sahara is concerned, *out of difficulty comes opportunity.*

That chance began in earnest in 1999 when, after more than three decades of military dictatorship, former General Olesegun Obasanjo became the first democratically elected Nigerian president in 26 years. Originally, in 1976—after the assassination of the military head of state General Murtala Mohammed—General Obasanjo (by virtue of being the deputy head-of-state) took over the reins. From that point, he governed Nigeria as a "militocracy" for three years and made a legitimate attempt to turn governance of an oil-rich nascent Nigeria over to the civilian regime of President Shehu Shagari. But this proved to be nothing more than "a good deed certain to be punished," because in practically no time the Shagari presidency descended into a nonstop run of corruption only to be overthrown by a military coup led by Colonel Muhammadu Buhari.

This in turn led to a run of *coups d'état* that saw about seven shifts in governmental musical chairs until Obasanjo was once again brought to power in a democratically held election in 1999. (Generally, the elections were looked upon as un-free and unfair. But Obasanjo's eight-year administration led an upward trend that helped return Nigeria to economic freedom and renewed diversification.)

Economic Growth and Debt Payment

Before Obasanjo's administration, Nigeria's GDP had been painfully anemic since 1987 and had only managed a 3 per % rise between 1990 and 2000. However, under

Obasanjo the growth rate doubled to 6 per cent per anum by the time he left office and continued to head "North." Helped in part by higher oil prices. Nigeria's foreign reserves rose from $2 billion in 1999 to $43 billion in the final year of the general's presidency in 2007. Along the way, Obasanjo was able to secure debt pardons from the Paris Club amounting to some $18 billion and paid off another $18 billion to help his native land become virtually debt-free. Most of these loans were accumulated from short-term trade arrears during the exchange control period. It's also important here to note that these loans were accumulated not out of corruption but during a period 1982-1985 when Nigeria operated exchange control regime that vested all foreign exchange transactions on the central bank of Nigeria.

Ultimately, Obasanjo's second administration (from 1999 to 2006) ushered in an era of great growth and restructuring for Nigeria that restored its credibility and brought its stock way up in all the ways that truly matter. Instituting massive reforms on everything from lowering trade barriers, to repairing roads and privatization of key industries, the Obasanjo regime also reversed the balance of trade from a minus 10.4% in the minus column (in 1999) to a plus 9.78% by the time his term had expired. It was also a period that saw Nigeria's GDP nearly triple from $54 billion USD in 1999 to $141 billion by 2008.

When Obasanjo finally stepped down in 2009, this was continued under the Goodluck Jonathan administration. However, the spate of corruption that had marred previous administrations ended up taking down the Jonathan administration as well. And in the 2015 election, the nation once again voted an "Ex-Military Leader" (Muhammadu Buhari) into office.

Initially Buhari's second term in office ushered in an era of reformation and a concerted effort to clean up both Nigeria's finances and its commercial credibility, as well as repairing the nation's damaged credibility due to previous corrupt governments. Until recently, Buhari had been making steady progress, if bumpy at times. Until mid-2016, when the wheels seem to come off the train, Buhari seemed to be making all the right moves. But in this two steps forward-one step back, volatile legacy of governance in the Sub-Sahara, we may be looking at a "hung jury" where the Buhari regime is concerned.

Nevertheless, when one steps back to look at its long term horizons, Nigeria has come a very long way in the last twenty years or so. It still has so very far to go.

There has been a global paradigm shift in the last two decades as well. Twenty years ago, few economists would have been willing to predict the emergence of Brazil, Russia, India, China & South Africa (the BRICS nations) as economic powerhouses to the degree that they have become in the new millennium. Although technically the European Union—an economic aggregate of 28 member states—has the world's largest collective GDP (at $18.52 trillion), in real terms as they apply China is rapidly gaining on the United States of America as the world's largest economy. In so doing it is staying on pace with what seems to be its monetary destiny. Just in the last six years it has leapfrogged past Japan, Germany, France and the United Kingdom.

MTN: A Waltz of Giants

South African Telecommunications giant MTN is a classic African success story...and more. On a continent where the challenges of infrastructure and ruralization have marginalized millions into isolated pockets of society, mobile networks have been the saving grace in helping transform the disenfranchised into advanced tech community networks.

In 2001, with the wave of privatization sweeping through the telecom industry in Nigeria, MTN was arguably in the right place at the right time. Adopting a customer-focused strategy from the outset, MTN set up as many outlets as possible for their subscribers to gain access to products and services. To boost its market share among rural, low-income consumers, MTN created services by establishing a "bricks and mortar" network of local agents, setting up kiosks in rural areas, and giving agents motorbikes to reach even the most remote places.

They also developed lower denominations when selling airtime to accommodate the low and unpredictable incomes of many African consumers, and introduced innovations like telemedicine and voice-based apps such as iCow and Xam Marse to provide rural farmers with real-time access to market prices through the internet on their mobile phones. Finally, MTN Mobile Money launched in 13 countries in November 2013 with more than thirteen million mobile money subscribers throughout 14 countries in the Sub-Sahara alone. This mobile internet banking system enabled customers to wire virtual cash to one another, either from simcard to simcard or from phone to phone. Driven by MTN's groundbreaking technology, mobile telecommunications have already proven to be the lifestyle game-changer in 24 Countries on the African Continent.

In ironic bit of government facilitation, when MTN won a bid for a mobile phone license to operate in Nigeria at a cost of $285 million, institutional investors were skeptical, because Nigeria had limited wireless capacity at the time and was considered a risky bet. But with a very visionary government "failsafe" to back their launch, the company gained 300,000 subscribers in its first year. Today the company has over 50 million subscribers. In 2015, MTN reported $22 billion USD in revenue out of which US $5 billion came from Nigeria. Nigeria is the most profitable subsidiary contributing 30% of the group's revenue.

According to United Nations Economic Data (UNED) the global economy Gross Domestic Product in 2014 was $77.27 trillion. Of this, the United States of America accounted for $17.348 trillion as the largest single national economy in the world. It was followed by China with a GDP of $10.357 trillion making it the second largest economy. Japan, the third largest, has $4.603 trillion GDP. Germany, now fourth, has a GDP of $3.873 trillion while France, at fifth, has $2.559 trillion GDP. The UK, which dominated the world for decades as the economy to beat, has now dropped to seventh in the committee of nations. And in just four years, Nigeria has taken a quantum leap into 21st position with a GDP of $594 billion (according to most estimates).

Since its return to democratic governance in 1999, Nigeria has attracted FDI capital ventures in legion, and is now making a measurable paradigm shift into a world-class economy. If policymakers can see beyond their noses to give Nigeria the economic blast-off it needs to recover from the missed opportunities in the late 1980s, they will get to be part of a tectonic shift that will shake the entire economy of the Sub-Sahara. Foreign investors can see opportunities that most Nigerians fail to grasp. *The challenges: lack of infrastructure, epileptic power supply, and an anemic industrial base are fast becoming opportunities for foreign investors.*

In 2014, US President Barack Obama declared Nigeria as the world's next economic success story, stressing that this was one of the major reasons his government was committed to helping the country build strong democratic institutions and remove constraints to trade and investment through the African Growth and Opportunity Act. Making this declaration at the US-Nigeria Trade and Investment Forum, an event organized by the Nigerians In Diaspora Organization (NIDOA) in Washington, DC, during the year, Obama said that his country expanded opportunities for Nigeria to effectively access markets and diversify its economy beyond a narrow reliance on natural resources. "As we support these efforts, the diaspora can play an important role in contributing to a strong, vibrant and economically prosperous Nigeria," Obama emphatically noted. That paradigm of Executive endorsement, though 3 years old, still holds value.

At the Reuters Africa Investors' Forum in Johannesburg earlier in 2015, foreign investors who have their businesses in Nigeria and other African countries were quoted as saying; "If you want to ride Africa's business boom, choose your country well and be ready for bumps on the road. But the momentum is upward and you will be rewarded if you stay the course." African policymakers and chief executives of companies operating in Africa are spreading this upbeat message, as interest in what was once dubbed the "hopeless continent" blossoms along with growth rates.

'Hooray for Nollywood!'

H ere's a little known factoid. In terms of feature films going out under the aegis of a single national industry, Hollywood is no longer Number 1. Since 2010 (India's) "Bollywood" now produces more actual releases yearly, including 1,989 feature films in 2015, and annual revenues of just over $8 billion (USD). Hollywood still holds the lead in annual box office gross with $10.8 billion (but with only a paltry 798 releases in 2015). But guess, who comes in at a solid Number 2 in total fictional feature films produced? That's right: Nollywood! The Nigerian film industry with 979 features and a growth pattern that can only be looked upon as "exponential" has absolutely infused the African Market with popular first run films...and parts of Asia as well.

A sobriquet for the Nigerian Film Industry, "Nollywood" is also logging in at just a notch over $1 billion in total sales. And to add to its recent cachet in the last 10 years, this Lagos based film community has been a solid staple of the Nigerian economy since the 1950s, having truly come into its own since 2001. Besides having a broad active audience in Africa, South America and the Caribbean, Nollywood is also attracting some very quality acting and directing talent from neighboring countries like Ghana and Cote d'Ivoire who are flooding this reinvented new creative center with innovative concepts, solid talent and funding.

During the year, Global X Funds listed the first Exchange Traded Fund (ETF) on the New York Stock Exchange to track Nigerian stocks. Recently Nigeria's Stock Exchange (NSE) disclosed that it is reviewing applications from some leading global investment banks to join its trading floor to take part in improving liquidity. Despite the falling Naira (still tied to oil prices), the index rose to over 9% in 2015. And though the average was down from the spectacular rise of 29% in 2013 and 24% in 2014, the upward trend continues and U.S. investors are looking to continue "heavy up" their investments in Africa's largest economy. This comes particularly into play since the nation's GDP has spiked from its 2010 levels of $212 billion to nearly tripling its output in just four years.

Today, foreign trade flows amounts to 65% of daily trades on the NSE. And despite the rollercoaster ride in 2016, Nigeria's economy has still managed to grow at a healthy rate of 7% in the last few years despite problems in its infrastructure. Once the African giant gets the power equation right, the economy will be able to leap frog into the Fourth Industrial Revolution.

Nigeria's Sphere of Influence: One may argue the point ad infinitum. But by all economic indicators as well as those demo-metric paradigms, Nigeria has become the most dynamic market in Africa, and the most attractive to FDI driven corporations and governments. What's more, it is the economic cup that runneth over onto its "sibling nations" and West African neighbors. Such nation-states as Cote d'Ivoire, Ghana, Sierra Leone, Cameroon and Niger have all felt the benefit of Nigeria's new advance guard of bullish billionaires, bringing an entire new dynamic of technology, energy and funding that breaks down barriers and builds prosperity.

Current Market Indicator: Buy and Hold… and be patient

Long-term benefits will be your reward.

Brass Island in the Nun River estuary of Southern Bayelsa State, Nigeria

South Africa's New Dichotomy

Cape Town — South Africa's Shiniest City

Even though downgraded to a BB+ rating for the Rand, South Africa is still a Standard & Poor's buy and hold— with a stable if perhaps stagnant future. Part of the reason is the fact that South Africa remains an economic Leviathan that cannot be denied. And despite the recent removal of Jacob Zuma from office for "stealing the future of the country," there is still something of an Africapitalist revolution in the works where businesses are recapturing the initiative through massive economic initiatives and building the economy through FDI capital.

Until 2013 South Africa was the largest African economy in terms of GDP. Figures as recent as those of 2016 showed that at $294.80 billion (USD) it had fallen far behind that of Nigeria and was recently passed by Egypt at $326 billion, not as much due to slow growth as the fact that countries like Nigeria and Angola have catapulted into economic prominence especially since the global economic meltdown of 2008.

Just behind Egypt and far ahead of both Tunisia and Morocco, South Africa is the #2 nation on the entire African Continent for what are referred to as *foreign arrivals.** Much of that is due to global commerce and business travelers. But South Africa— because of its ethnic balance, its generally temperate climate and especially its residual

---

* As recently as 2015, tourist friendly nations such as Kenya, Tanzania and Nigeria have not kept specific data on foreign arrivals into their countries. These records are now being reviewed and updated as the nations form new economic coalitions.

colonial connections with the British Empire—is still the African hotspot, despite the additional 3,000 travel miles often required to get "down under."

To further fuel the paradox, although its health care system is fairly good, recent surges of cases of HIV (a national pandemic) place its life expectancy rate at 62.1 years of age, ranking it 148th in the world, quite a fall from earlier rankings. And yet South Africa still has the 7th highest per capita income to GDP ratio in Africa with $13,165 per annum. (Per capita income Indexes are averaged out, relative to population. So single economy oil rich countries with smaller populations such as Libya, Algeria and Gabon will indicate a higher standard of living than actually exists.)

The South African Economy — A Delicate Balance

Any discussions of South Africa must first be examined in terms of its preemptive status in three distinct areas: 1) the good vs. evil mosaic of its complex political history; 2) its access to critical natural resources; 3) the status of its currency (the rand) in world financial markets. South Africa's rand is the sole African currency that represents some stability to the rest of the world. It remains among the 20 most traded currencies on international markets. So it still offers something of a safe-haven for financial institutions and investors looking for a bullion-based currency as a solid financial anchor.

In the purest sense, it is one of the youngest republics on the continent. As such, South Africa has had to deal with the hangover of a full century of apartheid, two decades of global economic sanctions, and finally some well-intended, occasionally naïve and frequently inept attempts to right the wrongs of the past. And at this point, it is essential to revisit that "twice-told tale" because there is so much political and economic subtext that escapes one's notice, even among people who have been exposed to it a dozen times.

Officially a "Republic" since 1961, South Africa maintained a strictly enforced regime of apartheid through to 1989. The implication for the establishment of apartheid was "separate but equal facilities, education and social programs for all." And of course, nothing of the sort was allowed to take place. In fact, the South African independence that occurred in 1961 was a release from British Colonial rule quickly followed by a political lock on the government by the deeply entrenched Afrikaans community, virtually all of whom were politically committed to the separation of the races that they believed was essential to the survival of the culture.

Numbering about 22% of the racial balance in the early 1960s, South Africa saw more than half its Caucasian population vacate in the 1970s—mostly expatriate Brits who fostered a white diaspora back to their native homelands in other commonwealth countries. They knew that the corruption of apartheid and the continued disenfran-chisement of the 78% black majority could not hold, and they suspected that a civil war would result between the emerging black population (and ANC) and the Afri-kaans who all agreed, "would fight to the death" to defend their birthright. They also felt the mounting pressure of world opinion as it hardened toward the Balkanization of the black and colored races in their country.

In the 1980s all but a handful of nations placed economic sanctions against South Africa, and only its vast reservoir of coveted natural resources and precious metals enabled it to hold together. Ultimately the "national paranoia" gave way to world pres-sure and stifling economic boycotts in 1989—enough to allow F. W. de Klerk broker a transition to open elections and release of Nelson Mandela from prison. Nelson Man-dela proved his greatness and the depth of his conversion during his 23 years in prison. And yet one cannot discount the politically savvy and well-navigated transition F. W. de Klerk created during the three years of his "transitional" government (with Thabo Mbeki as South Africa's first ever black Vice President).

The Mandela Legacy ...

There are truly times in history when one man is destined to lead a nation out of darkness. Nelson Mandela was the right man for his time. And no one could have done what he was able to accomplish with quite as much skill, timing, compassion, humanity and *savoir faire*. Inheriting a great deal of paranoia from the disenfranchised Afrikaans and a potential political power struggle between the ANC and the (Zulu) Inkatha Party, Mandela immediately set forth the *Truth and Reconciliation Act,* forgiving all crimes committed on both sides of the previous regimes, both government atrocities and any acts of rebellion or retribution.**

In the short term, the act and the National Reconciliation Commission set up to oversee it quelled animosity, inevitable political party conflicts and any immediate inclination toward mass reprisals. The (white) Afrikaans population felt somewhat secure. The 78% black majority and "coloured" races (9%) seemed sufficiently molli-

---

** It has become a truism that, "One man's terrorist is another man's freedom fighter." This has held true historically for centuries. Most recently, two Israeli Prime Ministers David Ben-Gurion and Menachem Begin ("The mad bomber of the Irgun.") were both "freedom fighters" in that nation's struggle for independence. So was Ireland's first president Eamon DeValera. And Jomo Kenyatta, "The George Washington of Kenya," was a de facto leader of its bloody Mau Mau rebellion in the 1950s.

fied and trustful of the process. And most important, the anticipated civil war that the whole world dreaded never took place.

In the first place, Mandela was smart enough to allow all privately held corporations and family industries not only to continue but also to thrive. Although presented with petitions to do so, he demurred on any recommendations to nationalize South Africa's vast natural resources or mining industries. In fact, in view of the corruption that accompanies most nationalized energy companies, privatization in South Africa has remained a standard. What's more, his reassurances to groups like the World Trade Organization and the IMF of South Africa's continuance of financial integrity kept its powerful financial backbone intact and lifted the value of the rand to its highest level in years.

The immediate result for South African businesses was an assurance to the world financial communities that its government would allow business and investment to flow as usual, and with minimal government impediment. In view of this yielding to private enterprise, Mandela nonetheless saw to it that South Africa provided social services in ways that worked, including free health care for the aged and for all children under 7 years of age (the sectors that needed it most).

When Nelson Mandela retired from public office in 1998, his longtime No. 2 (and one of the architects of the 1989 transition) Thabo Mbeki won a free election to replace him as South Africa's President. In its way, South Africa's growth into the Sub-Sahara's pre-eminent economic power took place on Mbeki's watch. From 1999 to 2008, South Africa opened extensive trade and exportation to China, Japan, Germany and the United States, and vaulted into a number 1 position in terms of national GDP.

Perhaps one of the most underrated political administrators in African history, Mbeki continued to keep South Africa on an even keel until he tendered his resignation in the face of corruption charges in 2008. Completely vindicated in 2010, Mbeki was nevertheless replaced by South Africa's 4th president Jacob Zuma who came to be the architect of South Africa's gradual but relentless unraveling in world markets, especially in the last six years before his eventual disgrace and resignation in 2018.

2010 to 2015 — The Bubble

Since the changeover and especially in the last two years, the political and economic climate in South Africa has come onto shaky ground. The Jacob Zuma presidency has been replete with financial corruption and scandal.

The General Assembly walked out en masse in November of 2015, and the World Bank momentarily considered dropping its Bond Ratings to junk. Foreign investors, cautious about ventures into South Africa in the best of times, have backed off in even

far greater numbers than usual. Despite some of the richest mineral deposits in the world, South Africa's annual growth rate has slowed to about 1.3%. And, in relation to the GDP, the Human Quality of Life Index (much higher under Mbeki and Mandela) has fallen severely to one of great disparity.

So much malfeasance had been sniffed out during Jacob Zuma's administration that it finally took emergency measures by surviving minister Patrick Gordhan in 2017, who worked out an uneasy alliance with South Africa's CEOs by providing them with a laundry list of economic reforms. With Zuma now forced into retirement, new president Cyril Ramaphosa has doubled down on efforts to work with the Economic Transformation Committee (ETC) on resolutions to build back the South African financial franchise by dealing with critical issues such as water shortages, diminished electrical energy grids and improving labor relations with strained unions. This initiative as part of the overall ANC National Development Plan is designed not only to restore outside investor confidence in South Africa but also to save the reputation and perhaps survival of the oldest surviving political party in South Africa.

As part of that "credibility" campaign, the South African NEC has implemented a program called *Invest-SA,* a robust program of financial incentives to attract foreign

South Africa's eGovernment!

One positive aspect of Jacob Zuma's legacy before leaving office in 2018 was announcement in 2016 that South Africa would become the first government in Africa to be virtually 100% accessible as a smart phone app. Even though only 54% of South Africans own a computer, nearly 70% have smart phones (especially Millennials). He did it to make amends for a spate of charges of political corruption, but it can easily be said, this might have been one his most visionary contributions in an otherwise picaresque 10-year career.

Ever aware of this, South Africa just became the first African government to have a live eGovernment Website nicknamed IMBIZO. On IMBIZO (A Zulu word meaning "gathering" or "political discussion") everyone with a smart phone can access daily updates, broadcasts and immediately apply for and receive their government ID cards, social services and benefits. The result has been the elimination of very long lines at government offices almost overnight, along with restoring South Africa's image as being ahead of the curve (even of most G 7 nations) on this particular aspect of technology. And yes! As it turns out, perception is reality: Access creates transparency. And transparency spawns public demands for accountability.

investment and reignite acquisitions from major financial institutions and venture capital.

South Africa's sphere of influence...

Notwithstanding the ongoing drama and the massive cleanup of political corruption being undertaken by the Ramaphosa administration South Africa is still the "S" in the aggregate of shakers and movers called the BRICS nations. And yet again South Africa (at 48th in the world) was still rated Number 2, behind Mauritius (at 30) among all African nations on the 2016 Legatum Prosperity Index. So one might observe that it has "nine lives" where its fiscal resilience is concerned. Despite the ostensible problems South Africa is having in terms of government stability the fundamentals are sound. Flagging global confidence and its financial integrity notwithstanding, South Africa has enough insiders and credible powerbrokers who believe the ship is currently being righted. And to those willing to be patient the rewards, both tangible and perennial, will be forthcoming.

One aspect of South Africa that is proving more significant than any other is the fact that it virtually "anchors" down Southern Africa. Its trading relationships and business influences in "satellite economies" such as Zambia, Namibia, Botswana and Mozambique have been both stabilizing and reassuring. It is, in every sense of the word, the banker of southern Africa—the one other nations look to for stability, trust, and (that hidden dragon of African growth) accessible credit.

Current Market Indicator: Buy and Hold (forever)

Unless hell freezes over or the sun sets in the East, South Africa (warts and all) will remain a bellwether for the economic future of the entire Sub Sahara.

Stellenbosch wine route and valley of vineyards, outside of Cape Town, South Africa.

KENYA

(Republic of Kenya)

'Freedom' by any other name...

Well, things are seldom dull in Nairobi these days. And as always seems to be the case, Kenya is at a crossroads yet again. And by the time this edition of the book is published we will know whether this pivotal giant in the Sub-Sahara has taken two steps forward or yet another step back.

As the government in power, it is incumbent upon current President Uhuru Kenyatta and the Jubilee Alliance to show Kenyans that they have successfully delivered on at least some of the promises that they made when they came into power in 2013. But even after winning a hotly contested 2017 Presidential election, they still have an uphill climb.

This has not been made any easier by the fact that party politics in Kenya have just gotten bizarre—even by the colorful standards of the Sub Sahara. This "Through the Looking Glass" lack of logic has been aggravated by the fact that Kenyatta, despite having won the election and a recount in November of 2017 is still being invalidated by an opposing party candidate Raila Odinga who refuses to concede the election. Rather than step down and acknowledge the democratic process Odinga recently staged his own inauguration by swearing himself in as "The People's Choice" as president. Written off as a "publicity stunt," Odinga's outrageous behavior has called into question both Uhuru Kenyatta's leadership and sense of authority. Kenyatta, showing remarkable restraint more than occasionally denounced in the press as "weakness" has chosen instead to deal with the nation's other more pressing problems.

Kenya is an important partner of the United States and other countries that are fighting transnational terrorism, especially al-Shabaab. As a key member of the Intergovernmental Authority on Development (IGAD) it has also played a critical role in IGAD's efforts to improve security and peace in war-torn South Sudan. Additionally, Kenya is a leading center for industrial production and is an economic powerhouse for the East Africa region. And Nairobi is the regional headquarters for many transnational corporations and international organizations. So even now, even with this delicate juggling act, the country has a strong influence on its less stable or more burdened neighbors.

And yet even though (the August 2017) elections were closely monitored by discrete independent observers, there remain accusations and counteraccusations from the CORD movement that the IBEC (Independent Boundaries and Electoral Commission) was totally bought and paid for by Kenyatta's Jubilee Alliance. Not surprisingly, protests—some violent—broke out in the days that followed, though none of them with the carnage or intensity of 2007.

Still, even in the weeks that followed, protests and chaos were the order of the day—a situation made even worse by the intense rise of al-Shabaab whose recent atrocities in the Northeast region of the country are putting them on course to rival ISIS as the most horrific and brutal radical jihadists in the world.

It's a shame things have taken this downward turn. And it makes the climb back to credibility even more difficult, because as recently as 2015 "The World Bank's 2013–14 'Doing Business' Report" asserted that sub-Saharan Africa has benefited more than other regions from regulatory improvement and that, "few countries offer greater promise than Kenya!"

This quote from a 2015 *Fortune Magazine* article bullishly summarized the new outlook toward Southern and Eastern Africa.

And for a time at least, Kenya had become the Sub-Sahara's recruitment poster Marine. It can still get back to that point, because—despite all the recent complications—Kenya remains the spearhead of the EAC (East African Community) and the one that other nations within their sphere of influence look to for stability and leadership.

All this innovation and ingenuity comes as a surprise to the statisticians and the "by-the-book" bean counters, because, when it comes to quality of life and the Index of Economic Opportunity, Kenya—on paper at least—comes off as looking pretty lousy.

Its $60.5 billion annual GDP, though a solid number 11 in Africa, has apparently flat-lined over the last five years. Its unemployment rate listed at 40% it ranks as one of the highest in the world. low even by Sub-Saharan Its literacy rating, though fair by African standards, comes in at a tepid 71%, and its *real PPI* per GDP ranking is only $1495 a year, standards. According to income the average Kenyan makes about $1.25 a day. And none of these figures are really quite accurate, mainly because the 25 million U-25 African Millennials ("Afrillennials") have quantum leapt "the mother country" into a different universe.

The most visible reasons are the three T's—*Technology, Telecommunications, and Tourism.* This comes with an emphasis on technology in all its aspects, because Kenya, perhaps more than any other African nation, is at the center of what has recently been labeled the "Silicon Savannah."

Contradicting the fact that Africa—despite its economically challenged middle class and cash-strapped small business—has one of the most exorbitant fees for internet use, technology in Kenya flourishes. And it does so because in East Africa in particular, technology is not a perk; it is a matter of survival. As necessity is the mother of invention, small businesses, farmers, rural merchants and especially Millennials are finding it indispensible in ways more developed nations tend to overlook.

Much of this includes IDEOS, or low-cost smart phones that are crossovers between and iPhone and a Blackberry. Selling for around $80 each (notwithstanding subscription subsidies), these IDEOS are both cost-effective and capable of allowing users to electronically network their business, their families, their homes and even their education entirely from a vast array of apps exclusive to their particular electronic personalities.

The 'I's' Have it:
Internet. Innovation. Intellectual Property.

Well, who would have thought? But nevertheless it's true. As of this moment, the leading nation in global mobile payments (per capita) is Kenya. 80% of all those with  cell phones use them to make payments on everything from bank deposits to rides in a taxi. About 60% of people making less than $2.50 a day have mobile phones. And they're learning quickly that electronic mobility translates into a great deal of personal freedom—of time, of movement and of safety. In fact it's fairly safe to say that mobile banking originated in Kenya.

Kenya's leading mobile technology company Safaricom™ caught onto to this whole notion several years ago. Especially with its *Sambaza* prepaid-minute *swap program* introduced in 2008 (where you can send thousands of minutes of calling time to someone else's app), and its M-PESA virtual money step up from Bitcoin and cellphone ATM instant access in more than 48,000 locations in 2016, Safaricom leads the way in mobile internet access and calling (see Chapter 4). Now, however, it is finally facing price wars from other Kenyan competitors such as Airtel and Zain, who now offer calling rates that are one-third of 2011 levels. (This is particularly liberating since, in many ways, poor and economically marginalized people in the Sub-Sahara have to pay exorbitant rates for cell-phone minutes and Internet access. In fact, it is not at all unusual for someone with a $30,000 a year income to pay as much as 15% of their total gross income just for access to their apps, their internet and their cellular technology. And, given the opportunities set before them, it is a surcharge they are more than willing to pay.)

One can credit many of these quantum leaps in technology to the vision and encouragement of Kenyan Minister of Communications and Information, Bitange Ndemo, who has proven to be something rare in a government official—a visionary. His best quality thus far has been one of lowering government restriction and "getting out of the way" of new tech companies as they flex their muscles, finding bumptious new ways to experiment, and "try new stuff." Branding his department as ICT4D (Information and Communications Technology For[4] Development), Ndemo has not only encouraged the development of technology companies and their solutions, but also incorporated them into government social services, opportunities for the poor and rural communities in Kenya…and as an active facilitator for new channels of education.

Companies such as iHub, a Kenyan non-profit started by Erik Hersman, are breaking new ground in every imaginable area of technology. As it has been set up as both a forerunner and a facilitator, iHub has created a tech network across East Africa that focuses on young African entrepreneurs—including web and mobile phone programmers, designers and researchers. Very creatively set up to be an open community co-venture, iHub is part vector for investors and venture capitalists, part incubator and part think tank for some of the most creative and innovative young minds in African technology. Just since 2011, the iHub hybrid and "university commons" has grown to more than 14,000 members and has led to the launching of about 150 tech companies in the Sub-Sahara.

Erik Hersman

One of the companies to come out of the iHub incubator is an educational "virtual classroom" called *Eneza Education*. Providing its own brand of e-tutor for rural Kenyan kids (11-18) who do not have easy access to middle and high schools, Eneza enables its subscribing students to learn courses in math, English, science, history and basic technology, solve problems and take over 2,400 quizzes and 20,000 drills and work models. Through Eneza, teachers can assign homework, receive reports on student performance and grade independent tests. Starting out modestly with about 100,000 subscribers in 2013, Eneza now has over 1 Million students in rural Africa, with a prediction for exponential growth to more than 50 million in at least 10 different African countries over the next five years.

Another spinoff of the iHub brain trust is a career app called *Mara Mentor.* For a price of $199 (and a hefty subscriber list) Mara Mentor is a "social enterprise vehicle" for emerging young entrepreneurs with emphasis on "women entrepreneurs," that creates career strategies business models to help them build their careers and their young companies. With about 500,000 subscribers already, Mara Mentor also channels them

M-FARM and iCow: The Virtual Farm!

A pair of emerging superstars coming out of the iHub think tank is looking like a very good way to revolutionize farming and ranching, not only for Kenya, Ethiopia, Tanzania and East Africa's bread belt, but also quite possibly for the world.

M-FARM is a mobile software solution that enables farmers and ranchers to get directly in touch with their markets. With M-Farm's agro-app, small farmers can get feed prices, order everything from food to fertilizer,

connecting farmers

make virtual veterinary contacts, learn the latest market prices for their products and even make direct contacts with potential buyers—all by means of a few key strokes on their smartphones. Besides the obvious advantage of not having to spend days traveling to and from market, M-Farm subscribers save money by cutting out middlemen and having to undergo merchant hassles at coops and conventions.

The agri-app iCow is a forerunner to M-FARM but somewhat more "farm specific" in that it goes directly to the actual online marketing of cattle, swine, sheep and goats in that it enables the farmer and rancher to determine feed and fertility cycles, look for possible veterinary issues, measure positive weight gain and connect with "free" advice from farm to market professionals. (Note: To accommodate the issue of possible illiteracy of some rural farmers, most of the apps mentioned here are provided by means of audio instructions and keystroke visuals for easier access no matter what someone's educational level might be.) It has become quickly apparent that the success of these software apps in East Africa will have long range positive implications in terms of global farming and virtual marketing of goods that not only spell "survival" for small farmers but also billions of dollars in savings to global markets.

over into another network called *MSM (Mara Social Media)* that gets young East and Southern Africa entrepreneurs together in an online chat environment to make new contacts and exchange ideas.

Through a combination of optimum P2P and B2B currency (M-PESA in this case) and government subsidy, a Kenyan company called *M-KOPA has developed a way to provide pay-as-you-go solar energy service to more than 200,000 households in Kenya with spillovers to other parts of rural East Africa.* Where many rural African homes have zero electricity and are compelled to run on kerosene, M-KOPA currently offers solar home systems for an initial deposit of only $35 (about 43¢ a day), all of which can be made on M-PESA mobile payments services. At this point M-KOPA is making projections by 2020 of reaching a global off-grid energy spending at $50 billion with East Africa counting for about 10% of the total market.

'Chinatown'

"Forget it Jake. It's Chinatown."
— *Chinatown* (1973)

The quote from the famous movie ironically describes what has often become the African approach to Foreign Direct Investment—especially where it defines China, the BRICS Nations and their interest in Kenya, because some things are better off being appreciated than they are being over-analyzed. And above all else, the best thing a government can do is to amend trade-restrictions, lower tariffs and eliminate all blocks to Foreign Direct Investment. And Kenya in the last dozen years has led the way in accomplishing this..

There is little doubt that one of the driving influences in the new Kenya has been the more than $8.5 billion investment in the national infrastructure by nations like China and Japan. China, with its "no strings policy" has been the largest source of FDI participation, including partnering with the Kenyan government on a cross-country railroad, shoring up its principal seaport at Mombasa, and providing dam and utility construction across the country.

Although many nations in the Sub-Sahara are starting to push back a bit on China's eager involvement and consider the Asian giant's investment to be much more conditional than it appears to be on paper, Kenya has shown no such reluctance and recently President Uhuru Kenyatta signed a new investment agreement with the Chinese for an additional $2.3 billion to go into new facilities, dams and energy production.

This renewed business partnership with China has a strong influence on many of Kenya's sibling nations in East Africa—such as Tanzania, Ethiopia and Uganda—who look to Kenya to be both forerunner and "crash-test dummy" for co-ventures with BRICS nations that will inevitably spillover to them.

It is a mantle of responsibility that Kenya assumes with some difficulty, even though its preeminent position is only logical. Kenya was the first nation in East Africa to win its complete independence (in 1963), and one of the first nations in the Sub-Sahara to manifest a homegrown government that displayed any real semblance of stability. Credit that to the 15-year presidency and strong leadership of the father of Kenyan democracy, Jomo Kenyatta. Kenyatta was one of those rare individuals everyone including Nelson Mandela looked to as the role model for how to transform a Colonial Protectorate into a Constitutional Parliamentary Republic.

In truth Jomo Kenyatta was a valiant military leader and skilled politician who proved to be better at liberating his country than he did at governing it. Beloved by all the people, he did manage the difficult task of extricating Kenya not only from British Colonial Rule but also wrangling a tricky extraction from influence by the Sultan of Zanzibar and later surviving the notorious Shifta Wars with Somali Separatists to the North and East.

Once elected for a 15 year run as unopposed President of Kenya, Kenyatta instituted a Parliamentary Unitary Republic (a euphemism for one party rule). And though he led Kenya directly toward the West and Capitalism, he made some serious mistakes in judgment along the way. Avowedly anti-communist and intent on land reform to return Kenya to the people of his nation, he also fell victim to his own love of luxury and to a continued tribalism that amounted to a kind of "old boys network," seeing to it that his Kikuyu friends were placed in major positions of power (which they immediately used to their advantage).

Once an enfeebled Kenyatta died in 1979, he was succeeded by a series of rather corrupt national leaders who did little to advance the Kenya's cause for nearly 25 years. In truth, the UN finally determined that the presidential race of 2002 was the first truly "free election" in Kenya. And perhaps the best advances for Kenya have been made in the last four years during the administration of Jomo Kenyatta's son, Uhuru Kenyatta.[†]

Despite accusations of corruption (a default position for political opposition in most African states), Uhuru Kenyatta's administration has gone farther faster in developing some key parts of the Kenyan Economy. Principal among them are several programs of what can only be called *Pragmatic Urbanism*. Buildup of urban infrastructure

---

[†]*Uhuru* is the Swahili word for "freedom."

and modernization of major cities began in earnest about 2009. As a result, Kenya's Capital, Nairobi, and its principal port city, Mombasa, have in the last 5 years become picture postcard cities that promote the notion of a newly urbanized Kenya.

These, along with the build up of Kisumu and other towns and cities around the famous Lake Victoria "Lake District" in the western part of the country have done a great deal to reveal Kenya in all its glorious potential—modernized, industrialized and conducive to the Millennial momentum that marks Kenya as a beacon of progress and new ideas.

Whether it continues on that lofty trajectory may rely entirely on that delicate balance between energized high technology, the Millennials it attracts and a government that appreciates the dynamics of both enough to get out of the way.

Kenya's Sphere of Influence: 2015 turned out to be a banner year for Kenya in a number of ways. For the first time ever, it hosted formal visitations from a sitting US President and a Catholic Pontiff. And it happened all in the same year. First Barack Obama (who demurred on his first scheduled visit to Kenya in 2009 due to security reasons) came and spent two days. Then Pope Francis I (the first since John XXIII in 1961) came in October. (Both are good indicators that Kenya's stock has risen high in world circles.) In fact, in the last five years—all UN and IEF metrics notwithstanding—Kenya has garnered a solid reputation as a very good place to do business (and now a fairly safe place to be).

The China Connection, the Japan validation, and increased interest from the US and UK have lifted Kenya's stature on the entire continent and have made it the #1 Anchor State in East Africa. Its symbiotic economic ties to Tanzania, Uganda, Rwanda and the newly emerging Ethiopia have helped to create a positive entrepreneurial environment in the East and more than that a sense of community and a tech network few other nations enjoy.

Especially significant has been the cooperation the Kenyan government has shown with new Internet technologies as part of its operational infrastructure and improvement of quality of life in less developed areas. It is a partnership that, if allowed to continue, can help lift the "Silicon Savannah" into being one of the most innovative and imitated tech centers in the world.

Current Market Indicator: Kenya is rated a Buy!

Despite a host of challenges, including a contested election of Uhuru Kenyatta to a second term as president, Kenya has a very strong franchise. And its rising class of Africapitalists are determined to keep it that way.

ETHIOPIA

(Federal Democratic Republic of Ethiopia)

*Ethiopia and Djibouti have launched the first fully electrified cross-border railway line in Africa.
It links Ethiopia's capital, Addis Ababa, to the Red Sea's Port of Djibouti.*

To gain some perspective, start here: According to most historians, Ethiopia rivals Egypt as the birthplace of Western Civilization. Identified as the ancient empire of Abyssinia (or Punt), it is the site of the oldest recorded hominid carbon dated back 4.2 million years. It is also the conceptual origin of a beverage called coffee, highly developed ancient architecture and the invention of coinage—or monetary exchange—as we know it. Through the leadership of Haile Selassie I ["The Lion of Judah"], Ethiopia was—until 1979—the oldest surviving autonomous "Empire" in the Western Hemisphere, and the second oldest in the world. (Now, only Japan remains.)

Partly in tribute to its longstanding credibility in the East African community and partly due to the fact that Addis Ababa is one of the most beautiful cities in the Sub-Sahara, Ethiopia has come to be one of major focal points for the convening of African organizations, legations and heads of state. In fact the main administrative capital of the African Union is in Addis Ababa where the AU Commission is permanently headquartered. A newly constructed power center, the AUCC Conference Center and Office Complex was inaugurated on 28 January 2012, during the 18th annual AU summit. The complex, built by China State Construction Corporation, was a gift from the Chinese government, and features a number of other facilities, including a 2,500-seat plenary hall and a 20-story office tower. The tower is precisely 99.9 meters high to signify the date—9 September 1999—when The Organization of African Unity voted to become the African Union.

The Ancient-Modern Paradox of the Lion Throne

Ethiopia has the most phenomenal history in that it has been both a valiant and courageous entity. It is the only nation anywhere to stand off and defeat a colonial aggressor state, regain its independence in 1881 and gain a treaty with all parties, including concessions. Once again, in the face of outside aggression such as invasion from Fascist Italy in World War II, it was a beacon of African courage and resistance. And it is in fact one of the 24 countries that met to found the original United Nations. As the largest land-locked nation in the Sub-Sahara (it is about the size of Bolivia), it comes in at the throat of the Blue Nile and houses a beautiful lake district and one of the most varied climates in the world.

A Bad Year and a Worse Reputation

To add to the living contradiction that Ethiopia has become, it has—by all Human Rights Watch Reports—done abysmally in the last 18 months since January 2016. Governed by the People's Revolutionary Democratic Front (PRDF) it gets a very bad rap for human rights violations. And Freedom House gives it a miserable 12 out of 100 ranking (100 being the freest) as being a state that is "not free." This perception is skewed in very much the same way Assisi's regime is maligned in Egypt.

In truth, the government of Mulatu Teshome finds itself in a political conundrum that is both unique and perilous. A predominantly Christian Nation (62%), Ethiopia is landlocked in the Horn of Africa by five of the most openly corrupt, hostile and radically Islamist nations in the world. Sudan, South Sudan, Eritrea, Djibouti and Somalia wrap around about 85% of its borders, leaving only Kenya as a kind of safety valve and channel to some semblance of civilized sanity.

This was not helped in the least by the resignation in February of 2018 by Prime Minister Hailemariam Desalegn, immediately followed by a State of Emergency declared by Ethiopia's parliament to quell recent protests and threats of revolt from outlying states for better representation.

The emergency measures ban protests and restricts publications that could be deemed to incite violence. Although President Mulatu Teshome still runs the show in Addis Ababa, the surprise resignation of his Number 2 managed to shake the matrix in every imaginable way—so much so US Secretary of State Rex Tillerson made a "courtesy call" to shore up relations with America's best ally in East Africa. Because in the opinions of many experts, if Ethiopia descends into a state of revolution, the entire Horn of Africa will be lost.

So translations to the democratic mindset of a civilized world are, from Ethiopia's perspective, not that easy to come by. That is where the problems start, but by no means where they end.

By all surface indications Ethiopia is at the bottom of all quality of life indexes. At 145 of 181 nations measured, it remains one of the poorest countries in the world. In direct contradiction to all this, the International Monetary Fund (IMF) rates Ethiopia one of the most dynamic economies in the Sub-Sahara, registering over 10% economic growth from 2004 through 2009…and about 8% up through 2013. As such, it has been the fastest-growing non-oil-producing African economy. Although growth has slowed somewhat since 2014, the outlook still looks pretty bullish, which leads one to ask the question: Where is this apparent uptick in economic activity coming from?

The answer comes in three parts: *Part 1: Youth.* Precisely 63% of Ethiopia's population is under 25 years of age. Still undereducated when compared to other nations of the Sub-Sahara, 55% of Ethiopian Millennials in 2015 were getting secondary education (as opposed to just 29% in 1995). Although 25% of the population under 30 is out of work, they do live in the virtual world of technology and smart phone apps. And spillover Internet access from Kenyan online education such as Eneza Education, Safaricom and M-Pesa are quickly bringing them up to speed. Cross connections with more bullish economies such as Uganda and Kenya have empowered them into a new awareness of Internet shopping, online education, and virtual money. And as youth always drives new markets, Ethiopia's very young, better-educated urbanizing youth seems to be propelling the country in the right direction.

Part 2: FDI commitment from some key nations. As one facet in a Rubix immediately triggers a solution in another, despite its political problems (much of them generated by its siege mentality in the face of Islamic extremism), Ethiopia is still managing to hold it together, economically. In 2016, much due to improvements in infrastructure, it showed up as number 2 in Africa's Top 10 in terms of total GDP growth.

What's more, Ethiopia's burgeoning youth driven economy with massive projected retail sales in the next 5 years, has drawn some serious Foreign Direct Investment from China, India, Turkey, Saudi Arabia and the United States. Recent reports from the IMF (noted earlier) and from the United Nations Conference on Trade and Development (UNCTAD) rated Ethiopia and Kenya the Number three and four African markets for new investment with an anticipated $6.1 billion in 2016. In that investment package, Ethiopia leads the way with a cash infusion of $4.5 billion (USD). Much of this has to do with the Ethiopian government's new policy of privatization of most industries, along with a lowering of all trade and tariff barriers, making this emerging market a very FDI friendly economy.

In an active ongoing portrait, China is right there at present, representing 15% of Ethiopia's total exports as well as more than 20% of its FDI participation.

'An All-Female Flight Night' on Ethiopian Air

Why didn't someone think of it before? The question was asked and then answered by Ethiopian Airlines who on November 19, 2015 made history by sending an all-female crew on a flight from Addis Ababa to Bangkok, Thailand.

The fully feminized flight Crew was the first in the 70-year history of the airline, and the crew turned out to be more than the pilot and co-pilot: It also included maintenance crew members and air traffic controllers. Needless to say it was a "statement flight." And it came from a surprising source—Ethiopian Air.

By no means the first to have female pilots (Women started piloting planes for American Airlines as far back as 1973) Ethiopian did make sure it was unprecedented. That was because every single person on the flight staff was a woman. A full female cabin crew, including master flight attendants also staffed cabin, ramp and airport operations, as well as onboard logistics, air safety and security jobs. The airline announced that it wanted to diversify and show the world the important jobs African women now hold. Ethiopian Airlines says about one-third of its employees are women.

But the number of female pilots is still below 10 percent. Just over five percent of all commercial airline pilots in 2010 were women. Still this goes a long way toward breaking the glass ceiling...including and especially the one in the sky.

The US slots in at third place as an export market (mainly for food and animals). And Saudi Arabia represents 9.1% of all exports, and 8% of all—mostly food and fuel tradeoffs—since Ethiopia has no petroleum reserves to speak of, and Saudi is agriculturally bereft. At this point, it is important to point out that, all common perceptions to the contrary, Ethiopia is one of the Sub-Sahara's two or three bread-basket nations, which leads us to Part 3 of this little puzzle.

Part 3: Agricultural production and diversity of natural resources. Well, we've all seen the photos and heard the news—gaunt starving children and food relief being sent to Ethiopia—droughts, desertification, "we are the world" concert benefits…and all that information is more than 25 years old. Yes, Ethiopia still has some issues of malnourishment, but by-and-large it now produces some of the world's most prolific crops, including coffee, beans, sugarcane, various oilseeds and an entire cornucopia of vegetables. And it doesn't stop at fruits and vegetables. Ethiopia is also heavily invested in swine and cattle production, and is in fact one of the world's Top 10 producers of beef cattle.

In a way, it seems inconceivable that this erstwhile "Live-Aid" poster child for food relief of the 1980s could now somehow be providing a broad range of agro-based commodities. And at least part of the reason is the new empowerment that comes from such programs as the One-Acre Fund (with internet access farming coming out of Kenya) plus the work of such brilliant new grow-crop entrepreneurs as Ethiopian Fitsun Hagos and Luna Farm Export PLC.

Upbeat and optimistic at all times, Fitsun Hagos spent the first 16 years of his life growing up in the Tigray region where the Ethiopian famine in the 1980s was at its worst. So he has always embraced a dedication to creating a self-determining network of farms that would be a showcase for the nation…and one that would be a beacon for food starved neighboring countries like Eritrea, Sudan, Somalia and Djibouti.

Although Luna leases the farmland from the Ethiopian Government (the Interior Ministry owns virtually all the farmland), Hagos and Luna's 400 employees have transformed their 100,000-acre farmland into the best of all possible worlds of organic crops and free-range cattle and swine, processed and brought to market in ways that are both prolific and profitable. In fact, their current farm-to-market techniques are not only prolific but also provide new production innovations that get finished product to countries in the Middle-East such as Saudi Arabia and UAE that have enhanced their market share and enabled them to seize major market initiatives in the Pan-African agribusinesses that are gaining in popularity in developing countries. These new eco-friendly breakthroughs and farm-to-finished-product techniques are projected to bring in $50 billion to $150 billion in new revenues by 2025.

Ethiopia's Sphere of Influence: Notwithstanding its powerful influence the EAC and its active involvement in COMESA, Ethiopia's primary mission in the last five years has been one of individuation. It has been in the process of becoming its own nation with its own destiny, and without outside influences on its economy, including being helped to death by USAID the IFA and other "well-meaning" dependency groups. Part of that process has been weaning the Ethiopian government off the process through the efforts of enterprising African Entrepreneurs to privatize Ethiopian business, agriculture and ownership of energy. Up to 2012, it was an uphill battle. But since that time the tectonic plates of commerce have shifted. FDI commitments have helped this erstwhile codependent country break new ground. And individual businesses startups have more than tripled in the last three years.

Current Market Indicator: Buy and Hold

Despite the external threat and internal crackdowns, economic tides are rolling in. Start to look for things to get better soon.

Summary

As far as the Four "Anchor Nations" of the Sub-Sahara are concerned, even the most dedicated investor will admit that we are very much like firewalkers, stepping gingerly yet as an act of faith. More players and new economies will rise to challenge for leadership within the next few years. Nations such as Namibia, Cote d'Ivoire, Mozambique, Botswana and Rwanda have made remarkable strides in recovery, economic stimulation and stable governance. And their economies have begun to reflect that the economic currents are trending in their favor.

So one can choose to welcome them to The Club with the belief that all boats are lifted with the tide. Or one can play the "Zero-Sum Game" and look for some other economy to fall back into the crowd. Then again, that defines the conundrum of investment. Are you a bull? Or Are you a bear? Are you a lion or meat?

Well as they say, "TIA" (This is Africa). And dinner awaits the bold.

CHAPTER 8

Twelve Africas:
Africa's Next Hottest Markets

I f we have learned anything by now it is this: Africa is the very definition of change. Today's major players hit bumps in the road that suddenly shakes the foundation beneath them and investor confidence right along with it. By the same token, a new election, a change of government or an uptick in social consciousness can suddenly lift a former troubled economy onto the Cloud 9 of renewed national energy and proportionate Foreign Direct Investment.

That has become the case for easily a dozen nations just since 2010. And it has happened to make all the difference. Nations with previously troubled destinies such as Rwanda, Botswana, Uganda, Cameroon and Cote d'Ivoire have become balanced, bullish, reliable participants in the rising tide of African Economies. And resource rich nations such as Mozambique and Tanzania have seen dramatic spikes in the last four years that are virtually unmatched in the Sub-Sahara.

There are myriad reasons. And they are often as seemingly unrelated as the countries that drive them. No question, every nation in Africa has a complex network of interconnection—one that forms a web of all the things they share in common.

First, virtually all of them have been subjected to Colonial rule, often by more than one European nation over the course of time.

Second, they have almost all been alternately helped then later hampered through "death by good intentions"—by the IMF, UNAID, USAID, The World Bank and a dozen other "foreign aid" organizations that are like the monetary version of a "Roach Motel." (Money goes in, but it doesn't come out.)

Third most governments, especially those in the Sub-Sahara, are less than 60 years old, and some are less than 20. More than half have undergone protracted political strife and civil wars that have lasted for decades. Ten of those have only been resolved in the last 15 years. And, in terms of national credibility, that has made all the difference.

Fourth, many economies are now looking to technology as a way out of the global ghetto—and it is working to some degree in all of them. Advanced technology coming out of Nigeria, South Africa and especially Kenya have proved liberating, not only to Millennials but also the entire world of commerce. Finally, we have the ultimate force to be reckoned with: the youth movement. UNICEF recently confirmed our estimates that 69% of the populations of the entire Sub-Sahara are under 30 years of age. That makes Africa the youngest continent on Planet Earth. Millennials and Gen Z's are the ones demanding education, technology and a better quality of life. And youth will be served.

At this point, we've already covered many of Africa's powerhouse nations. Now we redirect our attention to what we have to qualify as "The Comers, The Next Big Thing, the 'Developing Dozen,' and The Heirs Apparent." Since each story is unique and yet many are interconnected, we'll take our collection of rising stars in alphabetical order.

BOTSWANA
(Republic of Botswana)

Central business district, Gaborone, Botswana, 2017.

Botswana has the highest Index of Economic Freedom ranking of any nation on the African Continent. Start there. It also rates highest on the World Democracy Index at number 28, just a notch behind France and ahead of nations such as Portugal, Israel and Taiwan. This places Botswana at # 1 on the Continent and just behind Mauritius in the broad spectrum of African nations. This includes island nations such as Madagascar and the Seychelles. And that makes Botswana a course study in democracy in every entrepreneurial sense of the world.

The comparisons to France are appropriate here, because Botswana has the same approximate total area. It has, in Sub-Saharan terms, a very lush varied countryside in the Southwestern sector, a relatively pleasant climate and a certain *bon amité* that one might find on the Riviera. But imagine France with a population of only 2.24 million people, and then add in the fact that 70% of the rest of the country is smack in the middle of the Kalahari Desert.

Then again, comparisons to France often err because Botswana is an Anglophone nation like its neighbors South Africa and Zimbabwe. Unlike those two countries with their very troubled political histories, however, Botswana achieved its independence by mutual consent from the British Commonwealth in 1964, and somehow managed to get it right the first time.

First, the new government of Sereste Khama immediately managed to extricate itself from the talons of an apartheid-plagued South Africa and set the seat of the new Parliamentary Democracy in the city of Gaborone. From there, a series of balanced ecumenical regimes followed, along with a logical string of social programs, universal suffrage and a revamped system of Health and Education. In just 25 years, Botswana has increased its literacy rate from 69% in 1991 to 83.5% in 2015 with the greatest strides in education being made among women. The government has provided a series of seven very strongly situated vocational training schools across the country. And at the university level many private institutions are making scholarships affordable, available and winnable for students who show the determination to achieve higher education.*

Although its $15.6 billion GDP has flatlined a bit over the last ten years, Botswana still enjoys a solid PPI (quality of life index) of $7,140 per capita—one of the best "real indicators" in Africa. It shines where its support of national resources and wildlife are concerned, and has managed to successfully eliminate poaching almost entirely from its list of ecological challenges.

In truth, Botswana has worked hard to develop reforestation efforts in heretofore depleted areas and is actually one of the few countries in the world where some indigenous animal populations have either held their own or actually grown in the last 10 years. The Chobe National Park and the Moremi Game Reserve (in the Okavango Delta) are major tourist destinations, and African Elephant herds in those areas remain stable.

The World Transparency Index has just rated Botswana "the least corrupt nation in Africa," which is a classic example of being damned with faint praise. And though

---

* The religious influence of Botswana is 96% Christian. And having Christianity as the official state religion has enabled it to override any restrictions made upon women based upon gender.

the Index of Economic Freedom slams President Ian Khama of "creeping authoritarianism" (whatever that means) Botswana continues to get one of the highest ratings for good places to do business. Its competitive banking system is one of the most advanced in the world. And it has become one of the best brokers of virtual money in Southern Africa. Botswana's major ties both culturally and politically remain with South Africa, and the proximity has traditionally been an amicable one. This political symbiosis has helped both nations greatly as trading partners, solid financial networks and stabilizing influences for the rest of Southern and Eastern Africa.

Although only 12% of the land is considered arable, Botswana has long been a highly agrarian economy, and ranks 15th in cattle production. (About 50% of the Botswana population has at least one cow.) Exceeding even the reserves of South Africa, Botswana has now officially become the world's "diamond mine." And though the government owns 50% of all diamond production (split equally with DeBeers), it has aggressively courted FDI relationships, especially in the last 10 years. It has consistently lowered all trade barriers and tariffs. And its number one trading partner remains the USA. It helps that the nation also has newly discovered veins of copper, nickel and potash to contribute to the national treasury. And its trade balance now remains in the black by about $7 billion USD.

At the moment, and above all other nations, Botswana has been given an "A" bond rating and recommended by both Moody's and Standard and Poor's Indexes as "one of the best markets in Africa to do business." Botswana's *Pula* has held up perhaps better than any other currency since 2014, and the BSE is the best-rated stock exchange in Southern Africa, providing a rather robust 24% return on investment in the last two years.

The Bottom Line

Consistency and integrity win out in the end. Botswana is an island in the storm for the last 50 years and shows even newer signs of exponential growth. It is in fact, Southern Africa's safe harbor.

Current Market Indicator: A Strong Buy

CAMEROON

(République du Cameroun)

Cameroon is now erroneously looked upon as a "middle of the road" emerging economic empire in central Africa and openly embraces the commercial, cultural and political umbrella of its giant neighbor to the Northwest—Nigeria.

Despite a rather lousy rating on the Index of Economic Freedom and the Transparency Index, Cameroon has recently turned out to be rock solid politically, sociologically and in terms of a healthy robust economy.

The apparent challenge lies in the fact that President Paul Biya has governed the country since 1982. The good news is that President Paul Biya has governed Cameroon since 1982. (So let us attempt to quantify the seeming contradiction.) On the downside, critics observe that Biya is a classic case of "the Devil you know." To his credit — or perhaps his survival instincts — supporters say that he knows how to govern a country that is a constant cauldron of corruption and political agitation (especially in the north). In truth, political dissent is harshly dealt with, and repression of agitators is somewhat infamous. On average, however, quality of life among the general population—though far from perfect and somewhat the median for the Sub-Sahara—is stable and supportable. Life expectancy is one of the lowest on the continent (at 54 years of age), partly due to the fact that it generally has a health care system that is considered inadequate even by African standards. At present there are only 2 doctors for every 10,000 people, and bribery and corruption in health care networks have become a national scandal.

Cameroon is perhaps the most unapologetically Francophone nation on the entire continent of Africa. Its official language is French. English is the second most frequently spoken tongue. And about 64% of its citizens are bilingual. It manages nicely to fit itself into the Commonwealth of Nations and also Le Francophonié. And both these cultural affiliations serve it well when it comes to trade, tourism and all FDI ventures into the country.

Cameroon enjoys an annual nominal GDP that has enjoyed moderate growth in the last couple of years to about $29.7 billion. And its primary sources of income besides agriculture are what investors refer to as the four "C's" of Central Africa—cotton, cocoa, coffee and crude oil. Its principal trading partners for import and export are the "usual suspects" for prodigious West African nations—China, France, India, Spain, Netherlands and the USA.

In truth Cameroon—despite a rather sloppy government infrastructure—has really pulled it together when it comes to creating a "user friendly climate" for Foreign Direct Investment. In spite of that, 2016 FDI investment was only about $621 million, just a notch above the 2015 figure, so prospects seem to have flattened out. The good news accompanying all this is a 4.6% unemployment rate, which is one of the lowest in Africa.

One of the most alluring aspects of doing business in Cameroon has been its rather bullish financial system. In fact, it is now looked upon (perhaps erroneously) as the "Banker of Central Africa." In truth, Cameroon's financial corridors are the busiest in what is known as the CEMAC region.**

Offering one of the broadest bases of financial services in the region, Cameroon's banks are also 65% foreign owned and only make about a 3% profit versus 20% for most banks. At the moment, less than 6% of Cameroonians actually bank, but P2P smart phone and internet app banking is the fastest growing financial sector especially among its 25 and under Millennials.

Bottom line on Cameroon

Although it may not be the best country in Africa to live, it has become a great place to visit…and to do business. It's all about who(m) you know and what kind of investment you're looking to make.

 Current Market Indicator on Cameroon: Buy… carefully

** Economic and Monetary Union of Central Africa (CEMAC). This includes Angola, Burundi, Cameroon, Central African Republic, Chad, Democratic Republic of the Congo, Equatorial Guinea, Gabon, Sao Tomé and Principe and Rwanda.

CÔTE D'IVOIRE

(Republic of Côte d'Ivoire)

Abidjan — West Africa's Riviera

Cote d'Ivoire has enjoyed something of a major breakout since 2013—mainly because it finally stopped fighting what seemed to be a nonstop string of civil wars and has come to show a bit more national stability. In truth, Cote d' Ivoire simply has too much going for it in terms of natural resources and new infusions of FDI to stay down for long. It has just needed to open itself up to the opportunities. Now at last it has. With a $36.9 billion annual GDP, the year 2016 saw it become one of the top four most competitive markets in the Sub-Sahara, and it is still improving. As of mid-year 2017, it ranks a solid number 7 in Africa in terms of infrastructure.

It helps a great deal to have a new president who is trying to "do the right thing." And so far the Presidential Administration of Alassane Quatarra, since his government won free election in 2012, has been a proverbial new broom. As a result, Cote d'Ivoire has jumped to be one of the top ten African nations in terms of both Economic Freedom Index and the Democracy Index. Most striking among the improvements of the now seasoned Quatarra-Duncan administration has been the implementation of massive labor reform, including major advances toward the elimination of forced labor and child labor—especially from its Cocoa plantations—giving it a virtual clean slate from the US Department of Labor's list of violators. And its "zero tolerance" policy for government corruption, though still far from fully enforced, has at least cut down on a system of bribery and money laundering that was—under the regime of former president Laurent Gbagbo—something of a scandal.

That is something just short of a miracle, given the rather checkered past of this Francophone nation that is now looked upon as an anchor state, especially among its adjacent siblings such as Ghana, Sierra Leone and Guinea. I emphasize Francophone at this point because of the Colonial culture that the French style brings with it— more one of assimilation and socio-economic fusion—which has its benefits and its hindrances (a subject we will cover next in Chapter 9).

Slightly larger than the nation of Italy, Cote d'Ivoire is an anomaly in that it now popularly boasts what is rapidly becoming looked upon as the African "Riviera" at Abidjan. And it is the absolute port of choice for all its landlocked neighbors to the North, many of whom ship their goods for export through Cote d'Ivoire's coastline cities. It is Important to note that nations such as Mali, Burkina Faso and Chad are at choice when it comes to channeling their goods for overseas shipment, many have listed Cote d'Ivoire as a preferred port of call, due to its improved stability and integrity of contract.

One of the issues it has addressed successfully is its ability to stop the flow of armaments, drugs and conflict diamonds through its channels of distribution and out of its port cities. And a basic cleaning up of its image has helped bring a more stable climate and enhanced reputation for Abidjan and its other shipping centers.

Besides becoming a major tourist attraction and vacation spot for its African neighbors, and in addition to its exportation contracts that contribute more than $2.5 billion to the annual GDP, Cote d'Ivoire is also occasionally referred to as "The Chocolate Coast" due to its prolific $3.2 billion in cocoa production for major corporations such as Hershey (US) and Nestlé (Netherlands).

Still referred to in some sectors as "The Ivory Coast," (the Anglophone description of what was once the African capital of the Ivory Trade in the 18th, 19th and early 20th Centuries) Cote d'Ivoire has more actively embraced its French antecedents in the last 25 years, and it seems to have paid dividends. In the last five years, Cote d'Ivoire has, through its re-energized petroleum industry and solid financial center out of Abidjan, grown to be the third largest economy in West Africa. Its current real GDP of $34.5 billion with an annual growth rate of 6% places it just behind Ghana (at $39.2 billion GDP) but still a distant third to Nigeria whose $594 billion tops all African nations.

Although the Ivory Coast's long history of political instability has somewhat surprisingly caused the BRICS nations to be slow to engage it FDI co-ventures, the US and EU (especially the Netherlands and France) have been quick to come into what they consider a very good new place to do business.

At this point, Morocco continues to be Cote d'Ivoire's longest standing trading partner in Africa for exports in the Sub-Sahara and something of a mentor and "go-to" nation that—more than any other—has helped attract institutional investment channels and broker a healthy Bourse Régionale des Valeurs Mobilières SA (BRVM) stock exchange.***

This is due in part to a clever monetary move made by Cote d' Ivoire and 7 other Francophone nations around 1998 when they pegged the CFA *(Communuate Financiére Africaine)* to the Euro, leading to stable exchange rate and an enhanced ability to attract giant blocks of Foreign Direct Investment (FDI).

As recently as 2014, Morocco's exports to Cote d'Ivoire increased by 300% during the same year that Morocco and Ivory Coast signed 26 public-private partnerships and investment agreements. The agreements that had crowned the Moroccan-Ivorian Economic Forum held in Abidjan that year covered all areas of trade, maritime fisheries, investment, tourism, ICT, agriculture, housing, education, and training. What's more, Morocco's leading financial institution Attijariwafa Bank established a branch in Côte d'Ivoire as early as 2010 with a capital infusion of $250 million (USD) one of the first such coventures in the Sub-Sahara.

The Bottom Line

This is a classic case of "knowing the right people and establishing relationship," if you plan to do business here. At the moment, it is a hot new economy—but mainly for the aggressive investor. Given its past track record of corruption and civil strife, the faint of heart might want to wait a beat. Then again…it's all about who you know, and who you trust. (Isn't everything?)

 Current Market Indicator: Be Bold. Buy and Hold

***The Regional Stock Exchange (BRVM) is common to all eight countries of the West African Economic and Monetary Union (WAEMU) including the following: Benin, Burkina Faso, Cote D'ivoire, Guinea-Bissau, Mali, Niger, Senegal and Togo.

GABON

(République Gabonaise)

The dramatically slanted roof of this assembly hall on a hillside in Librevile, Gabon, incorporates Gabon's vibrant ecology to create a striking expression of a Green Gabon.

If Gabon had a national slogan it would be this: "Two Steps Forward. One Step Back." That is because this unexpected powerhouse is a success in spite of itself.

About the size of Poland, Gabon is resource-rich for its size. And because of tremendous oil and gas reserves, it is one of the richest economies in the Sub-Sahara with an annual GDP of $14.6 billion and a Purchasing Power Parity (PPP) of about $18.6 K per capita. This figure of course is a "red herring' characteristic of most oil rich nations with small populations. And since Gabon has only 1.66 million people, quality of life for the average Gabonese citizen would seem better than it really is. In truth, Gabon is politically and economically one of the most inconsistent nations in Africa. "Big Dumb Puppy-dog," might be a good metaphor, because it tries so hard to do the right thing and more often than not just trashes its own house.****

Gabon's vast oil reserves, prolific manganese mines and dense forestry, has led it to be a primary exporter of natural resources to its principal trading partners—USA, China, Hong Kong and South Africa. It has made decent attempts at industrializing in the last 10 years and has built up a number of textile plants, cement factories, chemical plants, shipyards and tobacco harvesting and cigarette factories.

**** "Big dumb puppy-dog," was the reference Johnny Depp made in 2008, alluding to USA's foreign policy in Asia and the Middle East—an irony many political observers believed to be correct.

The country is highly reliant on Foreign Direct Investment. And though it has a rather stringent tariff structure at 27%, it encourages businesses to come to the country, especially those willing to contribute to its industrial development.

Government inconsistency, however, has been a trademark of doing business here, and many manufacturers and retailers from the EU have come to build in Gabon only to leave in utter frustration a few years later.

In terms of political genealogy, President Ali Bongo Ondimba basically succeeded his (eponymous) father Omar Bongo Ondimba in 2009, when the former died in office after "governing" the country for 41 years. And though Gabon describes its government as a Presidential Republic, the Ondimba family has more or less ruled it as an undeclared absolute monarchy for over 50 years.

The strength of the Bongo-Ondimba administration has been that, though absolutist in many respects, it has governed with just a loose enough leash to avoid civil wars, attempted coups d'état and any long term civil strife that has plagued its troubled neighbors such as Cameroon and The Democratic Republic of the Congo.

Recently Ali Bongo has tried hard to engage in more transparency to help shore up public infrastructure for utilities, health and education. And thus far, he seems to be making steady if bumpy progress. Gabon at present has a respectable 84% literacy rate, but this too is a bit misleading since dropout rates of students before 6th grade are about 30%. Despite a seemingly bullish economy, unemployment sits at about 24% and, almost in defiance of a prolific GDP, the public debt is just below 26%, indicating fiscal mismanagement at practically every level. Despite its rich oil reserves Gabon is a profligate credit risk, and the Ondimba administration is constantly hitting up the IMF for loans for which they have shown scant propensity for repayment.

Although it recently sat as a non-permanent member of the UN Security Council in 2010-2012, the general FDI and IMF outlook on Gabon is one of caution, especially in view of tanking petroleum prices in 2015 and the fact that Gabon has not traditionally responded well to crisis environments.

This time, however, it might have to. Because like its mentor state Nigeria, Gabon needs to learn the lessons of spreading the economic bet to several new industries at once. Like any one-industry boom economy the truth ultimately comes home to roost—now more than ever, "It is diversify or die." Not so much of a threat as a glimpse of the future.

Current Market Indicator on Gabon: Hold

There's not much here to make Foreign Direct Investors feel bullish just yet.

GHANA

(The Republic of Ghana)

Petronia City, Oil and Gas Capital, Ghana.

Ghana has to be on everyone's list as the most improved nation in Africa. It is the second largest economy in Western Africa, and has for the last 25 years been considered a stabilizing political influence in the Sub-Sahara. That solid sense of political balance was set early on by its "Founding Father" Dr. Kwame Nkrumah, the liberator of Ghana who extracted it peacefully from British Colonial rule in 1957 and went on to walk that very fine line that kept it in balance for the next 20 years.

You may also credit that somewhat to its long having embraced a political stance of non-alignment, and the fact that its ambassador to the United Nations, Kofi Annan was elected its Secretary General in 1997. In so doing, he enjoyed a two-term ten-year run as one of the two hardest working Secretaries General in that international institution's rather irregular 70-year history. As former head of the World Health Organization before his appointment to post of UN Secretary General, Kofi Annan continued on his humanitarian mission, becoming an active, vocal and hands-on advocate of human rights.

Striking such a stance is not an entirely popular undertaking, especially since more than two out of every three of the United Nation's 193 member states get failing grades for alleged human rights violations. But Kofi Annan has always embraced a reputation for being outspoken where corruption is concerned.

Having one's own unannounced Secretary of State become one of the 10 most influential politicos in the world does tend to put a bit of moral pressure on the home country—especially when he goes on to win the Nobel Peace Prize in 2006 for accomplishing any number of bold human rights initiatives. In fact, Kofi Annan's credits include having revitalized the UN and returning it to its original peacemaking core of integrity, arbitrating conflicts between nations, and for engineering (behind the scenes) such initiatives as fighting hunger and providing underdeveloped nations with sustainable qualities of life. Along this bold path, Kofi Annan was individually acknowledged for having helped transform Nigeria from a military dictatorship into adopting well-monitored free civilian elections, and for holding larger member nations such as the USA, Russia and China accountable for their own human rights issues (such as massive imprisonment of citizens).

Due to a tradition of integrity especially in the last 25 years, Ghana has one of the best human rights ratings and is ranked as the #5 least corrupt among Africa's 54 member states. Attribute much of that to the 2012 election of John Dramani Mahama as one of a succession of fairly stable presidents in a nation that has seemed to strike the appropriate balance between good governance and private sector ambition.

At the moment, Ghana is one of the few countries in Africa that enjoys predominantly free universal health care, and its educational system is constantly improving to include a vast network of vocational schools as well as a burgeoning university system with a well-developed liberal arts curriculum.

Not only does Ghana enjoy a very diverse and balanced economy, it is constantly expanding areas in which it does thrive. The world's seventh largest producer of gold and the ninth largest producer of diamonds, it is currently cultivating one of the most prolific oil and natural gas fields in the world—the famed Jubilee Field—with over 300 billion metric tons of petroleum reserves.

Perhaps Ghana's most prolific new areas of growth are through technology. Its advances in cyberspace, Internet and telecommunications have grown to rival even Nigeria as a leader in smartphone and virtual money technology. Much of this accelerated innovation is coming from Ghana's state-owned super-tech giant Rig Communications, which—so far—is specializing in low cost tablet and smartphone manufacture at price points that most middle-income Ghanaians can afford.

In the last 10 years, Ghana has often been criticized for its lack of privatization, its high import tariffs and for the fact that, especially in areas such as technology and energy, it doesn't appear willing to loosen the leash.

So far, however, it has kept bureaucratic skullduggery to a minimum and its newest government sponsored economic satellite project, "Ghana: Vision 2020," promises to bring a paradigm shift to Sub Sahara technology. With this new initiative, Ghana has announced its intentions to achieve its goals of accelerated economic growth and improved quality of life for all its citizens, by reducing poverty through private investment, rapid and aggressive industrialization, and direct and "aggressive poverty-alleviation efforts." To its critics *GHANA: Vision 2020* appears to be just another ploy disguised to augment its cryptic nationalization of even more industries. Since Ghana's government already owns two out of every three major businesses in the nation, it would appear to be excessive. But, so far, the Dramani Mahama administration refuses to let down on what may appear to be a socialistic seizure of capital enterprise in the nation.

The final test of intention may come with the construction of something appropriately called *HOPE City,* Ghana's showcase multibillion-dollar technology center outside of Accra. Although construction is just under way, this tech and business center is due for a well-choreographed completion in 2020. And it will feature six-immense skyscrapers, including one that is 75 floors and 270 meters high—the tallest building on the African Continent. Predicted to office as many as 30,000 employees, HOPE City promises to be the "Lion of African tech," although detractors are betting that it might just as easily become its White Elephant.

At the moment, Ghana's neo-socialist infrastructure may have reached its point of critical mass. In the last three years, the nation's fiscal deficit has continued to be very high. In 2012, the deficit stood at 11.6 percent but dropped to 10.4 percent in 2013 and then to 9.4 percent in 2014. The high national overhead in 2012 was attributed to all of the following: the payment of accumulated arrears; significant drop in grants from donors; over-estimation of revenues from oil companies; larger than expected petroleum and utility subsidies; higher interest cost burden arising from the rise in short term domestic interest rates, and a GHC of about $1.1 billion is recorded in the budget as a "discrepancy."

It is also somewhat indicative of Ghana's attitude at the moment toward Foreign Direct Investment and the major FDI players from the EU, US and BRICS countries. Ghana's current intention (70% of it) is to grow from the inside out. But it is sticking its toe in the water through privatization of telecommunications, finance and solid consumer market expansions. So eventually, if not immediately, one has to look to Ghana to really start spreading its wings. Timing is everything; so one has to ask "Where and when?"

In the ultimate paradox, despite its deep deficit challenges, Ghana has one of the highest FDI commitment ratios of any nation not named Nigeria, Kenya or South Africa. In the year 2016 the projected investment from companies like Coca Cola, IBM, Deloitte & Touche and AT&T have exceeded $3.2 billion USD. A lot of other

Foreign Direct Investment is taking a serious look and asking all the right questions. The question is which way you are betting…and the smart money is going here.

Current Market Indicator on Ghana: Buy and hold

This should be the watchword, unless and until we see that privatization is the path of preference.

Accra has been listed among 35 Most Resilient Cities in the World.

MAURITIUS

(Republic of Mauritius)

Mauritius (as in delicious) is a classic example of the fact that small countries are the best opportunities for an optimal quality of life—provided they are well run. By every tool of measurement this island nation (occasionally referred to as "the African Hong Kong") is just that.

In truth, if one were to run a word association game and bring Mauritius into the conversation the first thing everyone would think of is "Free." It is a free market economy and a free port with the highest rating on the Index of Economic Freedom. It is the only nation in Africa rated by all indexes as an "Entirely Free Democracy." It provides free National Health Care for all of its 1.3 million citizens, and free education up to lower tertiary levels (the first two years of college).

A small island about twice the size of Hong Kong (or slightly larger than the peninsula state of Singapore), Mauritius boasts a surprising $13.5 billion nominal GDP and at $19,509 PPP, has the second highest per capita income in Africa while managing to thrive without a single minable mineral commodity or mass-market cash crop (an object lesson to resource rich African nations).

What's more, it has a 15% flat tax rate for corporations and individuals that everyone seems to like, a seductive .07% tariff on all import goods and recently elected the second woman president in the history of modern Africa, Ameenah Gurib. (Bibi Ameenah Firdausi Gurib-Fakim, is a PhD and biodiversity scientist who still holds her civilian title as Managing Director of CIDP Research Center for Phytotherapy Research). She is preceded by Monique Oshan Bellepeau who, in 1998, became modern Africa's first woman president.

Both women are of Indian-Pakistani origins. And in fact, Mauritius is 68% Indo-Mauritian, 25% Creole (black and mixed-race of African descent) about 2% European, and 5% Asian (Chinese). A non-religiously aligned government, it is the only nation in Africa where the main religion is Hindu (at 48%). As for the remainder, 37% are Christian, 17% are Muslim and about 4% are Buddhist.

Ameenah Gurib-Fakim,
President of Mauritius

Some experts tend to dismiss Mauritius as an anomaly, while others—because it is an island 500 miles out in the middle of the Indian Ocean—would tend to dismiss entirely its membership in the African community. And they would be wrong to do so.

In every sense of the word, Mauritius is the kind of member everyone wants in their club. And if people started writing off island communities, the nation of Indonesia would not, as such, exist. (This bias, though flawed, is frequent. In fact, the Seychelles and even Madagascar—an island about the size of Texas and only 200 miles off the coast of Mozambique—are more than occasionally written out of the African conversation when they should not be.)

People often debate the success of Mauritius, laying on the "Francophone vs. Anglophone" argument to give some credence and credit to its political substructure, moral compass and rule of law. And though Mauritius is decidedly French in its cultural undertones it experienced Dutch, French and English Colonial rule in its time—as it progressed from the 17th century through the 20th from a slave-trading nation to a haven for pirates to having to stave off Somali pirates in the 21st Century. Especially since its complete independence in 1992, it has used its cultural balance, its British way of conducting business and its French cultural traditions (along with a large India-Pakistani, Creole balance of race and workforce) to emerge as a highly astute international player, especially in areas of international trade, finance and intellectual property management.

Recently Mauritius even made appeals to the Maritime Protection Authority (MPA) to win ecological and economic control over its own Chagos Archipelago, a string of islands with some of the most prolific, precious and fragile coral beds in the world. Having been expropriated by the UK as an international environmental preserve, the Chagos had long been held by Mauritius as its own fishing ground and ocean garden as part of its territorial waters. Petitioning the MPA, Mauritius was granted full rights to that territory over the UK's protest. Meanwhile, the tiny nation has proved it can fish without over-fishing and also be a good custodian of the environment, thus promoting the small *mpa* — (a *marine protected environment*).

Mauritius has virtually no mining and only about 25% viable agriculture (mostly fruit and sugar). So, it has been forced by circumstance to be innovative in terms of its national commerce. It does have a moderately successful fishing industry, but has to import most of its convertible energy. It has, however, become a leader in technology, telecommunications, information technology, banking, financial services and "offshore enterprises" (a euphemism for the fact that it is a great tax shelter). It is also a very effective broker nation between Africa and Asia, evidenced by the fact that, in the last seven years, Mauritius has also attracted more than 9,000 offshore business entities, many of which have wanted networking channels between Europe, Africa and companies in India, China and Southeast Asia.

Other commercial avenues in which Mauritius now shines are in such areas as aviation development and finance, shipping and ship management, corporate establishment and licensing, international data processing and management, international finance and offshore funds management. In the final analysis, Mauritius has been graded as one of the most market friendly environments in Africa and the perfect haven for FDI ventures of all kinds.

Current Market Indicator: A Strong Buy

Despite recent impeachment proceedings set against Prime Minister Ameenah Gurib-Fakim (ones that experts predict she'll survive), Mauritius has set the bar high for most nations in Africa and the developing world.

Monument of Nature and UNESCO world heritage site, southwestern tip of Mauritius. Le Morne mountain symbolises slaves' struggle for freedom.

MOZAMBIQUE

(Republic of Mozambique)

U ntil recently, Mozambique has proved to be a textbook case study of the failure of "trickledown economics," because this resource rich nation with rapidly advancing urbanization and what was described by the World Bank as a "blistering pace of economic growth," has been utterly bereft of basic services for its wretchedly poor and underprivileged. It is still graded as one of the bottom 15 worst nations in the world where quality of life is concerned with a scandalous rate of "child malnutrition" at somewhere in the neighborhood of 46%. And no amount of economic progress can wash clean that stain on its national reputation.

By all appearances this began to change in 2012, and Mozambique has been one of the hottest new markets in the Sub-Sahara certainly in the last four years. The country—riven by civil war for 15 years from 1976 to 1990 and riddled by something of a kleptocracy for another 10 years—is finally poised for an economic breakout, largely due to some recent discoveries of vast new stores of mineral resources.

As of 2014, it started becoming one of the world's biggest coal exporters. And the recent discovery of two massive gas fields near its southern waters has turned the region into an energy power producer promising mega-field of cubic liters valued at $400 billion USD, just for starters. Add these new discoveries to one of the largest veins of aluminum in the world representing 31% of Mozambique's total GDP and you have the formula nation rich in spite of itself.

This mining boom has triggered something of a construction bonanza especially in the coastal areas. Mozambique's annual growth rate since 2012 has averaged 8.1%. Its money *the metical* has one of the best exchange rates against the US dollar of any monetary denomination in Africa. Mozambique has particularly attracted FDI investment from India (always a hot market for energy production), China and the EU, though South Africa (at 31%) continues to be its most prolific trading partner. With new oil and gas discoveries, major corporations such as Shell and BP have moved in for strategic partnerships. And industry experts predict a $200 to $400 billion infusion into the economy over the next 40 years.

Therein lie the blessing and the curse. Because with the new "gold-rush" mentality comes the danger of a kleptoconomy approach to boom-bust markets that usually has a 20 to 30 year window before the resources get siphoned away and contracts close.

Foreign Direct Investment has dropped off a bit since its 2015 peak. Still, 2017 saw more than $3.2 billion in FDI come in to build industry, manufacturing, IT and smart phones for Mozambique's tech hungry Afrillennials. And it has especially seen a rise in commercial real estate, shopping malls, building complexes and multiple unit housing for what has turned out to be a rush of diaspora from China, India, and the Portuguese homeland.

In the ultimate irony, the Portuguese—feeling a downturn in their own economy—are flooding back to Mozambique on common-country passports, taking high skilled jobs and living a rather lavish lifestyle relative to the fees paid them in Maputo.

Like Angola before it, Mozambique's ties to the colonial motherland, Portugal, has always been a conundrum of corruption and codependency. As poor as the Portuguese colonial system has been historically, they always manage to keep their hooks in longer than anyone else. And Mozambique only gained its independence in 1975 due to a military coup in the homeland followed by its own civil war between two political factions—the FRELIMO and RENAMO (a communist resistance front)—that finally led to free elections in 1996 won by the FRELIMO democratic front.

The "democratic" front governing Mozambique over the last 20 years has received mixed reviews at best. And though the new president Filipe Nyusi, sworn in after the 2014 election, has perennially promised new reforms, the country remains on the World Bank's and the IMF's "watch" list for the foreseeable future, at least until it proves its ability to take care of infrastructure, health and education for those who need it most.

The Bottom Line

Caution is the watchword. Even though it is enjoying a sudden spike in prosperity, an unrepentant lack of governmental reform—despite a B+ bond rating—appears both congenital and unresolved.

 Current Market Indicator: Hold

NAMIBIA

(Republic of Namibia)

Windhoek, Namibia

Namibia is currently on everyone's "good guy" list as one of the Sub-Sahara's better success stories. It is pretty much smack in the middle in all categories. Its annual GDP has virtually flatlined since the year 2000. Its PPI (Personal Prosperity Index) at $10,550 per capita, per anum is good but unchanged in the same period of time. Its average growth rate (5%) is solid but starting to trend downward. And it has, since its inception, been looked upon by outside investors as little more than a political and economic satellite of South Africa.

Historically this "South African" sibling connection makes sense. Namibia officially won its independence from South Africa in a parting of the ways in 1990 after a 12-year violent struggle to extricate itself from the apartheid regime in Pretoria. For once, the UN actually played a constructive role in brokering Namibia's national individuation, although it took the transitional administration of F. W. de Klerk to enable this to take place.[†]

Not surprisingly, for years the conversion value of the Namibian dollar has been directly tied to that of the South African rand. (The difference is that Namibia

---

† The "transitional" de Klerk administration—especially the influence of his Vice President Thabo Mbeki to mend fences and open South Africa up to becoming a positive influence in their geographic sphere—is a story that too often gets overlooked and truly needs to be told.

acknowledges the connection where other nations within the South African sphere of influence do not.) Since 1990, Namibia has enjoyed a stable if somewhat stodgy government that seems intent upon not making waves. Some of this is due to Namibia's acknowledged lack of survival basics such as water. With a large part of the country smack in the middle of the Kalahari Desert it is heavily reliant upon groundwater to sustain the 2.2 million people, and upon "shared" river waters on its borders with South Africa, Angola, Botswana and Zambia.

Since the 2014 election of President Hage Geinbob to a five-year term, however, Namibia has entered a new era of economic dynamism that is at least attracting new FDI from the US, China and South Africa, and causing other nations to take notice. In the last three years, Namibia has been very open to both expansion and modernization, especially where its approach to technology is concerned. In truth, the Foreign Investment Act of 1990 (FIA) was one of the first laws passed since Namibia constructed its national charter. The FIA is a de-facto guarantee for all Foreign Direct Investment that any private businesses coming to that country will never be "nationalized." And its stance as a free-market economy has been a part of its trade platform since day one.

Unfortunately, no EU or BRICS nation had taken much of an interest until the last two years, due mainly to some pretty stiff trade barriers. South Africa remains Namibia's principal trading partner for imports (84%) and exports (34%) with the USA coming in at a distant Number 2 in both categories. (And both nations enjoy some "favored nation" trade agreements that enable them to skip the customary encumbrances that have slowed so many others.)

Rich natural resources such as diamonds, copper, silver, lead and uranium have been a primary source of the nation's healthy $17 billion annual GDP. Its agricultural infrastructure is self-sustaining but little else. But tourism, telecommunications and finance have all been on the rise—so much so that in 2014 Bloomberg rated Namibia the most dynamic new market in Africa and one of the 15 hottest new economies in the world.

Recent shakeups in South Africa's government in 2015 to the present have had their ripple effects on the Namibian dollar. But as far as FDI ventures into the country are concerned (about $500 million in 2015) the outlook is decidedly sunny. And projections for the next two years promise to triple that amount.

 Current Market Indicator: Buy Namibia now!

RWANDA

(Republic of Rwanda)

Kigali, capital city of Rwanda.

William Faulkner once wrote that "Facts and the truth have very little to do with each other." Nothing underscores that more than the nation of Rwanda.

The fact is that more than 20 years after its "dark night of the soul," Rwanda is still living down one of the worst reputations in the Sub-Sahara, due primarily to one of the most violent and bloody civil wars in African history.[††]

The truth is that Rwanda is now the best political and economic turnaround story in the entire Sub-Sahara. A 2017 Investment Report by *Africa by the Numbers* rates

---

[††] By now, everyone has either seen the award-winning film, Hotel Rwanda. Either that, or they know the libretto. Based on the 1990-1994 Civil War that killed over 1.2 million native Tutsi and moderate Hutu tribe members, the war came about as a Tutsi led rebel attack by the Rwandan Patriotic Front (RPF) who had fled to neighboring Angola. Viewed as an act of overt aggression, the Tutsi rebel attack was a counterinsurgency in response to more than 30 years of persecution by the Hutu majority and resultant Tutsi diaspora to neighboring Angola, Uganda and Tanzania. The conflict came to a head in 1994 where it was finally settled by a UN resolution and the Criminal Tribunal For Rwanda (CTFR). Since that time, Rwanda has recovered remarkably and is a leading economic power. But when the film came out in 2004, it garnered actor Don Cheadle about 10 different best actor nominations and managed to open some old prejudices about Rwanda that were already 10 years old. Not the best PR for any nation, especially one trying so hard to rebuild its image.

Rwanda as having the best overall infrastructure in Africa, and a number 2 ranking (behind Mauritius) as Best African Countries for Ease of doing Business. It has the fifth best human rights rating in Africa by Amnesty International and Transparency International. Since the year 2000 alone, Rwanda has reduced its poverty rate from 59% to 42%. And as of 2016, it enjoys an arc of life expectancy that has, just in the last two decades, jumped from 46.6 to 61.2 years of age. Rwanda's GDP, though a modest $9.1 billion estimated for 2017 has more than doubled since the year 2000 with an annual growth rate of 8.3%, slowing only slightly since 2013.

It isn't just coincidence that all this can be traced back to the inauguration of three time president Paul Kagame in 2000. Often criticized for being authoritarian, the Kagame regime has been marked by strong leadership and a dedication to get Rwanda back into balance after decades in conflict. The fact that the Rwandan Constitution was revised in 2014 to permit him a third 7-year term in office, Kagame (a Tutsi) has been the real locus of power in Rwanda since the 1994 ceasefire.

One has to be impressed with Kagame's administration since he governs a rather unusual balance of land/population ratios when compared to other African nations. About the total area of the state of Massachusetts (or the island of Sicily) Rwanda has a population of more than 11.5 million people, which makes it among the most densely populated countries on two continents. Since he officially took over the country in 2000, Kagame has concentrated on rebuilding the country's infrastructure, solving energy issues by doubling electric capacity since 2005, assuring 71% literacy

President Paul Kagame

from primary and secondary education (nearly double the 1980 rate of 38%) and providing a National Health Program that covers 91% of all Rwandan citizens.

Rwanda has the fourth best "freedom" ranking of any nation in Africa, and—because of its Farm Bureau's active subsidies—enjoys the lowest unemployment rate anywhere in the world. (Less than 1%.) The rebooted Rwandan Republic also enjoys a runaway best gender-equal political representation with women comprising 63% of the voting members of the Lower House of Parliament (the largest female voting block of any government in the world).

Rwanda has been particularly active in coming into modern technology, communications, Internet and smart-phone marketing and virtual banking apps. Consulting with several international economic powerhouses such as Hong Kong, Singapore and Thailand to duplicate their successful business models, Kagame established the Rwanda Development Board that not only encourages FDI from interested nation-partners but also "fast-tracks" startup Rwanda corporations often within 72 hours.

Apparently, Kagame's strategy is working wonders. In the first half of 2016 alone, Rwanda has been rated by "Analyze Africa" as the #2 Best African Country to do Business (after Mauritius). And the World Bank bumped it up to the #3 Most Competitive Economy in Africa.

Credit much of this bullish rise in the economy to Rwanda's embrace of technology, telecommunications and the Internet. Recent cellphone contracts with telecom giants MTN and Tigo have seen to it that nearly 7 million Rwandans over 15 years of age have accessible functioning smart phones. And Internet contracts with SEACOM now have around 14.2 Internet users per 100 people—up about 700% in just five years. Rwanda is now #1 in the use of the Internet for educational purposes.

In 2018, Paul Kagame (now the nation's official head for 18 years) shows no signs of slowing down, and his August 4th landslide victory has stanched all intimations of opposition. Still, Kagame's traditional draconian methods when it comes to dealing with both dissenters and syndicated crime have garnered him some severe criticism from human rights watch organizations…but little among the Rwandan people themselves. Remembering the wholesale slaughter and chaos prior to 1994, the preferences for order and quality of life far outweigh any concerns over personal freedoms.

The best summation of Rwanda's irrevocable climb into true prominence can be best underscored by the recent blossoming Kigali Innovation City. Founded in June of 2016, this Rwandan solution to Africa's development includes a Think Tank partnership with such prestigious companies as Ericsson, MasterCard and the Government of Jersey to help the country leapfrog into what it calls "The Fourth Industrial Revolution." This quantum leap is being made through digital pathways provided to all citizens of Rwanda…and is the ultimate example of using technology to unshackle the (previously) isolated middle class of another rising African nation.

The Bottom Line on Rwanda

With stable progressive governance and an active, well-educated population of rising Millennials (more than 65% under 25), Rwanda has got to be the best untapped new market source in Africa. Still trading primarily to the US, China, Tanzania, Uganda and inside the Sub-Sahara, it is ripe for FDI explorations…and will more than welcome the opportunity.

 ## Current Market Indicator on Rwanda: A Strong Buy!

SENEGAL

(Republic of Senegal)

Trends are everything in the shifting sands of developing nations. So, when the beginning of 2017 saw Senegal make Africa's Top 10 on the Legatum Prosperity Index for the third year in a row, it had to be looked upon as a very good sign. The reasons are simple and direct: a continued cash surplus and a major leap in Personal Freedom. In the inevitable quantum leaps that some nations in the Sub-Sahara are they are also able to reverse their their fortunes almost in a matter of months. Following that pattern of turnarounds, Senegal is now acknowledged as one of Africa's overachievers.

That is refreshing to say the least, since this Francophone nation had something of a rollercoaster history prior to the year 2000. But advances in the last 15 years have been remarkable and all to the plus side. This is striking and something of an anomaly given the fact that Senegal has technically been in the midst of a rather strident Muslimization over the last 20 years. And Marabouts, religious leaders of various Muslim brotherhoods, exercise a strong political influence.

This was particularly true of the administration of the nation's previous president Abdoulaye Wade (from 2000 to 2011). But surprisingly, despite years of allegations of corruption, nepotism and violations of human rights, Senegal's fifth chief of state actually managed to become more moderate toward the end of his tenure, and though far from perfect, left office somewhat on good terms in 2012, graciously stepping down and turning over the reigns of government to current president Mackey Sall.

At present, Senegal has a quasi-democratic political culture, one of the more successful post-colonial democratic transitions in Africa. Local administrators are appointed by, and responsible to, the president. In 2009, during the latter years of the Wade regime, Freedom House downgraded Senegal's status from "Free" to "Partially

Free" based on increased centralization of power in the executive. Since the Spall government took over, however, it recovered its Free status in 2014.

Senegal is something of a political and socio-economic anomaly in that, although it is 94% Muslim it is largely a secular state that, despite various Muslim brotherhoods, strongly resists radical jihad and extrinsic influences from the Middle East. (As an example, Senegal recently severed all diplomatic ties to Iran and banned Iranian immigration when it was discovered in 2009 that the Khamenei regime was exporting terrorism and radical jihadist elements into their country.)

Senegal has more than 80 political parties. The unicameral parliament consists of the National Assembly, which has 150 seats. Senegal also boasts of an independent judiciary, although judicial corruption is occasionally a challenge to the legal system there. The nation's highest courts that deal with business issues are the constitutional council and the court of justice, members of which are named by the president.

After major monetary and economic reforms in 1994 where price freezes and economic subsidies were dismantled, the country has stabilized nicely and has a balanced economy with about 24% of the nation's GDP coming with natural oils and bituminous production but no measurable sources of crude oil. It also shows about 9% in gold reserves, another 8.5% in cement production and a rather prolific fishing industry that represents just over 15% of the Gross Domestic Product. The former capital of French West Africa is also home to banks and other institutions that serve all of Francophone nations in the Western Sub-Sahara. And Dakar remains the hub for shipping and transport in the region.

Senegal also enjoys one of the most robust tourist industries in Africa. From a relatively small industry at the introduction of the first Club Med resort in the 1970s, tourism has grown to be an important part of the Senegalese economy especially in the last five years. A leader in the union of nations of the Francophonié, Senegal not only attracts tourists from France but also other nations of the EU and the United States, which draws a relatively larger tourist share from Northern Europe and the Americas to its Dakar (Secret Beach) coastal resorts. In 2014, Senegal's foreign tourist visitors had reached 1.5 million attracted to luxury beach resorts, natural and historic sites, and it actively competes for tourist business with nearby Gambia.

One of Senegal's most prolific new industries lies in renewable energy sources, specifically driven by solar energy initiatives and Akon Lighting Africa.

The energy crisis in Africa, a problem for tens of millions, seems to have struck most severely in the western Sub-Sahara. It ruins school study, shortens viable industrial production and reduces retail business where it otherwise might flourish after dark. When power is available in nations like Liberia, The Gambia, and even the mega economy of Nigeria, it is often unreliable and power outages cause major problems of functionality.

Senegalese pop-star Akon, in partnership with Give 1 Project and Solektra Energy has created a series of small renewable energy through utilization of photovoltaic solar cells, as the most cost-effective solution to Africa's energy crisis. The Akon Lighting Africa project involves installing solar equipment in rural households in Senegal, Mali, Guinea, Gambia, Burkina Faso, Gabon, Congo and Cote d'Ivoire. Thus far it has already provided viable solar energy grids for more than 1 million homes and small businesses.

All in all Senegal, as a country, is on an upswing. Although its GDP is a modest $16.5 billion and its PPI is only $2555, it is trying to lower its clunky trade restrictions and stodgy bureaucratic approach to new business to accommodate more FDI participation from the EU, China and India. Senegal is embracing a policy of "gradualization" that is bringing it slowly but surely into one of the most reliable mid-sized states in Africa.

Current Market Indicator on Senegal is Buy and Hold

Good for the long term.

National Park Niokolo Koba in Senegal.

TANZANIA

(United Republic of Tanzania)

Dar es Salaam City Centre

As we have seen, Tanzania has that unique business environment that enables the Technology, Tourism and Telecommunications trifecta to "jump the shark" where rather poor, semi-corrupt governance is concerned. Ergo, Tanzania may not have very high ratings for good government. But it enjoys a strong association with Power brokers like neighboring Kenya, Nigeria and South Africa. And it seems to know enough to get out of its own way where free trade, lowered tariffs and business development are concerned.

Despite a shaky relationship between major industries and its apparent disregard of social services, Tanzania is in every other way a nation rapidly on the rise. Ranked one of the Top Ten Markets on the move by both Bloomberg and Standard and Poor's, the nation's GDP has spiked in the last 10 years to $51.9 billion—nearly double its rate since 2006. Although along with Kenya and Nigeria it declines to chart "arrivals" into the country, private estimates of its tourist traffic list in in the Top Three in the Sub-Sahara. At the moment, tourism in Tanzania—with the largest network of national parks in Africa—provides nearly 15% of its GDP and employs nearly 1.7 million of its 51 million people (and 36 million employable adults). The Bank of Tanzania is a major financial hub, and has averaged clearing more than 21.5 Trillion Tanzanian shillings since 2015 (about $32 billion USD). And Tanzania, along with Kenya, has become the East African hub for Bitcoin, M-Pesa and other virtual money transactions.

With nearly 7.7% annual growth, Tanzania boasts a dynamic market uptick and is looked upon favorably by its largest trading partners—United Arab Emirates, UK, South Africa, Switzerland and (especially) China.

Now, the East African sleeping giant is on the verge of becoming a major player in the oil and natural gas market. By all indications, the new Royal Dutch Shell, British Natural Gas Songo Songo exploration drilling expedition on Tanzania's south coast promises to make it an oil rich economy that could bump up its GDP by as much as an additional $36 billion by 2020 (to a projected) $90+ billion. To add to its positive market allure, FDI inflow into Tanzania has been a robust $2.1 billion in 2015, mostly through the Internet, financial and technology sectors.

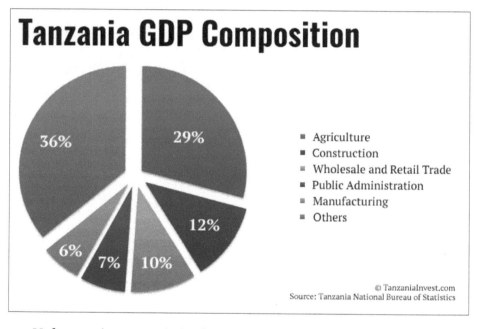

Tanzania GDP Composition

- Agriculture
- Construction
- Wholesale and Retail Trade
- Public Administration
- Manufacturing
- Others

© TanzaniaInvest.com
Source: Tanzania National Bureau of Statistics

Unfortunately precious little of this seems to trickle down to those who need it most, because despite its newfound prosperity, Tanzania is not a very good "top down" economy. In fact, the major criticism of the administrations prior to the present one has been the fact that practically none of the nation's considerable spike in GDP has benefitted the people who need it most. The average Tanzanian still earns less than $1.35 a day. And despite a literacy rate of 74% (about the African median), it is estimated that more than 2 million children in Tanzania receive no more than two or three years of schooling. Only 31% get secondary education, and less than 2.5% receive higher secondary and college level courses.

By contrast, President John Pombe Mugufuli (nicknamed "The Bulldozer") seems on a mission to level the playing field in all aspects of Tanzania's national character.

In fact, since taking office in July 2015, he has been on an active and very visible crusade to purge corruption and bribery from the Tanzanian government, as well as blatant government waste. In March 2016, he cancelled Tanzania's traditional "Freedom Day," and actually cut salaries of civil servants until they were willing to show more financial responsibility in government bureaus. As recently as the summer of 2017, he sent shockwaves through the mining community, including Africa's fourth-largest gold producer, with a series of actions he says are aimed at ensuring that mining companies pay their fair share of taxes. In so doing, he has threatened to close down all gold mines in the country if the companies in question delay meeting with the government to resolve allegations of tax evasion, kiting funds and money laundering.

On a more positive note, Mugufuli has openly courted Millennials, 53% of whom are under 18 years of age. Noting that Tanzania is an indicator of the rise of Africa's youth, he has made improvements in education a priority. Most of Mugufuli's early reforms have come in the national educational system, and at least some of them come in his effort to develop TZ21—Tanzania 21st Century. Launched in 2011, Tanzania 21st Century (TZ21) provides assistance to the Tanzanian Ministry of Education and vocational training to upgrade the learning curves for all primary school children in Tanzania and Zanzibar. In Mtwara and Zanzibar, the TZ21 program has focused almost exclusively on designing and expanding localized e-curricula (such as Eneza) in reading, math and science. It seems the government has finally gotten the message that educated Afrillennials are the wave of the future, the keys to advancing technology and the modernization of the country.

 Current Market Indicator: Buy and hold Tanzania.

Kilimanjaro

UGANDA

(Republic of Uganda)

Organic Tea Farm: Uganda is Africa's undisputed leader in organic farming.

It is a sad instance of the African character that some nations with great potential occasionally backslide. There is no stronger illustration of that than the recent decline and reboot of Uganda. This 360º conversion/reversion is attributable in large part to the thirty-year administration of President Yoweri Museveni whose National Resistance Movement offers a classic example of Lord Acton's maxim: "Power corrupts. Absolute power corrupts absolutely."

Museveni and the NRM came into power in 1986 after overthrowing the six-month regime of military strongman Tito Mikelo, whose singular claim to fame was his 1979 overthrow of infamous international bad boy General Idi Amin Dada (lately adjudged to be one of the 10 worst dictators in human history).[†††] Recently, under international pressure, the Museveni administration has promised free elections in 2016, something the President has done twice before in the past without actually honoring his commitment.

[†††] Ironically, when the Army overthrew Idi Amin, Milton Obote [Uganda's second president] was returned to office and restored Uganda's role in the world community by acquiring one of the best human rights ratings from the UN from 1980-1985. It was, however, not enough for Mikelo who ousted Obote in 1986, leading to the shortest administration (6 months) in the modern history of Uganda. Tito Mikelo was overthrown by the infamous "Ugandan Bush War" that ultimately propelled the Museveni government into 30 years of uninterrupted power.

So the UN, the WTO and other organizations are in a wait-and-see mode as to whether or not it lives up to its promises. All of this tends to overshadow the simple truth that Uganda is a nation truly rich in resources, natural landscape, forests and wild life. Uganda's vast landscape is characterized by fertile soils, regular rainfall, rich veins of copper, gold, nickel and iron and recently discovered oil fields. Coffee and cocoa plantations abound, and agriculture accounts for 70% of the nation's GDP.

Roughly the size of California with almost exactly the same population (37 million), Uganda is strategically situated in the very axis of Southwest Africa and conveniently borders the best parts of five other nations—Rwanda, South Sudan, Kenya, Democratic Republic of the Congo and Tanzania (with whom it shares Africa's most abundant lake region, including a very large portion of Lake Victoria). Uganda enjoys abundant wildlife and has finally begun stepping up long overdue prosecution of poachers in its national parks.

Generally, however, corruption in the government is considered an international disgrace, and human rights violations, prosecution of LGBT, and health issues have sent it hurling back to the abysmal stats under Idi Amin Dada that roiled the rest of the world from the early 1970s.

Ironically, in recent years the Museveni administration has finally done a respectable job of shoring up the country's infrastructure. Basic energy needs are met with great regularity. Education levels, though lower than the continental average, are improving, as is individual longevity to 63.5 years. It recently set up a *National Programme of Poverty Reduction,* and it seems to be gaining traction.

Currently Uganda is working to attract Foreign Direct Investment in setting up value-added manufacturing and agro-processing facilities. Even though Uganda has a vibrant farm system, the majority of its agricultural products—such as tobacco, fish and coffee—are exported in raw form, and sold back to it as finished products at import prices. Added value from crop-to-shelf and food preservation could potentially reverse billions in losses caused by spoilage and lack of markets, particularly for seasonal fruits and vegetables.

One area in which Uganda shines is in Certified Organic Farms. Right now it has 400,000 hectares of organic farms, including thousands of small family farms. And in many ways, with more than 18% of all its farm products organically grown, Uganda has set a new standard for Organic Farming throughout the developing world. (See Chapter 5.)

More than anything, Uganda has been rapidly urbanizing and has attracted strong Foreign Direct Investment in such areas as energy, telecommunications, and virtual technologies. In fact, nine different tech giants have come in with apps, programs and services in just the last 2 years, much of it focused on the country's phenomenal youth demographic. As of 2014, more than 50% of Uganda's population of 37 million reported in under the age of 15, and 71% is under the age of 25, making it the youngest nation in the world. That means this young country is facing a supreme challenge to education, social services and expectations of infrastructure. And that's where technology is taking over: in truth, all the wonders of electronics, telecommunication, Internet and apps that are the only means this ruthless momentum of youth has of connecting not only to itself but also the rest of the world. Youth will be served. And in this case it is actually forcing Uganda into hyper-drive when it comes to modernization, starting with increased access to electronic government services.

Today, Uganda notably serves as a strong economic and financial hub for neighboring nations such as Rwanda, Democratic Republic of Congo and South Sudan. And new FDI capital infusions in the year 2016 look to total more than $1.2 billion USD. Climbing back into respectability, Uganda is once again an active member of EAC, COMESA and WTO, despite a rather wretched imbalance in public debt. And

Museveni Inauguration: A Protest

You can't just write it off as a difference of opinion. But it is definitely a difference in philosophies and perhaps a perception of personal ethics. We refer to the mass walkout of the Diplomats from the US, Canada and most of the EU when Uganda's President Yoweri Museveni was sworn in for a fourth term (as a flouting of that nation's Constitution and amid accusations of massive voter fraud). It wasn't so much that they disapproved of Museveni's flaunting of Uganda's Constitutional limits to two terms in office as they apparently objected to his invitation extended to Sudan's head of State Omar al-Bashir, who currently tops the International Criminal Court's wanted list for human rights violations and crimes against humanity. In his acceptance speech the longtime Ugandan head of state described the ICC as a "bunch of useless people," which may be as accurate as it is insulting.

Yoweri Museveni

Perhaps characteristic of their acceptance of less-than-perfect governance in the Sub-Sahara, the Museveni inauguration was attended by the heads of State of Chad, Ethiopia, Kenya, South Africa, Tanzania, Zimbabwe, and South Sudan. Write this off not so much as an engagement of Realpolitik where tolerance for governance in the Sub-Sahara is concerned (which it is), as it is Africa's way of telling the G 8 nations to "mind your own business." So defiance, in this case, was a matter of individuation and autonomy for Africa that overrides any moral scruples that might have entered into the mix.

its $24 Billion GDP is more of an indication of its abundant natural resources than any astute financial infrastructure or visionary governance.

The Bottom Line

In Uganda's case of growth and progress, "There are more roses than thorns." And that might prove the perfect metaphor for this country's progress and development. Political changes seem to be in the wind, and economic shifts are definitely on the uptick. Only time and a pang of social conscience along with way will tell the tale.

 Current Market Indicator: Buy and Hold.

Good for the long term, if they don't get in their own way.

View from the above of the Capital city Kampala in Uganda.

ZAMBIA

(Republic of Zambia)

An elephant visits the reception desk at the Mfuwe Lodge in Zambia.

Zambia is a textbook study of how quickly nations in the Sub-Sahara may experience a reversal of fortune. We say that evidenced by the fact that in 2010, the World Bank named this southern African nation "One of the World's Fastest Economically Reformed Countries." Until the year 2000 it hadn't done so well. But, as they say, "The past is prologue."

Originally included in the infamous "African Scramble" of 1885, this area (about the size of Texas) was originally put under the control of the British South Africa Company that managed a favorable if highly exploitive "mineral rights contract" with the Bantu Chief of the Lozi, where it was later named Borotziland-Northwestern-Rhodesia, but only after strip-mining away a large part of that territory's prodigious copper deposits. Later, it combined with Northwestern Rhodesia to be reformed in 1923 as Northern Rhodesia, a self-governing part of the British Commonwealth. Then again in 1953 it was reformed into Rhodesia and Nayasaland—all before it finally gained its independence from British colonial rule in 1964 with its ultimate incarnation as Zambia.

So, one might accurately observe that the nation went through something of an identity crisis all the way up to its independence in 1964.

Although it might not seem like it upon first glance, Zambia today is one of the most politically stable countries in Southern Africa. It ranks number 16 out of 44 nations in the Sub-Sahara and number 106 out of 185 in terms of economic and personal freedom. That may not wow the locals in Europe and North America, but it has made tremendous strides in terms of developing countries.

Beginning with the presidency of Kenneth Kaunda that lasted in a one party system for nearly 30 years (1962-1991), Zambia has been unique in that it is one of the few countries in the Sub-Sahara that has avoided virtually any tribal conflict, civil war, or a major political upheaval. Kaunda's UNIP functioned as a Unitary Constitutional Republic (one party system) without major interruption until 1991. As a tribute to Zambia's stability, it has only had six presidents in its 60 plus year history as a nation.

Although most of the country's leaders have been acceptably "opportunistic" where their governance versus accumulation of wealth is concerned, it appears that the greatest strides were made during the presidency of Levy Mwanawasa from 2002 until his death in 2008.

Mwanawasa was the first Zambian president of note to openly campaign against bureaucratic corruption, and to address several public programs of health and education for the poor. He also actively restructured the economy to lower inflation and national debt by spreading Zambia's economic profile into a broad level of diversity and away from the damning brand of being "one industry" economy (copper). While making improvements across the board, Levy Mwanawasa actually ramped up the tourist industry in this landlocked nation, and made several cities such as Livingstone (near Victoria Falls) into tourist showcases.

Mwanawasa was also the first internationally active head of state in Zambia as well as the first leader in the Sub-Sahara to slam Zimbabwe's Robert Mugabe for his blatant corruption (something no one up to that time had done.) And he turned out to be the man who opened the gate to trade with China. As Chairman of the Southern African Development Community, Levy Mwanawasa did more to put Zambia on the map than any leader before or since. And today, thanks to his efforts, the Common Market for Southern and Eastern Africa (COMESA) is headquartered in the nation's capital of Lusaka.

Since Mwanawasa's untimely passing in 2008, Zambia has had a steady but unspectacular time of it keeping the momentum going. After a brief but effective Presidency of Michael Sata that ended in his untimely death in 2014, Zambia saw Edgar Lungu of the Patriotic Front narrowly win a January 2015. And Zambia is revising its constitution with a new set of referenda that are being put to a vote in the 2016 elections in October. A recent slump in copper prices has made Zambia's national money, the *kwacha,* one of the world's worst-performing currencies since 2014. But world demand fluctuates a great deal from year to year—and there will always be a demand.

Even though Zambia is still a bit gummy in terms of chartering foreign businesses coming in to invest for the first time, the recent infusion of cash and trade agreements from the Sub-Sahara's number one sugar daddy China has made a tremendous positive impact in the last six years. China, due to its own economic woes since 2014, has backed off a bit. But Zambia's relationship with its neighbor South Africa has been both stable and supportive, and (at 34% of all imports and exports) the Pretoria government remains the country's most reliable trading partner.

And the Zambian government has ramped up modernization of the nation in terms of building infrastructure—especially roads and public utilities.

Despite a healthy $24.9 billion GDP that places it squarely in Africa's top 20 economies and against the grain of a respectable (if deceptive) $5990 per capita income, 62% of the population of Zambia still lives just below the poverty line. So many improvements in quality of life need to be made, and soon.

At present, Zambia is still fighting the image of it being a one-industry economy. And new discoveries of copper veins have lifted it into one the world's top three producers. Still, Zambia has enjoyed an FDI cash infusion in the last year of just under $3 billion, much of it coming from corporations in China, the EU and the US who are bringing in business in anticipation of the youth boom in Southern Africa.

There are a couple of bright spots that dovetail into that confident approach to the market. One is the fact that Zambia is now the one of the most rapidly urbanizing nations in the Sub-Sahara, with 44% of the population in one of two-dozen cities that are now over 200,000 in population. Lusaka is number 1 with more than 1,800,000 inhabitants, with Kitwe and Chipata, numbers 2 and 3 and 600,000 and 500,000 respectively.

The second major factor toward a bullish future in Zambia is the young Millennial population. With approximately 80% of the nation under 35, it is the fourth youngest nation in the world. And they are driving the market. And now Millennials in the capital have come out with their own youth-driven magazine called *Y Magazine*.

Primarily a digital publication for reasons of cost and market sense, *Y Magazine* focuses on showcasing diverse lifestyles, trends and cultural shifts among Southern Africa's U-35 marketplace. With 4 out of 5 people born after 1980, Zambia leads the way in this very young market and is poised to generate an estimated $1.3 trillion in consumer spending by 2020 in Africa alone.

Following in the spirit of Levy Mwanawasa, Zambia seems to be improving. But it still needs to find the will to work its way out of the middle. Then again, like so much of Africa it looks as if the Millennials—given the leverage to do so—will show the way.

Current Market Indicator on Zambia: Hold

(Until Copper prices stabilize or they find more ways to diversify, it's dodgy.)

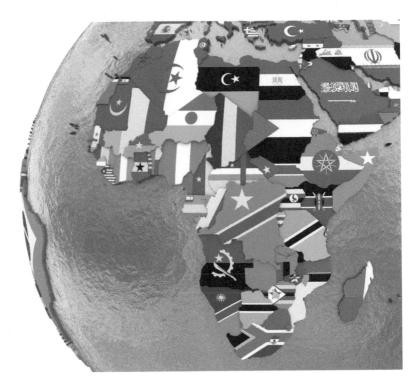

Summary

There are 54 nations in Africa and just as many scenarios for success or failure. We have taken here what we consider to be some of the most interesting, intriguing, challenging...and generally the most promising. The others, at least some of them, are worth examination too, if for no other reason than to avoid detours, provide warnings, and issue "travel advisory" signs for new investors along the way.

CHAPTER 9

The Colonial Legacy: Peeling Away 'The Onion'

"They were conquerors, and for that you want only brute force—
nothing to boast of, when you have it, since your strength is just an accident
arising from the weakness of others."

— Joseph Conrad, *Heart of Darkness*

J oseph Conrad is the English pen name of a Polish author and novelist named *Józef Teodor Konrad Korzeniowski.* And he was noted for two things. First, Conrad is famous for being perhaps the only living novelist who actually had a better command of English than his own native tongue—one he was able to translate into rich, sentient and often disturbing prose. Second, in indelible terms, Joseph Conrad was—more than any other writer of his time—able to communicate man's inhumanity to man, none more graphically depictive than his saga, *Heart of Darkness.* Penned in 1886, Conrad's masterpiece was a mirror held up to the brutal reconfiguration, exploitation, and enslavement of an entire nation— what came to be known as "The Belgian Congo"—by King Leopold II of Belgium and a core of colonial specialists who proved to be vicious predators, overseers and mass murderers that would rival anything conjured up by Hitler's Third Reich.

Granted, the example we are leading with will seem both melodramatic and extreme. It is also entirely accurate, comprises one of the greatest "cover-ups" in human history, and is indicative of the fact that Colonialism as it applies to the continent of Africa seldom did anyone any favors.

We are addressing a matter of degrees here. And though the intention of this book is to put a positive face on doing business in the Africa of today, it must also clean out some closets leading up to the present. Because it is the only way anyone coming to live, work, learn of, or even visit this continent will be able to have a passable understanding of the intricate cultural tapestry that has woven its way into the genealogy of every African nation.

In essence the colonization of Africa never took place because it was never intended to do so. Unlike the United States and Canada that grew into extensions of "Mother England," or nations such as Mexico, Colombia and Argentina that became replications of Spain, the colonial influences in Africa had an entirely different effect—primarily due to the disparity of race, culture and the imbalanced perceptions of what constitutes "civilization."

Welcome to the Onion!

We refer to this chapter as 'The Onion," for all the reasons the metaphor implies. To understand the African at all is to be able to peel back its layers, and to realize—more than any other part of the world—how the brand of colonialism established here left imprints without culture, left legacies without tradition, and more often than not took a great deal without leaving something of value in return. (This has not always been the case. There have been exceptions. And yet, as in the eternal cliché, those are the ones that prove the rule.)

As we examine the African Colonial Legacy more in depth, we need to break it down into *Two Eras* and what will turn out to be *Four Colonial Models.* By understanding them, you will be able to quickly grasp why Africa has become the political, economic, ethnic and cultural Rubix it is in this New Millennium. So when you realize that by studying 54 different countries you will find exactly that number of "colonial imprints" that render each unique, you'll experience just a sample of the labyrinth that lies ahead.

The Two Colonial Eras: These are actually fairly simple to divide into the Pre 1884 Berlin Conference, and the Post 1884-85 Berlin Conference—aka "The Scramble for Africa."

The Pre-Berlin Conference Era — 1568–1884

Nothing emphasizes the difference in the Two Africa's more emphatically than this period in history. In the North of Africa—especially Egypt, Libya, Algeria and

Tunisia, but also Ethiopia and Sudan—the Sultanates, Caliphates and Islamic vassal states had been set in place for centuries beginning with the reign of Suleiman the Magnificent in 1566. So, when the Berlin Conference came into being and Africa was being partitioned, many of the nations in the North were already well versed in the political maneuverings to which they would be exposed. Their civilizations were well positioned. They were already aware of the Realpolitik of the new Europe. And they also had the backing of their religious brotherhood of Mohamed. (No European power was going to be foolish enough to ride roughshod over any of the Northern African states and run the risk of incurring the wrath of the entire nation of Islam.)

The rest of this era is marked a cynical if simplistic approach to Africa—primarily by explorers in the Sub-Sahara—as a quick fix commodity venture in ivory and slavery. At the time, the most rapacious slave traders were the very Muslims from the Ottoman Empire (especially from "Arabia") who had civilized and unified the Northern nations.

Pouring down through the Horn of Africa and across to the Eastern Coast, Arab slave-traders looked upon all unbelievers as commodities not unlike ivory or gold. Subsequently, they regarded the "savage blacks" of the Sub-Sahara as too primitive to educate and convert and as such considered them no less an animal than an elephant, a lion or a gazelle.

For nearly three centuries, the Arabs were joined in this slave trade by the Portuguese, the Spanish, and the English (until 1807). The Portuguese and Spanish were especially prolific in this kind of commerce, capturing and selling millions of slaves over a 300-year period. Engaging in gold and barter agreements often with rival tribes from places such as "The Gold Coast" (now Ghana), Nigeria, Ivory Coast, Mali, Mauritania and Angola, these slave trading countries would often buy entire villages of captive Africans. Once purchased they would send them off wholesale as forced labor to sugar plantations in Brazil and the Caribbean Islands and the cotton fields of the Southern United States. A sizeable market also existed in Europe, especially, England, France, Holland and Belgium at least until the beginning of the 19th Century.

Otherwise, commodities such as ivory, spices and rare animals were harvested through animal slaughter and taken to nations of Europe and the "New World" where they were prizes in the societies of the day—very much like the detachment that accompanies harvesting an ocean bed or mining on an alien planet—a thing to be done and gone, with little thought of consequence to the regions being exploited.

Political reformations in Europe ended the African slave trade. France was the first to drop out (due in part to the French Revolution in 1784). The French were followed by the English in 1807, the independent kingdom of Brazil in 1821, and the rest of Europe a few years thereafter, ending a robust "industry" that had thrived for

400 years. When the US finally shut down all slave trade in 1865 the only slavers that remained were bootleg operations by Portugal to certain vestigial sectors of the world, including some Arab nations, uncharted parts of Eastern Africa and small pockets in Asia.

Officially slave trading—except in rare pockets of Muslim influence—was pronounced to be at an end by the 1880s. But abuse and misuse takes many forms, and little changes inside them. By the middle of the 19th Century, the Industrial Age was in full swing in Europe and North America. So the entire world perspective of Africa became one of the final frontier for many strategic natural resources—as well as an uncharted universe for the bold.

Gold had been discovered in Southern Africa—diamonds and emeralds as well. More than that, it was about to become a rich source of industrial crops such as coffee, cocoa and especially rubber (along with some copper and gold). Most major nations sent surveyors to different parts of the continent, and everyone came back with glowing reports of this resource rich continent.

In truth, the winds of war over territorial rights to Africa were blowing when Portugal, the weakest of the nations, prevailed upon Germany and Chancellor Otto Von Bismarck to host a twelve nation summit where they in fact divvied up Africa piece by piece…by piece.

The Berlin Conference of 1884: 'The African Scramble'

In what has become to be known as the Berlin Conference (or the "Congo Conference"), ten nations came to the table: Britain, France, Italy, Belgium, the Netherlands, Germany, Russia, Denmark, Austria-Hungary and Spain.

The conference, which took months, created The Berlin Act, which was a lofty expression of intent to civilize "The Dark Continent." In reality, was little more than a smoke screen for a coopted land grab that the nations had set forth to partition the entire continent as a mutually beneficial treaty of exploitation.*

According to the charter of the Berlin Act, the participating nations agreed to the following accords: 1) The Principle of Equal Right to validate annexation agree-

---

* *"The Dark Continent"* was the pejorative planted on Africa by journalist, explorer, and shameless self-promoter Sir Henry Morton Stanley. And the sobriquet stuck. One of the more controversial figures in the history of African exploration, Stanley was justly credited for finding noted humanitarian Dr. John Livingstone, for having possibly discovered the source of the Nile, and for his daring, ruthless explorations into "Darkest Africa" where he was actually employed as a "consultant" to pave the way for King Leopold of Belgium's "Free Congo State," that was anything but…

ing to honor all territorial claims; 2) the Principle of
Notification, (basically first come first served followed
by an assertion of sovereignty; 3) Free Trade between
nations; 4) Free Trade in the Congo (an area about the
size of Argentina); 5) Free Access to the Congo Rivers
and in fact all waterways; 6) The Final Absolute Abolition of Slavery.

(**Note:** To no one's surprise, the last of these initiatives was a matter of semantics because slavery had
already been universally abolished 20 years earlier. But
there were other states of being such as forced labor,
contract labor, sweatshop labor and child labor that
were euphemisms for an institutionalized repression all
over the western world. And—where Africa was concerned—it was a thinly disguised
disenfranchisement of native peoples that would continue as a brutal repression for
decades to come.)

Offering the deep seeded implication of "Christian conversion" and civilization of
these primitive peoples in what came to be described as "The White Man's Burden."**
The remaining seven geopolitical powers embarked on a campaign of unadulterated
imperialism while the rest of the world looked on with a tone of disinterested consent.

("Of course!" came the subtext of muted approval. "It was a difficult task at best,
and best managed with just the right blend of political pragmatism and ruthless compassion. Otherwise how else could these "benighted peoples in these primitive parts
of the world be brought into the light of modern civilization?")

In truth, when the Berlin Act went into effect, the entire continent of Africa
was split up into colonial protectorates. And not a single region, above or below the
Sahara, would be spared.

Of all the nations attending the conference, five demurred from participating
in the African acquisitions. Denmark declined for reasons of national principals of
non-intervention. Russia thought the geographic reach would spread them too thin.
Austria-Hungary felt they had come too late to the conference to stake any legitimate
claims. And the Dutch—due to the financial ruin of the Dutch East India Company
(VOC) and its rivalry with the English a century earlier—had lost all taste for acquisition. (They did, however, manage a massive diaspora of Dutch farmers, "Boers," to the

** "The White Man's Burden" was a poem originally penned by British author Rudyard Kipling to commemorate
Queen Victoria's Diamond Jubilee in 1899, reflecting the responsibility of civilization to aid and built the undeveloped
nations and repressed peoples of the world. It was almost immediately perverted by politicos with an eye toward global
exploitation, and adapted as a kind of slogan to justify a new wave of aggressive expansionism, acquisition and political
dominance in the guise of alliance. This not only applied to the land grab on the continent of Africa, it also defined it.

Trans Vaal of South Africa, where they would remain a thorn in the side of the British for the next sixty years.)

That left seven nations with an active role in the new territorial imperative. And to the one, they acted upon it with all deliberate speed.

Britain took the largest bands of real estate, including East Africa, Southern Africa, Nigeria and the Gold Coast. France took what came to be known as French West Africa (including most of what came to be known as the Sahara Desert), Cote d'Ivoire, Togo, Benin, Senegal and Cameroon. Portugal assumed control of what became Angola, Zimbabwe and Mozambique. Germany seized control of what would become Namibia and Tanzania. Spain had a postage stamp of a nation in Equatorial Guinea. And Belgium trumped all by laying immediate claim to what came to be known as The Belgian Congo (Democratic Republic of the Congo, the Congo and a small pocket territory that would later become Rwanda).

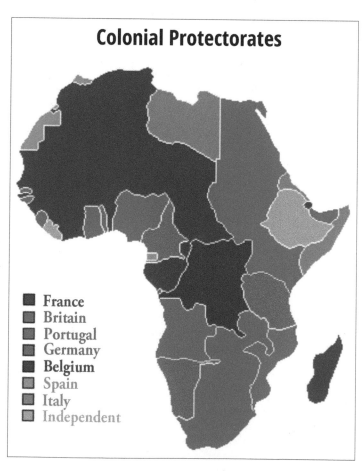

Colonial Protectorates

- ■ France
- ■ Britain
- ■ Portugal
- ■ Germany
- ■ **Belgium**
- ■ Spain
- ■ Italy
- ■ Independent

Italy, after a series of clumsy treaties, tried to strong-arm its way into the ancient Empire of Abyssinia and—military incompetents that they proved to be—were trounced at the battle of Adwa in 1896 by the forces of Haile Selassie. Shortly afterward, they were driven from the shores of East Africa for good, leaving Ethiopia (the seat of Western Civilization) as the sole African nation entirely free to conduct its own governance for another sixty years.

Other nation/states in the Sahara and Sub-Sahara did not fare so well. And out of the greatest mass acquisition of land in the history of the modern world, several different styles of colonial governance were soon brought to the forefront of geopolitical consciousness. Each would make its indelible imprint on the African psyche that has carried through to this day. Some offered more viable alternatives than others, though all would leave their scars.

The plans of acquisition from all the participating Berlin Conference nations and The African Scramble that followed—no matter what the ultimate model—had some distinct imperialist characteristics in common. And the political and economic pressures that came with them tended to provoke African leaders into a kind of reflexive pushback that more than occasionally met with armed repression.

During and after the Berlin Conference various European countries sent out agents to sign so-called treaties of protection with the leaders of African states, empires and "kingdoms." To the surprise of no one, these treaties favored all participating European nations at the expense of Africans. The African nations were left with the Hobson's choice of having to sign away their sovereignty, even though it was not proposed to them ostensibly in that context.

In carefully worded circuitous language, the treaties were presented to African leaders as mere diplomatic and commercial friendship treaties. (But they were never directed to read the fine print.) So after discovering that they had in effect been defrauded by European powers imposing political authority in their lands, African rulers and tribal chiefs tried to organize militarily to resist the seizure of their lands and the imposition of colonial domination.

This equal and opposite reaction to the imperialist scheme was, for the most part scattered, regionalized and utterly inadequate—especially when confronted by the new war machines that European nations had built up during the new Industrial Age—ones they were more than willing to try. What's more, the rebellions that took place in these disparate territories of the Sub-Sahara were not coordinated in the least. So their overthrow was already a *fait accompli*.

Ill timed, isolated and disorganized, they were scattered over months, years and even decades…and for the most part they became textbook examples of Sun Tzu's *Art of War*… or how to divide and conquer. The challenge to the participating nations would soon be finding out who would succeed at it—and who among them was best at putting their treaties into play.

Nations more experienced in establishing their Colonial models (e.g. The French and the English) had already learned from past mistakes and had solid plans in place to function as territorial "Administrators." The decadent Portuguese and novice Belgians would ultimately have learning curves of their own. All would have myriad consequences on the continent they meant to possess, and the fallout would take the next 140 years to be sorted out.

Purists will insist that there have been only two basic models for the colonial domination of African states: 1) Assimilation or Centralized Government (aka the Francophone system); 2) Indirect Rule through Provincial Networks (aka the Anglophone system). We acknowledge these two matrixes as being structurally correct, and most successful colonial programs have followed either one governmental design or the other. In truth, they often came into being later through some form of compromise where other systems that had failed finally adapted them as a means of damage control.

From this perspective of the 19th Century African Scramble there were Four Distinct Colonial Models that served as foundations for all others. And though hybrids were occasionally formed out of any two of them, each had its own set of rules, political guidelines and forms of self-justification. All of them were established upon certain steps of acquisition to give them legitimacy: In prearranged diplomatic initiatives, each acquisitive European nation would meet with appointed (often self-appointed) leaders of a given territory or established political state and pay chartering fees or outright purchases of rights to territory. In lieu of such official arrangements, they would initiate contracts that would enable regional leaders, Sultans or suzerains to benefit from the harvesting of natural resources. In return, they would set forth much alluded to civilizing influences, offering capitalistic industrialization, Legitimate Trade and Commerce, education, some form of centralized government replete with social services and military and political "stability."***

The French Model (Francophone)

Direct rule. Assimilative. Centralized. Culturally inclusive. Instructive. Organized. Civilized. Structured. Labyrinthine. Punitive. Ultimately exclusionary.

The Francophone system of assimilation entailed the cultural embrace of an entire nation, including the superimposition of the home government onto

---

*** Terms such as *Civilizing Influence* and *Legitimate Trade and Commerce* soon became euphemisms for imperialism and economic exploitation on an unprecedented scale.

the existing culture with the promise of ultimate acceptance, citizenship and full participation. The French, for their part, established a highly centralized administrative model influenced by their national tradition of extreme administrative centralism. In simple terms, they promised the moon, entailing full inclusion, *provided the territory under contract managed to jump through all the bureaucratic hoops.* Invariably, the occupied peoples would fail at some level. So in turn they would ultimately be subjected to total French governance with none of the benefits of citizenship.

The British Model (Anglophone)

Indirect Rule. Representative. Provincial. Democratic. Arms length. Proper division of labor and responsibility. Delegation of authority. Local governance. Double standards for law and labor force. Socially biased. Administratively rigid. Culturally Divisive.

The British colonies were often subdivided into provinces headed by provincial commissioners or residents, and then into districts headed by district officers or district commissioners. Laws and policies on taxation, public works, forced labor, mining, agricultural production, and other matters were made in London or in the colonial capital and then passed down to the lower administrative branches for enforcement.

Despite attempts to portray the use of indirect rule as an expression of British administrative genius, it was nothing of the sort. It was a pragmatic and cynical model based partly on using existing functional institutions, while setting the rest on Britain's unwillingness to provide the resources necessary to administer its own vast empire. In setting up this kind of structure, British rule was ultimately a declaration that the colonized states should themselves pay for their own colonial domination. It also meant that all local leaders had been marginalized so that they could exercise authority only at the whims of British Colonial officials. (In other words, they had virtually forfeited all autonomy.)

The Portuguese Model

Exploitive. Expedient. Exploratory. Underdeveloped. Popularly opposed. Industrially dependent. Transitory.

At the beginning of the Berlin Conference, the Portuguese had put down deeper roots in the Sub-Sahara than any other European nation. But their traditions of slave trading for 300 years left their cause unpopular and structurally weak.

Among all the participating nations in the 1884 Berlin Conference, Portugal had the longest standing colonial empire. They had been circumnavigating the globe since

Magellan, and settling nations in the new world such as Brazil, the Canary Islands, Ceylon (now Sri Lanka), and the "African Gold Coast," including what would later become Angola and Mozambique. But their colonization was based upon exploitation of local treasuries and upon the vast global slave market that originally opened up in the 16ᵗʰ Century. So they had no system in place to modernize, and never really did.

The German/Belgian Model

Imperialistic. Derivative. Paternalistic. Repressive. Exploitive. Genocidal.

The official Belgian attitude was one of paternalism: Indigenous Africans were to be "cared for and trained as if they were children." They had no role in legislation, but traditional rulers were used as agents to collect taxes and recruit labour. All labor was forced or coerced. Uncooperative rulers were deposed. Rebellious tribes or nations were put down by instant, aggressive military force. The Belgian/German model immediately set up in the notorious Belgian Free State (Belgian Congo). Later they would settle in German East Africa, which included Tanganyika (what would become Tanzania and Rwanda), and what would soon become Zambia in Southern Africa.

The Belgian/German Model Applied: The Free Congo State. Proudly proclaiming itself as a "Civilizing Influence," the Belgian model appeared to be a caring if co-dependent parent/child relationship that from a distance seemed idyllic. In application it was a draconian regime that became one of the most egregious human rights catastrophes in world history.

It was established by Belgian King Leopold II—a young royal from the newest nation in the Europe of that time, driven by political ambition, personal greed, and a need to "make his mark." (Indeed he did.) When his own parliament refused to subsidize the acquisition, King Leopold vowed to finance it himself with the understanding that he alone would reap the rewards from his "investment in colonization." As avaricious as he was ambitious, Leopold immediately set about to create what was called the *Congo Free State*. To be sure, it was anything but… Leopold's way of bringing civilization was to follow the Otto Von Bismarck German philosophy of pacifying the land with a heavy military presence. Having set in place treaties laced with bribes to tribal chiefs, he sent down "administrators" to activate the contracts, a few clergymen and 19,000 Belgian Civil Guard (the equivalent of two army divisions) to encourage the natives to honor the *Association Internationale Africaine*, a treaty that included production agreements to harvest ivory, palm oil, and especially rubber.

By the 1880s and the height of the new Industrial Era, the demand for rubber as a commodity had skyrocketed. The Congo in the heart of the central African jungles had the most prolific indigenous rubber trees in the world. And yet they still couldn't produce it fast enough to meet demand. In order to maximize his investment, Leopold invoked military pressure inspired by Bismarck and draconian plantation techniques reminiscent of the sugar fields of the West Indies (noted for severe disciplines).

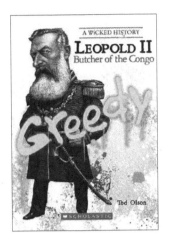

In truth, the Congo Free State was nothing more than an army of occupation, political repression and economic enslavement of an African territory the size of Argentina. Leopold's Belgian Guards would march into village after village, separate families, conscript the men into "press gangs" and leave the women and children behind to fend for themselves. Working 16-hour days, the men were forced to harvest sap from rubber plants. And failure to meet quotas would mean beatings, amputation of limbs and even death. Rebellions by small villages met with complete annihilation. Women and children, left behind by the tens of thousands, had no ability to hunt or grow crops and often simply starved to death.

Despite windfall profits in the first three years, the policies of exploitation in the Congo Free State were so brutally severe that, after ten years, the population of that region had dropped from an estimated 22 million people to just over 10 million—the majority dying from disease, starvation, neglect, torture, internment and mass-murder.[†]

Originally hailed as "The Builder King" and "The Great Colonizer," Leopold could not keep the lid on his atrocities forever. Finally in 1909 he was denounced by the Councils of Europe and essentially forced into retirement. At that point, the Belgian government tried to make amends by sending down missionaries, political reformation and a group of "companies" intent on rebuilding the infrastructure. In so doing they created a new entity called the Belgian Congo. And to no one's surprise they really made a mess of it.

The Belgian Congo, German East Africa, Namibia and the seeds of Apartheid.

The new Belgian Model in 1909 was a strategy called "the trinity"—*state, missionary*

[†] According to every standard of evaluation, the Free Congo State remains one of the five greatest crimes against humanity in history. With an estimated 11.5 million victims of the Belgian occupation it nearly doubles Hitler's pogrom against the Jews and political prisoners and rests just a notch or two under Stalin's 18 million starved and frozen to death in the Siberian Gulags. Of course, Mao Tze Tung's estimated decimation of 42 million Chinese by starvation, slaughter and economic abandonment remains the all-time record for mass murder.

and private company interests—to help repair the damage done and restore the Congo through gradual civilization. Although less brutal and exploitive than the

Free Congo State of Leopold, the long-term results were the same. The individual companies acted as their own regional state franchises, set their own rules determined on production, and had their own militias to enforce worker "inefficiencies." Oddly following the British Model of regional governors (and tribal corruption), they also kept the vestiges of the German hybrid, which was one of colonial separatism, utter segregation and brutal repression of tribal uprisings.

Ironically, the German Model that the Belgians imitated in part was not only brutally repressive but also surprisingly inept.

As it turned out, Leopold's idol and Europe's new strongman Otto Von Bismarck was something of a flop where applications of his colonial models were concerned. Intent only on production and making little effort to identify with the locals, the German model was simply intent on enforced civilization without any attempts at assimilation of the local cultures. Setting up strongholds in the Lake Districts of Tanganyika, the Germans set up companies to exploit the vast resources there (coffee and palm oil plantations), while really failing to grasp the depth of commitment it would require.

As opposed to Leopold II who loaded up with settlers, overseers, and entire armies to "pacify" the Congo, Bismarck sent down a few hundred settlers, a few hundred laborers and about three thousand military "administrators" to set in place the territory of German East Africa. It was a study in colonial arrogance and a failed business model. Logistically unable to cope with the challenges of their new territory Bismarck's colonial administrators found themselves trying to govern a country that was about twice the size of modern day Germany replete with some of the most perplexing terrain in the world—a geographical mashup of drought-ravaged plains and dense jungles. Unfamiliar with the terrain, improperly equipped for the modern harvesting of the rubber and utterly unfamiliar with the hegemony of local tribes, the Germans simply didn't have the structure in place to ever make it work.

Brutal repressions by the military simply lacked the force of numbers, and eventually met with so much tribal resistance that the German forces around 1894 had to solicit the assistance of the nearby British garrisons to help put it down.

That strategy eventually backfired on the Second Reich a few years later during World War I when the British (masters of tribal alliances by then) sent their Army to Tanganyika in 1917 to join with the tribes and drive the "Huns" out of the country for good.

Attempting an ambitious swath of colonization, Bismarck simultaneously tried the same strategy in "German Southwest Africa" (what would later become Namibia) with even more damaging long-term results. Making scant effort to entice the locals with even the façade of civilization, the German strategy simply dropped mining companies and rubber plantations down into the market, made contracts for what appeared to be salaries to laborers, which were nothing more than a sham, and then set the machinery of exploitation grinding into operation.

Ignoring the fact that the Berlin Act's *prime directive* was the absolute commitment by all parties to the abolition of slavery, Germany—host nation for the accords—didn't even bother to honor its own charter. Although the Germans didn't officially create any new slave colonies, they thought nothing of leaving all existing slave holdings comfortably in place, until they simply played themselves out. That of course took decades, and in their place the German companies would hire workers, pay them with "company" tokens and then charge them the same tokens for their daily rations of food.

Once again the German Colonial Model in Southern Africa (Zambia) came to experience the same logistical issues as those in German East Africa. So, in due time, the spirited Herero and Namaqua tribesmen in 1904 rose up against them in great numbers. By that time, Bismarck had learned his lessons from Tanganyika and sent down enough troops to quell the rebellion and did so with brutal force. Inside of three years the Germans had not only slaughtered over 120,000 warriors in a vicious manner of extermination, but also introduced concentration camps for the captured that proved to be the precursor to the Nazi holocaust techniques of WWII. Afterward the Germans established a complete partitioning of the territory, sectioning off tribes, then whites and blacks in separate communities in what proved to be the precise model for Apartheid adopted by South Africa a few years later.

Ironically, it was South Africa who rode to the rescue in 1917 *(vis a vis* the British brigades stationed there), driving out the Germans as a strategic side-bar to winning World War I.[††] At this point, it should come as no surprise that the British were past masters at this, looking—by contrast to other models—as a godsend to the newly formed nations of the Sub-Sahara, and using that platform of trust to establish their own "benign" framework for colonial government.

The German/Belgian Legacy. One of the major points of this chapter is to illustrate in very graphic terms just how pervasive and indelible the colonial influences on Africa proved to be. More often than not, they take generations to adjust to, reconfigure and (very often) overcome.

[††] One thing at which the Brits proved very adept was acting as White Knights (every pun intended) and riding to the rescue. Especially among African territories, desperate for anything even resembling civility, these orchestrated rescue missions enabled them to gain trust with the locals and establish Colonial contracts and territorial alliances after the fact.

In our examination of the Four Colonial Models, we are taking the worst first, because they leave large scars and little room for interpretation. Upon examinations, the depredations, genocide and draconian rule of the Belgians and Germans left the "Belgian Congo" a vicious mosaic of corruption, tribal conflict and—above all else— mistrust of the West. This has been so much the case, that this beautiful resource-rich Eden in the very heart of Africa has become crippled seemingly beyond recovery. Surviving the worst genocide in African history this lush nation still has the worst human rights record of any nation in Africa, the lowest per capita income (at less than $1 a day), and yet manages to produce a remarkable $53 billion in national GDP.

One can only imagine the accomplishments that might have been generated had it been permitted even an equal footing with some of the African nations that graduated out of the Anglophone or Francophone Colonial Models.

As it is, the Democratic Republic of the Congo has graduated out of decades of civil strife spinning out of its original petition for independence in 1960. It began with the usurpation of its first popularly elected president Patrice Lumumba inside his first year in office and was followed in the coming years by a vicious power struggle between several factions and the partitioning of that vast piece of real estate. Ousted (by an ideologically driven United States and an inept, exiting Belgium) Lumumba was assassinated due to his flirtation with the Soviet Union and Eastern Block nations of Europe. That de facto *coup d'état* was followed by a series of presidents and conflicts that saw the Congo taken over by the government of Mobutu Sese Seko, turned into Zaire for nearly 25 years and then reorganized into its present state.

Not that the Germans and Belgians were terrible colonial models when applying their Apartheid philosophies of rapacious colonialism, they even botched their imitations of the British model as evidenced by Germany's manipulations of the tribes in what would become the tiny nation of Rwanda.

As one of their parting shots in East Africa, the German governor there stepped into a tribal conflict between the local Hutu and Tutsi nations, choosing to favor the Tutsis, thus generating a tribal diaspora among the Hutus to nearby Tanganyika— something they neither forgave nor forgot.[†††]

As an equal and opposite reaction, it led—80 years later—to the bloody, protracted Rwandan civil war from 1994-1997, leading one to the inescapable conclusion that the European colonization of Africa has had ripple effects that take us

---

[†††] Until the late 19th century, which is to say, until European colonization, Tutsis (the minority) represented the aristocratic upper classes; Hutus were the peasant masses. The Europeans brought with them an idea of "Race Science," by which they took this traditional structure and made it even more extreme and more polarized into an almost apartheid-like system. Ethnic identity cards were issued. Tutsis were privileged for all things, and Hutus were really made into a highly oppressed mass.

to this moment 150 years later and will probably continue to do so for decades to come.

Angola, Mozambique and the Portuguese "Backfire." At this point, it might be said (in the *Star Wars* metaphor) that if the German/Belgian Model was the Darth Vader of colonialism, the Portuguese Model was Jabba the Hut.

Although their initiatives in the Berlin Act of 1885 were officially approved by the monarchy, Portugal received little public support from their own home nation and, in fact, felt a rising tide of "republican resistance" from the opposition party that would seize power ten years later.

So by nature the Portuguese set in motion an antiquated model of governance that was 300 years old—one built on transitory platforms that never worked very well in the first place. It's not that they didn't want their Colonial empire to succeed. It was more the fact that theirs was a concept long past its political pull date. What's more Portugal, as a political *force majeure,* had lost virtually all its global stature. By the mid-19th Century its world territories had been ripped away by other nations, one by one, until it only had its lands in the Sub-Sahara and Brazil.

The Portugal of the late 19th century had no industry as such, and had grown dependent primarily upon British factories to carry out their end line production of products. Such tropical raw materials like vegetable oils, cotton, cocoa and rubber had to be shipped to facilities in the south of England for final manufacture. So the Portuguese mining companies and plantations became little more than middlemen.

In addition, the Portuguese military—both army and navy—had been watered down over the centuries, and had degenerated to a level of ineptitude so perverse that it could arguably be matched only by the Italians.

It is ironic in the extreme that Portugal was one of the charter nations of the 1884 Berlin Conference. It had done so to use this convention as leverage to legitimize its longstanding claims on the African Continent. Once it received its charter, it immediately moved to obtain dominion over the nations of southeast, south central and southwest Africa (Mozambique, Zimbabwe [Rhodesia] and Angola in this case).

Perceived as feckless out of the gate, Portugal almost immediately had its territorial rights challenged by the British who eventually seized what they would come to call Rhodesia along with exclusive water rights to the Congo and Zambezi rivers to be shared with all other charter nations.

Portugal's settlement of Angola and Mozambique tried to follow the German overlord model of repression, forced labor and intimidation but invariably fell apart due to a lack of discipline, infrastructure and increased tribal mistrust. It is important here to remember that the Portuguese had a presence in Africa that went back 300 years. And what they had installed up to that point were mostly bases for the capture, sale and exportation of slaves to Brazil and the West Indies.

They had long held seaports in places such as Sao Tome & Principe, Cape Verde Islands, and Luanda (in Angola) for the expressed purpose of transporting slaves and ivory. Their centuries old "trade arrangements" and contracts with the Sultan of Zanzibar were again based primarily on slave trading. So their viable economic anchors on the East Coast of Africa (Mozambique) had lost their longstanding leverage. As such, the Portuguese overlords were already regarded by the locals on both coasts with a sizable measure of fear and loathing—not to mention mistrust. (This wasn't helped in the least by Portuguese attempts to sidestep the constraints placed on the slave trade using under-the-table deals with Arab traders well into the early 20th Century. Most were shut down or prosecuted. But some illegitimate trading continued up through the time of World War I.)

To strain matters further, when the Portuguese trading companies in Angola tried to superimpose their "Brazilian" diaspora that had succeeded for nearly a century onto their band across Southern Africa, they met with abject failure. Portuguese laborer, attracted to Brazil, simply couldn't be induced to come to Africa. Portuguese settlers only came in trickles. Many who did come returned home after a year or two. And finally the plantations and operations were forced to make contracts with The British South Africa Company who provided labor and essentially took over their day-to-day business. The move seemed to have worked for a few decades, since some of the Portuguese, lured by better (British) contracts, and improved working conditions, did migrate in the early 20th century—to the point that Angola in particular has a rather large mestizo population with some significant political influence in the country.

The Portuguese Legacy: Despite their administrative failures in both territories and their disappointing attempts to lure their workers to Africa, the Portuguese managed with the help of the British to hold onto their territories longer than any other European nation. And only in the mid-1970s did they finally pull the hooks out enough to see them become the nations of Angola and Mozambique—both of whom successfully petitioned for independence in 1975 (two of the last African nations to do so).

Not surprisingly, the political vestiges of corruption, repression, forced labor and botched diaspora left its scars on the political psyche of both Angola and Mozambique. Ripped apart by political divisions that were not only tribal but also influenced by the outgoing government, both nations found themselves locked in civil wars that went on for decades—neither recovering entirely until this century.

To this day, Mozambique and Angola have been names synonymous with civil strife, civil war and kleptocracy. And even today Mozambique (despite a blistering

...Colonial empires have philosophies and legacies that leave deep implants on the national psyches of the nations they colonize.

economic recovery in the last 10 years) has garnered one of the worst records of human rights violations in the Sub-Sahara. Angola, a nation that endured the longest civil conflict in African history, recently discovered the second largest oil reserves in the Sub-Sahara and the third largest in Africa and has, because of that single commodity, been able to recover somewhat from generations of bad management, abuse and colonial oppression. (Ironically, the Jose Eduardo Dos Santos administration has turned the diaspora tables back on his mother country. And in the last 10 years, Angola has seen a reverse migration of Portuguese workers coming to improve their quality of life in this new and very young country. To a lesser extent Mozambique has also managed to turn the tables on Portugal and has enjoyed a considerable reverse diaspora of its own, bringing a new migrant colony back to Africa.)

At this point, it should be obvious that colonial empires have philosophies and legacies that leave deep implants on the national psyches of the nations they colonize. This examination of models that don't work leads us to look at the ones that have succeeded at least to the degree that any Colonial philosophy can.

The French (Francophone) Model: Simply put, the Francophone Colonial philosophy is one of inclusion. It is all embracing and seductive but can be, and often is, misleading. (How very...French.)

France built its powerbase in their colonies quickly and by showing all the indicators of a "friendly takeover." After establishing rapport with local leaders, the French colonial administrators would immediately establish a highly centralized administrative system that was influenced by their ideology of colonialism and their national tradition of extreme administrative centralism. Their inclusive ideology explicitly claimed that they were on a "civilizing mission" to lift the benighted "natives" out of backwardness to the new status of what they referred to as civilized French Africans.

To achieve this, the French used the policy of assimilation. Philosophies of inclusion can be highly pervasive in both good and bad ways. In what appears to be a good way, it offers acculturation and education and the fulfillment of some formal conditions. If they played inside the lines and followed the rules set by the French

Colonial regime, "Selected Natives and Tribes" would have the opportunity to become "civilized French Africans." That was the carrot. And in many Francophone frontier nations it was a profound motivator, at least at the commencement of colonization.

In practice over time the stringent conditions set for citizenship made it all but impossible for most colonial subjects to become French nationals. For example, potential citizens were supposed to speak fluent French, to have served the French meritoriously, and to have won an award (either civilian or military) along with several other pathways to citizenship, one of which would be invariably blocked.

If the colonials did manage, through some miracle of intention, to achieve French citizenship, they would have French rights and could only be tried by French courts, not under *justice indigénat* (the French colonial doctrine whereby colonial "subjects" could be tried by French administrative officials or military commanders and sentenced to two years of forced labor without due process). However, since France would not provide the educational system to train all its colonized subjects to speak French and would not establish administrative and social systems to employ its entire colonial workforce, assimilation was more of an imperialist posture than a serious political objective.

In terms of the actual administrative system in its various African colonies— Algeria, Tunisia, and Morocco in North Africa, and Senegal, French Guinea, French Sudan, Upper Volta and others in West Africa, as well as Gabon, Congo-Brazzaville, Ubangi-Shari in Central Africa—the French used a system of direct rule.

They also created a series of federations in West Africa and Central Africa. In the colonial capitals, the governors were responsible to the Minister of Colonies in Paris. Most laws and policies were sent from Paris, and the governors who ruled with general councils were expected to enforce them in line with France's centralist traditions. The colonies were also subdivided into smaller administrative units as follows: 1) *Cercles* under *un commandant du Cercles*, subdivisions under Chef de Subdivisions; 2) at the next level, *Cantons* were administered by African chiefs who adjudicated through a rather confusing mash up of French Law under the Code Napoleon with local tribal laws.

While France tried to maintain this highly centralized system, in some parts of its colonies where it encountered strongly established centralized state systems, the French were compelled to adopt the policy of association, a system of governing that operated in alliance with preexisting African institutions and leaders. Thus it was somewhat like British indirect rule, although the French still remained committed to the doctrine of assimilation. In the association system, local governments were run with African rulers that the French organized at three levels and grades: Chef de Province (Provincial Chief); Chef de Canton (District Chiefs), And Chef de Village

Significantly less brutal and repressive than the German/ Belgian Model and far less corrupt and feckless than the Portuguese model, the Francophone Colonial Model maintained order for a longer period of time.

(Village Chief). In practice, the French system combined elements of direct administration and indirect rule, which might be interpreted as a tip of the hat to the British or Anglophone model.

Even more than the Anglophone Colonial Model, the Francophone Model of assimilation worked more effectively in nations with established societies already civilized to some degree. That meant the North African Francophone countries like Algeria, (French) Morocco and Tunisia—already civilized through Islam in the 9th century and the Ottoman occupations of the 16th century—experienced genuine forms of assimilation, citizenship and the international passports of France. Colonies in the Sub-Sahara had very little chance at the brass ring of citizenship, and it became obvious to everyone that this was never their intention.

Cameroon, Gabon, French Guiana, Senegal and others—95% indigenous tribes with no written language of their own—were unable to develop a viable platform from which to jump onto the fast track of French inclusion. (And the French very well knew this going in.) That meant they would be subject to the ruthless *Canton* level of administration, replete with tribalism, favoritism and corruption. And in that way they were no different than the Brits.

Significantly less brutal and repressive than the German/Belgian Model and far less corrupt and feckless than the Portuguese model, the Francophone Colonial Model maintained order for a longer period of time. Decades later, however, the wheels would come off this train. Rebellions, though less frequent would arise. But to their credit, the French had brought their culture into the Sub-Sahara at least to the effect that revolutions, when they came, were less intense and occasionally even led to a civilized solution. To their credit, to this day, the French have kept their oar in the water with almost every nation they have colonized. In so doing the French legacy has become like an amicable divorce, complete with visiting rights and conjugal visits—something in political terms that the French have mastered over the centuries.

The British (Anglophone) Model. On paper at least, the Anglophone model of Colonialism appears to have been the most successful—at least for the Brits. We've already noted that the British Model is based on Indirect Rule and provincial governance that, on the surface, appears to be an appropriate delegation of responsibility and proportionate empowerment of indigenous peoples. And as is very often the case, looks can be deceiving.

In Nigeria, West Africa, the Gold Coast (Ghana), Kenya and Tanganyika (Tanzania) in East Africa, and Rhodesia and Uganda in the South, Britain managed to hold its colonies at the central, provincial, and regional or district levels. In terms of structure there was invariably a Governor-General who resided in the colonial capital. He governed in cooperation with an appointed executive council and a legislative council of local and foreign "administrators." The governor was responsible to the Colonial Office and the Colonial Secretary in London, from whom policies, and programs were received. He made some local laws and policies, however. Colonial policies and directives were implemented through a central administrative organization or a colonial secretariat, with officers responsible for different departments such as Revenue, Agriculture, Trade, Transport, Health, Education and myriad others.

The British colonies were often subdivided into provinces headed by Provincial Commissioners or residents, and then into districts headed by district officers or district commissioners. Laws and policies on taxation, public works, forced labor, mining, agricultural production, and other matters were made in London or in the Colonial Capital and then passed down to the lower administrative levels for enforcement.

Ultimately it was at the provincial and district levels that the British established the true roots of *Indirect Rule.* At its core, it operated in alliance with preexisting political leaderships and institutions, enabling them to have the security of being in charge of their own destiny. This perception was often illusory, but it always worked in the beginning. And as the British had learned rather well order in the beginning was tantamount to success.

The theory and practice of indirect rule is commonly associated with Lord Lugard who was first the British High Commissioner for Northern Nigeria and later Governor-General of Nigeria. In his surveys of Northern Africa, Lugard found that the Hausa/Fulani emirates had an established and functional system in that region. So he very cleverly adapted this administrative model to his ends. On the surface, it appeared just and respectful; beneath the surface it was cheap and convenient, expedient and highly exploitive. (This led to a deep-seeded mistrust among the educated Southerners and the less educated Northerners. As such it fit very nicely inside the British plan of "colonial leveraging" by pitting one regional tribe against another.)

Somewhat like the Francophone model, but simpler, the Anglophone system provided four major institutions: *1) Native authority* made up of the local ruler; *2) The Colonial Official,* and the administrative staff; *3) The Native Treasury,* which collected revenues to pay for the local administrative staff and services; 4) *The Native Courts* that purportedly administered a long list of native laws and customs. In such a structure, justice came at several levels, and by all appearances provided a level playing field. At least at one level the traditional legal system of the colonized that was used by the courts to adjudicate cases was always locked into place, so that the locals felt at least some form of justice would be at their disposal.

That was the common illusion, and the British had learned well from their experiences from the British East India Company in India, Afghanistan and the American Revolution. By now, they acknowledged the importance of setting this infrastructure in place as soon as possible and that the representation—both legal and administrative—had to go deep into every colony, especially at the provincial and local levels.

What they always failed to include was "the fine print" that excluded all independent business entities from being subjected to the same set of rules. In several instances, especially the infamous British South Africa Company (that included the southern half of the Sub-Sahara), companies were simply allowed to operate under a different set of rules. They set their own labor contracts, established their own work regulations, and even enacted rewards and punishments for indigenous labor. Labor, though nothing as severe as the German/Belgian models, was often forced; and payment to workers was little more than a daily pittance. So the sweatshops that were the scandals of British society in the 1850s had simply been exported south and inflicted upon indigenous tribes who were left with limited alternatives and a labyrinthine court system they could never hope to navigate with any degree of success.

As in the Francophone system of colonial governance, the Anglophone model of indirect rule worked quite well in areas that had long-established centralized state systems. Well-established city-states, kingdoms, and even sophisticated Chiefdoms (such as the Zulu) managed to cope with these structured systems of government. But even here the fact that the ultimate authority rested with British officials meant that the indigenous African leadership had, at all levels, been vassalized. Arbitration between entities almost always favored the colonists and British companies, leaving little or no recourse to the tribes.

With the new Anglophone systems in place, the social umbilical cords that tied locals to the old system had effectively been pacified and rendered moot. Some astute African leaders maneuvered and ruled as best they could. Very often, however, local leaders used the new colonial setting to become tyrants and oppressors. Realizing that the British were now their court of last resort, they felt they could manipulate the colonial system to their benefit; and most of the time they were right.

At this point it is important to remember that in the 1880s the British Empire was at its zenith. They were the master colonists and literally, "The sun never set on the British Empire." Credit almost all of this to their sense of Realpolitik. Results were all that mattered, and to the pragmatic went the spoils.

No one before or since had mastered the Colonial Game better than the Brits. And if they had learned one art of governance in the decades since the East India Company of the mid-18th Century it had been the rule of *divide and conquer*—in this case playing one faction off against the other. In every colonial experiment in the Sub-Sahara the English overlords always used tribal rivalries to their advantage and favored the local indigenous tribes that, they felt, wielded the most power.

By the time the national leaders of the nations in the Sub-Sahara had caught on and petitioned for their freedom, nations like Britain and France came to the table willing to accommodate them under a strict set of "favored nation" conditions. By the 1960s when a majority of African nations became independent, the cost of administrating some of these territories had become logistically cumbersome and costly. So they granted independence, but kept them in the Commonwealth—with all the favored trade agreements and their companies well entrenched. Despite some "nationalization" of industry, by-and-large for the Brits it was very much a case of having one's cake and eating it too.

As far as the ripples they left behind, the laws of karma applied to the Commonwealth in every sense of the meaning. Tribal conflicts, civil wars and government corruption surfaced everywhere from Kenya to Nigeria to South Africa to Zimbabwe, many of them taking scores of years to sort out. In some cases like Nigeria the result had a happy-ending. Others like Zimbabwe have become the poster children for the ruination of nations, well-entrenched dictatorships and a loss of clear horizons.

Upon close examination, the Colonial system with the least long-term problems has been the more or less inclusive Francophone Model. Still we are talking about varying versions of "wrong," so caution is the byword.

Historically, no matter what colonial system was put in place, they all ultimately manifested by becoming alien, bureaucratic, dictatorial and corruptive. They distorted African political organizations, ultimately undermining their moral authority and political legitimacy as governing structures.

If this indeed was "civilization" it came at a very dear cost. And the national political "entities" left behind, especially those in the Sub-Sahara have only recently been able to lift themselves out of the fog of it.

Islam and Christianity: The African Conundrum

As is so often the case created inside the African conundrum, religion becomes the contradiction that defines the rule. And as we separate the two major eras of Colonial Africa into the Pre and Post Berlin Conference periods, and as we partition Africa into the Sahara and Sub-Sahara, we also need to take a hard look at the influences of Islam and Christianity and how they made their influence felt.

The Muslim faith came to the North of Africa in two phases, the major one coming with the rule of the Ottoman Empire of Suleiman the Magnificent in the early 16th Century. As a historical theory that "the man makes the religion" Suleiman might well have been the best Ambassador Islam ever had. Reinforcing the Muslim conquests of Northern Africa from the 7th Century, he overtook Egypt, Libya, Algeria, Tunisia and Morocco, as well as Somalia, Abyssinia and other nations on the Horn of Africa. And yet in the process of doing so Suleiman adopted the spirit of the religion, making it all inclusive, all embracing humanitarian and (relatively) color blind.

Noted for his equanimity, fairness and uncanny sense of justice Suleiman turned Islam into the club everyone wanted to join. And even though his successors later perverted the religion— including slavery—to the level that prevails today, Islam's influence in the North Africa of the 19th Century left the nations there buffered by stronger network of cultural connection. So when the Berlin Conference "Colonizers" came to set their African contracts, they were forced to deal with a group of nations that had a stronger sense of self.

Christianity arrived in a different guise. Although they had some historical presence in North Africa (especially with the Coptic Christians in Egypt)—and though the Moors and Christian had been battling for centuries over the soul of Spain— Christian missionaries often accompanied the nations of the Berlin Conference as part of the "bad cop/good cop" façade that came with "civilization."

Many came with good intentions and some traces of compassion. But most were viewed by the indigenous tribes as merely a part of the package—a reprieve from oppression but little more than that. When one is being struck with a whip and religious conversion is the only way to make it stop, one will do anything to end the pain. What turned the tide for Christianity in the Sub-Sahara

CONTINUED ON NEXT PAGE

Islam and Christianity: The African Conundrum CONTINUED

was the relentless activity of Christian ministries to shut down the brutal oppression against the indigenous peoples.

This was particularly true in the Belgian Congo and in areas of Portuguese rule when the clerics reported to the heads of state of the "dark depredations down under." The Brits and French both realizing that religion was, in fact, the opiate of the masses, granted the Catholic Church and the Church of England considerable leverage in "civilizing" the locals. In fact, the Christian schools for the locals were the best ways to learn language and culture. So the tribal leaders saw the benefits and used them to their advantage.)*

Ultimately, as the Law of Compensation arrives, the Christian influence served as a cultural building block in the Sub-Sahara after the Berlin Conference of 1884 much in the same way the Muslim influence of the Ottoman Empire in North Africa had served prior to that time. Even though the sensationalist headlines would make it appear otherwise, the nations of the Sub-Sahara do remarkably well when it comes to balancing their religious preferences in everyday life. Although some nations like Botswana are 90% Christian and others like Somalia are 90% Muslim, the balance in the Sub-Sahara is about 53% Christian to 39% Muslim, with 8% being either Buddhist, Hindu or tribal religions. It is not uncommon in the Sub-Sahara for a nation like Nigeria, that is 58% Christian, to have a Muslim head of state (Muhammadu Buhari) and conversely.

The recent exception to all of this is the eastern Sub-Sahara where Muslim militant extremists have successfully infiltrated the entire Horn of Africa. Al Shabaab is little more than a Muslim Mafia that has successfully subsumed Somalia and has made its presence a factor in the two vicious civil wars in Sudan, where wholesale persecution of Christian blacks in the South by Arab Muslims in the North led to the eventual secession of South Sudan (Africa's newest nation). Djibouti and Eritrea are little more than corrupt sultanates with very limited human rights and breeding grounds for radical jihadi infiltrations into neighboring Ethiopia. Ethiopia—a Christian island surrounded by a sea of Islamic extremism has rendered the kingdom of Haile Selassie a nation under siege, forced by circumstance to adopt a draconian repression of all political dissent.

---

* To that extent in Nigeria for example, missionaries translated the Bible into three main languages—Yoruba, Hausa and Igbo— to gain more leverage with the local population. The end result was 'highly educated' Nigerians came from the Southern region. The Missionaries could not penetrate the North (the region was ruled by Emirs and the local Islamic Caliphs who did not take lightly to citizens of their "nation" being educated; this would eventually give rise to a break-away faction –Boko Haram (which translates to-Western Education is SIN.)

Summary

Perhaps the greatest burden of the European colonial government models is that they left an incomplete ideological hodgepodge for the new nations of Africa to sort out—so much so that only in the last two decades have these new burgeoning economies truly been able to make sense of it, and find their own national identities.

Still, even today, these same young nations are having aid heaped upon them by the very "European benefactors" who exploited them in the first place. In what might well be looked upon as "guilt money," the EU and the UN (as well as the USA) almost annually descend on the Sub-Sahara with subsidies, grants and low recourse loans going out to those "good little governments" that somehow meet their standards. Is all this AID a good thing or just one more layer of The Onion—one where another level of corruption might be found?

That is something we will endeavor to answer in the next chapter. So stick around and turn the page. The best is yet to come.

CHAPTER 10

FOREIGN AID:
'Death by Good Intentions...'

"...Foreign aid to a country that doesn't also engage in significant amounts of foreign trade is more likely to end up in the pockets of dictators and cronies."

— Brien Behlendorf, WTO/*World Economic Forum*

It might be accurately noted that Colonialism *officially* came to an end with the initiation of the United Nations Declaration of Decolonization. It should also come as a surprise to no one that the colonial influence didn't end on the spot once the Declaration was officially "activated" in 1960.

By early 1961 a punch list of Seven Initiatives spelling out every nation's independence and self-determination was immediately set into place. And it was quickly adapted as a guideline for every nascent government on the African Continent. Between 1958 and 1977 more than 39 African nations launched their petitions for independence with another dozen splitting off into new political entities by the early 1990s. Those included virtually every nation in the Sub-Sahara from Cameroon, Congo, Central African Republic and Nigeria in 1960-61 all the way up to the Republic of Namibia in 1990 (actually split off as a separate political entity out of the charter for a new South Africa in 1991).

The majority of nations achieved their independence in the first ten years between 1960 and 1970, although a few such as Guinea and Ghana had done so as early as 1956. And while these new sapling national governments were coming into being, they were soon to become the objects of a new kind of political tug-of-war—a Cold

War in this case—between "The Free World" and the trenchant new Marxism of the Soviet Bloc nations.

Faced in some area with what amounted to the political/philosophical equivalent of speed-dating, it didn't take long for savvy leaders in many of these new African political entities to realize that they could quickly build both political leverage and funding by choosing their allies carefully—by playing both ends against the middle—and by taking the best political and economic package deal as a part of the process of "becoming."

In a way, this precedent had been originally set in Northern Africa in 1956 by Egypt's President Gamal Abdel Nasser in what amounted to something of a Hobson's choice. Nasser, who arguably ran one of the more politically progressive governments on the African continent felt sufficiently betrayed by his former "patrons" in the UK and France over the Suez Canal Crisis to set down his Most-Favored Nation trade treaties with the Soviet Bloc in a decidedly anti-Western political strategy. The move, looked upon as traitorous by former allies like the USA and cynical by many others in Europe, was actually one of political survival, and it paved the way to a new kind of "independence" available to other African Nations that played out in a dozen different scenarios.

One of the offshoots of this "defection" from European and Western influence was the terrorist model of Muammar Gadhafi in Libya that eventually became Africa's first de-facto "rogue nation." He was joined later by Idi Amin Dada in Uganda and eventually by "revolutionary" governments in places like Somalia and Djibouti. But these were in fact extreme examples of the kind of ideological spinoffs and alliances that came out of African independence.

In so many other instances, the "Free World" led by the US, the UK and France would rush aid—financial, humanitarian, and military—into any newly forming African nation (some headed by some unspeakably wicked military dictators) as long as they openly declared themselves to be a "democratic republic" and/or avowedly "anti-communist." This scenario played out in every nation from Nigeria to Niger to Kenya to the Congo (later Zaire) to Cote d' Ivoire, Sierra Leone, and Central African Republic. Eastern Bloc nations made their socialist imprints on nations such as Tanzania, Madagascar (which for 20 years became the Malagasy Republic) and Ethiopia.

More often than not, it would be a cynical power struggle between the two spheres of influence—so much so that they might lead to several changes of government followed by protracted civil wars that would last for decades. Such was the case in the Congo (following the assassination of Patrice Lumumba and the rise of Mobuto Sese Seko), Angola (which turned into a triangulated conflict between the US backed

UNITA and the Marxist MPLA) and Sudan where the Soviet backed rebels from the SCP held sway well into the mid-1970s.

Add into this mix the late-coming but relentless onslaught of radicalized Islamic Jihad (well-funded from Iran, Yemen and other oil-rich nations of the Middle East) in places like Sudan, Somalia, Mali and Mauritania and one begins to bear witness to the crazy-salad of money, food, weapons and economic leveraging poured into the entire continent of Africa well into the 1990s.

This ongoing ideological battle for the hearts and minds of a burgeoning Africa raged for thirty-three years from 1960 to 1993. And it led to a layering of tens of billions of dollars in aid money from the US led NATO Bloc and weapons and political leveraging from the 'Warsaw pact" Soviet Bloc nations, most of it funneled into the hands of dictators and military juntas with little more than 8% of it reaching anything resembling humanitarian aid or going toward the building of an infrastructure.

In fact, the rise of unrepentant kleptocracies in the Sub-Sahara such as those of President Mobutu Sese Seko in Zaire, Military strongman Sani Abacha in Nigeria and Robert Mugabe in Zimbabwe (only recently overthrown by former henchman Emmerson Mnangagwa) epitomize the modern Kleptocrat supported by the "Western Bloc" nations that included several African governments.*

In many cases, the aid and alliances from the former Colonial empires in Europe (along with the United States) only required that the official African government declare itself a "republic" or a "democracy" or a "democratic republic," try to hold free and fair elections and establish some form of bicameral system of government. In fact, during the 1960s through the 1980s in particular there was a proliferation of what came to be nicknamed *DINOS (Democracies In Name Only)* that remained in power only because they could be counted on not to be Communist or Socialist/Marxist. This was by no means limited to Africa and included nations in Central America, South America and Asia.

Applied to Africa, the models failed miserably because they were not, by even the most liberal definition, democracies. As we will soon see, Democracy is a middle class concept. And loosely configured emerging nations forced to subsist for centuries inside a rigged colonial system have no tangible way of functioning inside its rather sophisticated structure.

---

* *Kleptocracy* is a Greek root word implying government officials who used their high office for personal gain. Apparently Socrates first used the term in his outspoken criticism of the Oligarchy in Athens. And it came into greatest prominence in 1891 in Mexico when referring to the government of President Porfirio Diaz, and several other corrupt administrations that followed. There are any number of "name-tagged" kleptocracies, including those of Papa Doc Duvalier in Haiti, Gedrik Suharto in Indonesia and former Philippine President Ferdinand Marcos.

During the 1960s and 1970s, Eastern Bloc nations dug into their African "affiliates" with a different set of talons. Those involved some military and financial manipulation of men and materials, but invariably included an entire team of "advisors" coming into the host nation with a full agenda and ultimately a great deal of control. Not merely content with economic leverage, the Soviet Bloc nations usually insisted on complete infiltration of ideology and teaching tools, including Marxist models that they implemented for the host nations to follow.

East African nations such as Tanzania, Madagascar, Sudan and Ethiopia tried the "Soviet Model" of socialism at various stages of their development, and all of them met with long term outcomes that could only be described as failures. Within a dozen years or so, these Marxist hybrids were abandoned and replaced by representative governments that—though corrupt and dysfunctional in some instances—at least presented some distant drum of a better life to come.

Any purely socialist model of government, if it is to succeed at all, must have two qualities in common at the outset: 1) a total level of commitment to the end objective of shared economic prosperity; 2) absolute integrity in the fulfillment of that social model without any lapses in execution. With that strict set of criteria firmly in mind, there have only been seven nations in the world that have successfully executed a socialist form of government, and five of those have been in what are called the Nordic model. (More often than not the socialist/Marxist concept of government breaks down through corruption at some level, especially when it comes to black marketeering and a subsequent devaluation of human rights.)

In both instances as they apply to Africa, the socialist states and democracies that were superimposed on the Sub-Sahara were complete failures because the power-broker nations of the world only addressed the African enigma in purely political terms. In so doing—by turning Africa into a flashpoint of political ideologies—they simply layered one kind of colonial rule on top of another. Not surprisingly, the ideological struggles for the Soul of Africa also found themselves accompanied by some very practical—if not entirely cold blooded—economic considerations.

Particular favorites were played by the West eager to rush in with military and economic aid to "commodity rich" nations such as Nigeria, South Africa, Zambia and Kenya. And even as they shored up these political and economic alliances, it was evident that their "investments" were ones of commoditization. Mining and resource extraction, "boomtown" environments almost always create false springs of economic activity that carry with them limited lifespans, ghost towns and little or no economic legacy in the wake of their departure.

As far as reaching those in need—the poor, uneducated and disenfranchised who really might have benefitted from the human basic needs of food, shelter, health care and some form of daily income— the governments, restructured to deal with a new economic reality—offered few benefits if any. And what would end up happening in the aftermath of the "rape and run" short term spike mining bubble economies would be a decade of restructuring, and a lot of good intentions rather badly put in place.

'Live Aid!' A Dead End: The Ethiopian Parable

Many people believe that parables are one of the best forms of teaching. I happen to be one of them. So, we will catalyze this chapter on Foreign Aid by referring to a short but stormy episode of people from the US, UK and Europe trying to help a war-torn African nation that ended up in a debacle of good intentions gone wrong.

The nation was Ethiopia. The year was 1985. The noble effort was something called Live-Aid. Anyone who has been around the planet for more than 30 years prob-

ably remembers the episode well. Although the entire "charitable" undertaking represented little more than lunch money in terms of actual aid provided to a country in any given year, this rush of humanitarian support and phenomenal PR was a star-studded media event so shiny and so alluring that it even had its own theme song, as several recordings of "We Are the World" echoed across the global airwaves, literally for months on end.

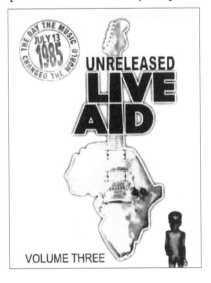

If you weren't born yet or have simply forgotten, a planned series of Live-Aid Concerts were set in place to benefit the poor and starving victims of a war-torn Ethiopia. Yes that "Ethiopia!"

Here we were in the early 1980s at the cornerstone of Western civilization—the Empire of Haile Selassie I, the liberator of Abyssinia, the shield against the Italian *Fascisti* and the Lion King of the only free nation to come out of the African scramble— and we were all forced to watch it become the political pawn in a violent civil war.

This Ethiopian Civil War marked what was known as the Derg Era—a deadly conflict called The Red Terror—named after the Derg leader Mengtsu Haile Mariam. In 1976, Haile Mariam had seized power and managed to lock the nation into a socialist strangle hold that amounted to little more than an "exploitation by warlord." When The People's Liberation Front (TPLF) rose up against Miriam in 1982, he brought in "military advisors" from practically every Warsaw Pact Nation (USSR, East

Germany, Romania, South Yemen and North Korea), including 15,000 Cuban troops flown in expressly for the occupation.** What resulted in the next three years was a savage civil war that cost nearly 500,000 lives, many of them civilians, women and children due to disease, starvation and neglect. Uprisings against the Red Rule sprang up especially in the Northern areas of Tigray and Eritrea, in a death match that finally came to a head around the late spring of 1985.

With the global influence of the Soviet Union already on the wane, the Ethiopian conflict became a political metaphor as one of the last ditch stands of Evil (warlords in this case) against the unified forces of Good. And soon enough the plight of the young and starving Ethiopian children became a cause celébre throughout a network of major world music icons.

In April of 1985, a team of rockstars headed by ace British music promoter Harvey Goldsmith, Culture Club superstar Boy George and (stateside) folk legend Joan Baez decided to use their celebrity leverage to coordinate the largest, most grandiose two-city Rock Concert fundraiser in history of the modern world—Live Aid. This "Free Concert" in two venues was to be broadcast consecutively in New York and London (and coordinated by BBC and ABC television).

Soon enough, the momentum for the event and its broad-sweeping philanthropic implications caught on with an entire echelon of rock-superstars. Such British icons as Paul McCartney, Mick Jagger and the Rolling Stones got on board with pledges to appear, and major American music legends Michael Jackson and Lionel Richie teamed up to compose the memorable humanitarian anthem, "We Are the World."

In a couple of weeks, everyone in the world was treated to various renditions of "We Are the World," promoted in extended commercials and featuring what seemed to be every hot music star in the world, and there you had it: Country icon Willie Nelson locking arms with David Bowie locking arms with Tina Turner doing an elbow loop with Stevie Wonder *et al.* in an endless celebrity daisy-chain pointing to the "free" live concert/telethon coming to the airwaves in July at Wembley Stadium and the JFK Center.

Unfortunately it didn't take long before the Live Aid movement became a debacle that would have made the Tower of Babel look like masterpiece of coordination. Originally intended to be a benefit for the war-ravaged nation of Ethiopia, Live Aid found itself suddenly being questioned as to the "narrowness of its focus," while the concerts themselves soon descended into an ego juggling act to see which celebrity

---

** One of Cuba's primary revenue streams from 1959-1991 was the exportation of military troops and weapons to support Marxist dictators all over the world—from Angola to Nicaragua—funding and logistical support provided by the USSR and The People's Republic of China.

groups performed when and who would have to share the stage with whom. (Some over-the-hill music groups saw this as an opportunity to resurrect their careers while many superstars felt put upon by getting to turf wars over something they were already doing for free.)

By the time the charity concerts were finally broadcast in July 1985, half the original cast had either stepped down or stayed away. Major headliners like Bruce Springsteen, Dianna Ross and Cher simply avoided the entire affair. (Prince cancelled but sent a video.) Michael Jackson and Stevie Wonder ended up boycotting the final event due to the "politics of participation." In England the entire evening descended into a rumor mill about the Beatles reuniting, and the promoters found out in painful ways that free charity events attracted mainly drugged out "freeloaders," and ended up raising less than $5 million on both sides of the ocean, virtual pocket change even back in 1985.

Proceeds from the song, "We Are the World," did manage to scrape up another $47 million plus about $58 million from licensing and promotional "memorabilia." So ultimately just over a $110 million was finally collected to go to the war-ravaged nation. But by that time other cause groups were getting involved, including one to channel help to "all of Africa" and also feed "the poor and needy farmers"...in the good old USA.

Originally set up with an atrocious sense of logistics, the money from Live-Aid, along with tons of food, was supposed to be channeled to The People's Liberation Front (TPLF) and through them to the millions of starving and needy.

Having put on the Live-Aid event and gathering what funds remained after rerouting the monies in a dozen different directions into some tangential expenses, slightly more than $60 million remained to get to the right groups in Ethiopia, which the people in charge were virtually clueless to undertake. One of the complications of getting anything to Ethiopia now remained with the fact that it had, by that time, become the world's largest landlocked nation. So any shipment of food and material ended up rotting on the docks of Eritrean port cities. And millions in funds actually got redirected to the warlords in Tigray who were playing both sides against the middle, while the majority of the aid monies reportedly ended up in the hands of the "Red Terror," Mengtsu Haile Mariam himself. (The very person everyone was trying to defeat.)

Ultimately, it is estimated that of the approximately $111 million raised by Live-Aid, less than $4 million in food and funds actually ended up in the hands of those who needed it.

On the surface, of course, this famous fiasco might seem a bit extreme. Once analyzed it is, in so many ways, symptomatic of the wasted funds that have come to

Africa just in the last 60 years since most of these nations achieved their independence. In fact, it is estimated that the foreign aid provided to Africa in all its various forms has totaled more than $1.1 trillion (USD) since 1961. And yet in real terms less than 12% has ever been applied directly to purpose. Here at least are a dozen reasons why:

The Millennium Challenge Corporation: The Truth About "AID"

There is a very aggressive US funding agency that manages to come off, intended or not, with the bullish personality of a hedge fund. It is called the *Millennium Challenge Corporation.* It is dedicated exclusively to funding developing nations that meet its extensive criteria. And in the 10 or so years of its existence it has already acquired a reputation for doing some pretty hard business, using its sources as stringently as any major credit ratings system.

First established by US President George Bush in 2004, Millennium Challenge Corporation (MCC) has attempted to provide effective aid for "qualifying nations" with appropriate accountability on several levels by vetting each country receiving monies through a *17 Point Program*—a kind of government report card if you will.

Petitioning nations are placed into one of two categories: 1) Compact Countries and 2) Threshold Countries. For a nation to be eligible as a Compact Country, it must show improvement in 11 of the 17 established criteria for good governance, including such qualities as *Civil Liberties, Human Rights, Government Effectiveness, Rule of Law, Control of Corruption, Public Health Expenditure, Natural Resource Management, Inflation Reduction* and many others. Petitioning nations showing significant progress in 9 of the 17 established directives might be considered as Threshold Countries. As such, they are eligible for funding on a smaller scale with limited range and a tighter window of controls.

In 2008 there were 25 Compact Countries, including such African nations as Benin, Burkina Faso, Cape Verde, Ghana, Lesotho, Madagascar, Malawi, Mali, Morocco, Mozambique Senegal and Tanzania. Among the "Threshold Countries" one could also count Kenya, Liberia, Niger, Rwanda and Zambia.

Notably missing from the petitioning political entities were Nigeria, South Africa, Egypt, Angola, Libya and other resource rich nations whose combined national revenues represented nearly 40% of all African GDP and who simply didn't need the scrutiny.

Even a quick glance at the list of Compact Countries raises a whole list of red flags, because such nations as Mali, Malawi and Mauritania appear on no one's list of "Most Improved Nations." And nations such as Burundi, Niger and Liberia are hardly Sub-Sahara superstars. So it might appear that some governments are either cooking the books or going through some kind of radical political facelift to get the MCC's blessing for its highly regimented transfer of funds. More often than not, the funds in question amount to only a few hundred million $USD and seldom reach more than $1 billion. They almost always come out of the US Congressional "soup kitchen" for developing nations. And the recipients are seldom if ever awarded all the funds they have requested.

The good news is that the majority of the countries challenged to lift their standards have risen to the occasion by improving their overall performance by as much as 25%. And even though the Millennium Challenge Corporation is linked to some notably conservative groups such as the Heritage Foundation (with its Index of Economic Equality), the fact is that this is the only complex system ever set in place to demand a set of criteria to be met by nations seeking funds. And because it is such traditional Foreign Aid funding behemoths such as UNAID, USAID and the International Monetary Fund (IMF) are not only taking notice but also using the MCC as a benchmark for their own lending parameters.

When you examine contributors across the board, there are dozens of different international lending organizations that offer no-recourse humanitarian aid to a long list of developing nations ostensibly "in need." Limited in funds, these groups have—until the last ten years or so—been notoriously slipshod in their requirements for funds. And for decades infamous kleptocracies from Haiti to Zimbabwe have managed to tap into billions with practically zero cost accounting to track their expenditures.

The IMF is a different creature altogether. Founded in 1944 and based in Washington DC the International Monetary Fund is the bully on the financial block. Established under the aegis of the World Bank and an immense international network of financial organizations, it offers long-term funding with every expectation of repayment in full. It has had to do so, because history has taught it the necessity of fiscal responsibility—the hard way.

During a brief period when it was headed by former US Defense Secretary Robert McNamara in 1973, the IMF made adventurous loans to a number of emerging market nations only to have Argentina (the largest debtor among them at the time) default on $128 billion of outstanding debt. When the IMF forgave Argentina its shortfall, it set off a cascade of defaults from a dozen other nations. Chile, Cameroon, Nigeria, Niger, South Korea, Bangladesh and Mexico—all announced their defaults inside the next six weeks—provoking a chain reaction that nearly tanked the fragile world financial system at the time. This brought on a major restructuring of loans and an entire new set of standards by which the IMF would hold the whip hand over nations attempting to renege on their commitments.

Now virtually every nation in the world uses the IMF data banks, including either GDDS (General Data Dissemination System) or Special Data Dissemination Standards (SDDS) for more financially lucrative advanced nations. When applied in today's financial environment, an IMF loan gives that global financial body terrifying leverage over any borrower nation, including clamp-downs on national banks, freezing funds, devaluation of currencies, and even forcing bankruptcies.*** So, even though most nations rely upon the IMF at some level for financial support and backing, it is a Faustian pact for many that few if any nations enjoy.

To some degree the MCC has lightened the burden on both ends by acting as both vetting source and financial "crash test dummy" for emerging economies. But in reality even that only solves one of the many challenges of foreign aid to African nations—as some small measure of insurance against corruption and for holding governments accountable for the representation of funds.

It has also come to prove more than ever that Foreign Aid as it applies to African governments does virtually nothing to build their economies. In fact it only serves to head a long list of things that don't work. From the colonial "codependent" umbilical cord to the Ideological (Democracy/Marxist) power struggle and the monetarily manipulated "Death by Generosity," Foreign Aid has proved to be the final nail in the coffin of emerging nations for all the reasons listed below that you didn't know you needed to know…until now.

First, there is the obvious network of corruption. This is the kind of "trickle-down" economics that never trickles down. Everyone from heads of self-proclaimed "humanitarian groups" to corrupt bureaucrats siphon off funds for everything from jobs to education and health care, leaving behind only window dressing that passes itself off for progress. By all the available credible metrics less than 8% of all foreign aid actually reaches those who really need it. And even when it does it provides little more than a Band-Aid for the real problem.

Second is the code of dependency that Foreign Aid creates. There is a Maasai warrior proverb that tells us: "A fed lion doesn't hunt." Governments, social services and the people

---

*** Yes! Even though some global financial institutions such as Goldman Sachs and AIG are "too big to fail," most nations and national governments are not. Just ask Greece, Italy and Spain. In 2014 these nations teetered on the edge of a bankruptcy forced on them by the IMF, until the EU interceded on their behalf and decided to bail them out, placing the European Economic Union on shaky ground ever since.

themselves cultivate a sense of entitlement toward the discretionary funds they receive and become sloppy in their application of them. *In truth, Foreign aid is addictive.* Whether it is food banks (SNAPS programs) or provisions for basic needs, people and the mini-mart philanthropies that support them become "waiting machines" that lose all incentive to become self-sufficient, seek higher education or pursue new careers. They turn into parasites. They subsist.

Third, Foreign Aid causes governments to atrophy. Even in functioning republics and conservative democracies, the national government is the largest employer. Yes, bureaucracies too require manpower and employ millions in most cases. As health and human services expand, you need government employees to run them—just as you do for education, the environment, utilities, the military, police and fire. Aid dependent governments are merely channels for money and end up neither building nor expanding infrastructure. Oversight as to the expenditure of aid often brings in its own overseers and does little to add jobs at the regional and local level.

Fourth, Aid of any kind creates a temporary bubble economy with no long-term horizons. Whether it is health clinics, medical and food relief facilities (such as Doctors Without Borders, the Red Cross, UNICEF and other generous but limited lifespan organizations) the commerce created only lasts as long as they do. All of them arrive with a limited presence and a specific pull date. And once they are removed there is a snapback that very often leaves the situation just as dire as they found it.

Fifth, Foreign Aid tends to eviscerate consumerism. Families on relief are just getting by; they are making ends meet and little else. They are not exactly brimming over with discretionary income. Little or no aid goes toward funding educational institutions or creating "job fairs." It doesn't build malls, underwrite car dealers or buy iPads for school children. It seldom if ever challenges a country to seek a pathway toward literacy. Even on a continent where 50% of the population is under 18, foreign aid brings no system of credit or means with which to purchase lifestyle-enhancing technology.

Sixth, Foreign Aid tends to paralyze economies. It stunts growth, decimates small local businesses and supports flaccid local governments that do nothing to improve either their standards or their services. Unless specifically earmarked to do so, no foreign aid ever goes into small business loans, loans to corporations, foster farms and coops or improve the efficiency of local industry. When it comes in many instances, it shows up as a contingency of foreign contracts that come on a twenty-year commodity raid and then leave only hulls of resources in their wake. (As an example, until five years ago Ethiopia had been the largest recipient of foreign aid on the continent of Africa. And to this day it has the lowest literacy rate [at 41%], the worst longevity [at 52 years] and one of the lowest per capita incomes in the Sub-Sahara at $1.10 a day. Only recently has it been revived by the influx of FDI from China and India ... and through the rise of technology due to demand from its Millennials.)

Seventh, Foreign Aid is all about control. Ultimately, even with the best intentions, it steals a nation's soul. A great deal of foreign aid is free recourse, which is addictive enough. A great of it entails long-term loans, whether from MCC or USAID and as such either entails a great deal of oversight (such as the MCC report card system) or repressive micromanagement such as that offered by the International Monetary Fund (IMF). Ultimately this stifles the initiative of the countries receiving funds because they are simply too preoccupied with jumping through hoops to encourage local business and dare the uncharted world of capital expansion. In that regard, they take the safe haven of expanding government bureaucracy by nationalizing strategic industries such as petroleum, natural gas, fuel, energy, utilities and other mining, leaving virtually no inroads to the virtue of capitalism.

Eighth, governments never pay back foreign aid loans. The people do. It's just Economics 101: Large corporations never pay taxes; they pass them onto the consumer. If you tax petroleum by the barrel, they charge for it at the pump. If you tax imports on retail goods, the added fees are paid for at the point of purchase. The same applies to debt retirement by nations. (Example: Recent IMF loans to Ghana were paid off by levying an annual $110 "surcharge" to tax-paying citizens. And Ghana has learned the lesson the hard way about the "Faustian Pact" of foreign aid in that they have had to "denationalize" their industries, 70% of which have been government owned, in order to grow to a level resembling their ultimate potential. In other words, though well run, Ghana has realized that it must become capitalistic in order to grow to its full potential. That means attracting Foreign Direct Investment.)

Ironically, one of the good things to come out of the Millennium Challenge Corporation's 17 Point system was the final item on its Report Card: *Ability to Attract Investment.* This implies, though does not specify, Foreign Direct Investment. It did seem to say to the participating Compact Nations that this was "the final criteria" for becoming a viable trading nation and reliable partner. Some nations like Ghana, Namibia and Botswana really got the message. Others are picking it up. And since we offer a document that is both pragmatic and resourceful we use that final touching point to launch the rest of our economic argument.

Summary: Now that we know what needs fixing, how do we fix it?

Never a fan of the backbencher's strategy that articulates the problem without coming up with solution, I follow this chapter by offering a simple Five Step Program that works—that brings hope, initiative, imagination and a solid business model. At least a few African nations have already embraced it. And no it's nothing terribly original inasmuch as it is a Rubix that may be constructed easily and with a few simple but disciplined twists of the block.

Those twists and turns come in the next chapters. And they involve Capitalism, Democracy, and FDI participation—"Enlightened Autocracy" and the help of a few good friends...not necessarily in that order.

CHAPTER 11

STICKS, BRICS and (No) STRINGS:
Africa's Building Blocks

"For me…the really inspiring tales are in the private sector: those daring entrepreneurs who take a chance, uprooting their lives in the West to build something in Africa. These guys are the pioneers, the innovators, the visionaries—and they are lighting a spark and setting the standard."

— Ashish Thakkar, *The Lion Awakes*

Before we begin what I hope will be a very positive chapter on how to get things done in the world's hottest market, we will make one last disclaimer. Feckless AID and bad loans are not exclusive to Africa. They have proven to be a global pandemic, and we need a different approach—starting here, starting now.

A classic example of nations throwing good money after bad has to be the COP 21 "Climate Change" Conference in Paris in November 2015. Hosted by France and co-sponsored by the World Bank, the COP 21 Conference is officially entitled the United Nations Climate Change Convention, *Conference of Parties* (hence the acronym). This 21st official convening—COP 21—included 6,000 representatives from over 195 nations to address this apparent ecological challenge to the wellbeing of planet earth.

One of the pillars of this climate summit's corrective framework is the scientific theory that carbon emissions (specifically CO_2) are the runaway cause of global warming. Since the warmest 15 years in the planet's history have come in this century, there can be little doubt that the planet is heating up. What compounds the issue is that the

COP summits on climate change have tipped the focus (if not the obsession) so heavily toward carbon emissions that they have ignored some of the immediate threats to the global ecology that truly deserve equal time.

Contamination of our oceans and rivers, industrial pollution of our air and air currents, shortages of water, serious cutbacks in the world's food supply (some due to drought), and finally the utter decimation of our oceans, our coral and our world's aquatic life—all these crises and more present a clear and present danger that the nations at COP 21 seem to think can be fixed by addressing the usual suspects called "greenhouse gases."

So once again—and the bottom line to all of this—our global community has come together to throw vast sums of money at a challenge it has failed to grasp in its entirety. That, on the surface, would seem unbalanced enough. The rest of the riddle may be answered in the absurdity of who is throwing money at whom and for what?

Bad COP. Good COP.

First of all, the rules of greenhouse gasses are simple. The top two nations: The United States and China are responsible for 38% of the world's greenhouse gas emissions—China 26% to the US's 12%. The other top six polluting nations (and geographic area) also include India, Russia, the EU and Japan. These combine to produce a total of 59% of the world's total noxious emissions. All of them have "pledged" to reduce their nation's carbon output by the year 2020, though none of them—certainly not China, and certainly not India—have designed a specific grid that would hold the strict tenets of that pledge. In other words, they'll just do the best they can (with absolutely no oversight and zero penalty for failing to do so).

At the same time what these top polluting nations will do between now and the year 2020 is use the World Bank's money to throw approximately $100 billion (USD) a year at developing nations to help them form effective programs to fend off climate change in their own countries and offset its effects such as drought. Included in this carbon lending program is an estimated $16 billion a year for African countries, which all seems very good on paper. But let's be realistic, shall we? Of the major high carbon emissions, only two are African nations log into the Top 25: South Africa at 12, due to its heavy mining industries, and Egypt at 18 due to its large population and heavy shipping in and around the Suez.

So...where does all this COP money come from? Where does it go? And who qualifies for the loans? At this point, no one has the answers—only the intention and promises of directives to be fulfilled. Thus far, none of the questions are being answered except with "the hope" that the initiatives established at COP 21 will be met by actions taken at COP 22 set up in Marrakech, Morocco sometime in 2016.

In chat rooms and at conference tables, a good many promises are being made to help nations build solar power plants and provide drought prevention models for the African farm belt from Cote d'Ivoire to Tanzania. But those in the North have born witness to failed solar energy programs funded out of Europe. And energy initiatives have hit Southern Africa from Namibia to Mozambique—many of which have been left to founder incomplete. So, now African nations must approach new ventures with the caution French author Honóre d' Balzac once gave to second marriages: "A triumph of hope over experience."

Everyone enjoys the thought of "free money." And there is little doubt that when the COP 22 funding convention comes to Marrakesh, some expedient borrower nations will show up at the trough to receive ecology grants for power plants and conservation programs—for which they will submit their "wish lists." But without solid business models the COP 22 initiatives will strike a Sophie's Choice—or what critics have insisted are "Funds provided by the clueless to be used by the irresponsible." The other, and far more accurate analogy would be "Guilt money from hoarders thrown at the hapless and the hopeless." Either way, the scenario—unless some Critical Mass in G-22 consciousness takes place—is a bleak one.

Even under the best of circumstances, COP 21 monies promise to turn into nothing more than financial codependency in an endless loop. And more African nations have come to realize, at last, that in the end there are no free lunches. Payment always comes due, and often in ways that satisfy no one.

What nations in the Sub-Sahara in particular have learned—much of it by trial and error—is that certain basics are essential to a successful, burgeoning economy and a solid positive future. We call it STICKS, BRICS, and [No] STRINGS: Africa's Building Blocks.

STICKS

Yes it is an acronym. It's also a set of building blocks. And any solid economy in Africa has come to use them over time, not necessarily in the order we stipulate.

As originally established STICKS stands for the following: *Stability, Technology, Infrastructure, Credit, Kinetic resource, Strategic alliances.* Taken in order as individual banners, the words imply a fair share of high intent combined with a sophisticated socio-political "national" model. But as we will soon see, one did not necessarily follow the other in a perfect evolutionary stream.

Just as each nation in Africa has its own story to tell, the major players in the Sub-Sahara rose to prominence by turning all the clicks in their lock on success at different times on the clock. So neither alphabetic structure nor chronology of social enlightenment offers any specific Genesis to create the winning formula. Still, the Synergy of Success does have a specific set of ingredients, however scrambled, that seem to work.

Stability. The term, stability, when describing a nation-state will almost always imply political stability. And a type of government—democracy, monarchy, socialist republic or dictatorship—is not necessarily as important as enlightened leadership. One might have the carefully constructed Republican model formed out of the 20 plus year supervision of De Klerk, Mandela, and Thabo Mbeki in South Africa from 1988 to 2009. Or one might find the "secret sauce" of a fast-track modernization born out of the quiet autocracy of a Paul Kagame that has helped Rwanda rebuild and rebirth itself since 1997. Then again, one might be galvanized by the Dr. Kwame Nkrumah inspired Social Democratic model of Ghana, the Democratic Matriarchy of Mauritius (with 3 women presidents in a row), or the enlightened monarchy of Morocco's Mohammed VI. However you try to frame the success, *Four Elements* all these styles of governance have in common are 1) an adherence to order, 2) an acute sense of social justice, 3) a determination not only to sense trends (such as technology) but also to adjust to them, and 4) an embrace of creative capitalism in all its many forms.

Technology. Virtually since the turn of the New Millennium (and especially since 2010), technology has to be considered the great economic leveler in Africa in general and in the Sub-Sahara in particular. And now more than ever it is equated to personal freedom at every strata of society. Primitive, rural, agrarian, Sub-Saharan Africa has been—for generations—plagued by immobility, a lack of logistics to and from market, inadequate access to modern transportation, poor infrastructure of roads, war, robbery and civil conflicts that have virtually held captive the poor of most nations.

Now, the point-and-click universe brings virtual banking, app market bidding and sales, and fingertip electronic classrooms that are educating entire nations of Millennials often with optional applications that are very often free. It has reset the social structure of entire civilizations. And even countries previously left on the political rubbish heap—such as Somalia, Djibouti and Malawi—are finding new routes to resurrection in this.

Through technology and smart-phone/tablet apps, both the poor subsistence farmer and the hedge fund billionaire now have equal access to the same level playing field—the worldwide web super-information super highway. Now African Millennials *(Afrillennials)* get to choose an online course of study, get to solicit student loans, get to buy and sell basic agricultural contracts and plan their futures with things like monthly billing, auto-pay, low interest financial transactions and electronic credit.

Infrastructure. Ultimately, African nations only succeed when they pay attention to the basics—health care, education, social services, transportation, utilities, national business development, and bottom-up rebuilding of the economy, all the while paying attention to the poorest first. This has been an extremely difficult pill for governments in the Sub-Sahara to swallow. But they are starting to get the message for a handful of reasons: First, the Afrillennials coming up *en masse* are agitating to receive basic human services such as health, education and welfare. At this point, by sheer force of numbers they will not be denied, and governments that continue to ignore them will not be in business long. Second, technology is allowing government to function at a lower cost. Third, African governments that have shored up their basic services—Mauritius, The Seychelles, Ghana, Rwanda, Cote d'Ivoire, Botswana, and Namibia to name a few—have suddenly found that they are far more attractive to FDI commitment at all levels—especially those interested in manufacturing and consumer sales. Fourth, for too long, resource-rich nations such as Nigeria, Sudan, Angola, Mozambique and Ethiopia that have ignored even the basic establishment of infrastructure—(electric) power grids, basic utilities such as natural gas, water and sanitation—continue to do so at their own peril.

(Some heads of state such as Muhammadu Buhari in Nigeria are experiencing massive protests and backlash for their failure to clean up the infrastructure failures of previous administrations. And recently in Madagascar the entire cabinet of President Hery Rajaonarimampianina tendered their collective resignations because he had reneged on his campaign commitment to rebuild that country's streets, rails and highways in a timely manner.)

Credit. "I believe in you. I have faith in you. I trust you." When you think about the words as they are expressed in these simple sentences, they represent that special surge of self-respect any individual feels the first time they are extended credit— by a bank, a venturesome telecom, a savvy retailer or insightful consortium. Smart marketers have recognized this and are making the most of it. And it has begun to pay huge dividends. This is something that the average African citizen has been denied most of his or her life. Since the average per capita income in 28 of the 44 plus nations of the Sub-Sahara is less than $2 a day...and since 70% of the population in those nations are "small farmers" dependent upon subsistence agriculture—literally hand to mouth—it is safe to say that at least 65% must deal with the harsh realities of cash and carry just to get through the week. Now they're being told they no longer have to. Now, someone has said, "I trust you."

We now have empirical evidence that entire societies have been built on fresh foundations of credit. This was the case in the United States of the 1970s and 1980s when the availability of soft credit sent the economy skyrocketing to 400% of its previous GDP value. In fact, it can be argued that credit pulled the USA out of a 30-year financial funk into a rich (if spendthrift) consumer society. As a counterpoint, the case can be made that they overset the bar, especially when the global credit orgy affected Europe in the 1980s and 1990s. But the basics apply—that credit expands consciousness and exponential growth are consequences of optimized purchasing power. And Africa—especially in the Sub-Sahara—has had nowhere to go but up.

As the economies stand in most nations of Africa since the year 2010, technology has intersected with credit in the best of all possible worlds. Canny entrepreneurs like Atlas Mara's Bob Diamond and Ashish Thakkar have built flexible credit into the matrix of all their banking relationships and all financial transactions—whether it is to startup businesses, major corporations or married Afrillennials starting their first checking account.

Retail and tech giants such as MTN (South Africa), Safaricom and spinoffs from iHub (out of Kenya) have set such a lively credit cornucopia that African Millennials have now come not only to accept, but also to expect as a normal part of their standard business package.

Above all else, credit creates optimism, within limits. A $2 billion loan to Gambia from the World Bank is of course a sought after, if impersonal, grant. A Credit line for $2 billion from ATT or $5 billion worth of Chinese FDI from Sinopec into Tanzania, Zambia and Mozambique is worth a great deal more in job creation and tangible, long-term horizons—plus all the intangibles of an elevated national pride and the self-esteem that accompanies a burgeoning economy.

Kinetic resources. Oil is a kinetic resource [Nigeria, Libya, Angola and Gabon]. It creates movement, employment, dynamism and immediate and long-term prosperity. So are copper, platinum and gold [South Africa, Ghana, Zambia and Namibia]. Then again, technology—the right kind of technology such as M-PESA from Safaricom—is a kinetic resource with hundreds if not thousands of permutations. So are intelligently placed financial resources, banking and investment [South Africa]. Cocoa can be a kinetic resource [Cote d'Ivoire and Cameroon]. Tourism can become the same kind of resource if properly promoted, as has been the case in Tanzania.

Experts point to commodity rich nations such as Nigeria or Angola, South Africa, Namibia or Sudan, and then pigeonhole them as "single industry" economies almost as a means of condemnation. The fact is that kinetic resource is a starting point but by no means a finishing line. Having some of the broadest and deepest oil reserves in Africa may give Nigeria's national treasury some deep pockets and help create an entire legion of overnight millionaires. But it goes nowhere if the government does nothing to build social services, solid infrastructure and diversification. A dynamic economy only remains dynamic if industries germane to the nation are developed, encouraged and expanded. Nigeria may be oil-rich. It is also the rising hub of technology, internet commerce, finance, fashion and the third largest film/entertainment community in the world. South Africa may be the unchallenged mining center of platinum in the world, but it has also become Africa's solid fiduciary center at all levels of banking and finance. Namibia with large reserves of copper and titanium has also become a trading center. And Mauritius, with no Kinetic resource native to the small island chain, has created its own in the form of offering an international "Safe Haven" to world businesses. Rwanda has recovered from death throes and civil war to become a locus of power for new advances in technology.

The bottom line is also a matter of simple logic. Every nation in Africa has a Kinetic resource it can develop and use to diversify. The only states that remain in peril are those who refuse to modernize—either through repressive government or excessive corruption across the board. We're happy to note that those are on the wane. And though they may always exist on a Continent with 54 diverse states at different levels of evolution, the trend is definitely upward—to widen and to deepen.

Strategic alliances come in many forms. They can come as a new bank from Atlas Capital (Atlas Mara) opening up to fill the financial hole left from the exit of Barclay's Financial. They can come in the form of a Sinopec Contract to drill in new fields off the shores of Mozambique.

The most visible "strategic alliance" comes in the form of trade agreements and economic unions such as exist all through Africa both in the Sahara and Sub-Sahara. Some groups such as the SADC (Southern African Development Community) have formed a fairly solid trade alliance led by South Africa but also inclusive of a group of emerging economies such as Mauritius, Seychelles, Swaziland, Madagascar, Mozambique, Angola, Botswana, Rwanda, Tanzania, Uganda and Zimbabwe. Others like ECOWAS (The Economic Community of West African States) offer a multi-faceted shared government, shared defense network and a respective border pact between Nigeria, Niger, Cameroon, Cote d'Ivoire, Ghana, Guinea, Gambia, Burkina Faso, Benin, Cape Verde and others. And that economic community works as a "bloc nation" to bring in major investors from China, Malaysia and (more recently) India.

Oftentimes these confederations are little more than window dressing and accomplish very little. On other occasions, however, they have proved highly beneficial, especially when it comes to offering complementary technologies and developmental models for improving government networking and role models. Most often, however—and this is certainly true in the last decade and a half—the best strategic alliances have come through Foreign Direct Investment and some very bullish co-ventures, especially from India, China and what are known as the BRICS nations.* When one takes into consideration all the Building Blocks for a solid emerging African Nation STICKS must by all forces of logic precede the BRICS.

BRICS

The BRICS Nations—Brazil-Russia-India-China and South Africa—are most remarkable for three things: 1) they have proven to be the hottest economic markets of
the last twenty years; 2) they represent nearly 40% of the world's population and along with Japan) nearly 25% of its GDP; 3) they have basically broken the chain of parochialism that has been a hangover economic model so characteristic of countries doing business in Africa for over 65 years.

Part of the reason they have proven to be simpatico trading partners for Africa lies in the fact that in three of the four cases they too were—in the course of their nation's history—on the receiving end of the Imperial Colonial Matrix.

In truth Russia, though never a part of the African Scramble as such, has yet to reenter a serious new phase of investment in Africa ever since the USSR lost the ideological battle for those contested nations throughout the cold war years of 1950-1989. Russia, gingerly sticking its toe in the water in some Southern African nations has only participated nominally through its involvement in BRIC affiliated investment groups. (Recently it was announced in the Russian press that, having pretty well played out

---

* *BRICS Nations: Brazil, Russia, India, China and South Africa.* Looked upon around the turn of 2000 as some of the world's hottest economic markets, the BRICS nations have gone through something of a readjustment in the last three years. Brazil, especially, has hit a period of economic downturn and political upheaval. India has been bombarded internationally with charges of civil rights violations. And China is an absolute crapshoot where its overbuilt, overpriced real-estate market is concerned. Still, they remain some of the driving forces in the world economy and long-term investment partners for Africa, and along with the United States, France and Malaysia they lead the way in developing trade and commerce in the Sub-Sahara. Finally, we come to South Africa. Recently added to the mix due to its rise into a position of prominence as one of the world's top 25 economies, it offers the insider's advantage to other African nations—the trust of the bullish neighbor to the South.

their other financial forays mainly into Asia and South America, Russia was perched to look to Africa as its "next big market." Not exactly a strategy that is causing African nations to line up.)

Of the remaining three BRICS nations, *India* has been the only one that was, to some extent, culturally anchored here. At 1.3 million of South Africa's 44 million people, Indians already represent 2.9% of the population there. And the island nation of Mauritius is the only nation in African sphere where they have a plurality of the population (at 41%) that are ethnically either Indian or mixed-race Indian and creole. At present the South African city of Durban boasts the largest Indian population (more than 400,000) outside India itself. And the trade relations with South Africa, despite the latter's political miasma, have recently climbed to historic highs.

Coming in later than China and the United States, India has—since 2013—become the single most bullish investor in Africa at every level, except total gross revenues. Although it admittedly has seemed to work its way into the Sub-Sahara from a geographic perspective (taking the nations whose coastlines form along the shared Indian Ocean first) India has shown a particular proclivity toward trading with the resource-rich nations of southeast Africa and southern Africa as its major commercial partners.

Most immediately in need of natural gas, petroleum and other forms of energy for its burgeoning 1.3 billion population, India has been especially attracted to nations rich in mineral deposits such as South Africa and the seemingly inexhaustible natural gas reserves available in Mozambique. More recently the vast oil fields discovered on the coast of Tanzania have sent Indian developmental companies into that nation with promising contracts. And India is one of the first countries outside of the United States and Japan to bring in large automotive plants for its two major brands into South Africa and Zambia.

India has also brought a number of retail, franchise and construction contracts to East Africa, and at the moment is a close second in new projects brought to Africa with more than 255 (as of 2015). As of March 2017, they were finally surpassed by China with 293 FDI projects, $108 plus in investments—$82 billion in exports and $54.3 billion in imports in 2016.

Not entirely immersing itself into the Africa economy until 2009, *Brazil* is a late entry into the African market. And yet it has cultural ties to the Sub-Sahara that have, from the beginning, made it a natural fit. Since Brazil was formed out of Portuguese Colonialism. And with 7.6% (approximately 16 million) of its population as black and another 43% as mixed black/white race (mulatto) descendants of African slaves, that South American nation has the largest "African" population outside of Africa itself.

Due to its links to the other nations of the Portuguese "colonial sphere" it comes as no surprise that Brazil has done most of its active business with Mozambique and Angola. In 2010, a rich new vein of coal discovered in Mozambique sent the Brazilian conglomerate, Vale, over to set up mining operations. Through its commitment to mine the rich mineral veins of Mozambique, Vale is working with Odebrecht, a Brazilian construction company, to develop coal reserves, build a power station and construct rail and port infrastructure to bring the black rock to export markets. This is typical of the "boomtown" exploitation of other African nations in the past—a highly energized ad hoc infrastructure of refineries and rail, all geared to a finite timespan complete with a pull date and little left behind in terms of economic "legacy." But in this case, the world's fourth largest nation seems to have gotten the message its relationship with Africa should engage in long-term horizons.

Starting with trade agreements in 2008, Brazil now imports 31% of its petroleum products from Angola's resource-rich oil fields. It has set up additional oil and gas import contracts with Nigeria and Algeria. And it has been generating its own South American diaspora of migrant workers and contractors flooding in to take advantage of this multi-billion dollar Brazilian investment. And now it is cultivating mining relationships with Zambia and banking and tech set ups in South Africa.

By now, the world's eighth largest economy has found markets for its food producers in countries such as Egypt and Libya, helping to boost Sao Paolo's exports in the North of Africa from $7.9 billion in 2009 to nearly $14 billion by 2014.

In 2015, Brazil has had to trim foreign investment due to renewed political turmoil, corruption scandals over the 2016 Olympic, ongoing health challenges due to HIV and its role in the Zika virus pandemic. Experiencing a ripple effect resulting in something of an economic downturn, Brazil is also reeling from a spate of ongoing political scandals. In a way it is understandable because Brazil's bullish economy is one of the youngest in the world and as such is one of the most volatile. It should, however, recover nicely, and once it does the platform for African trade is now in place...and promises even greater expansion ahead.

By sheer force of proximity, *South Africa's* position as a BRICS nation is unique in that it is both buyer and seller into the economies of the rest of the Sub-Sahara. Not only is it Africa's banker (along with Morocco) in so many ways, it has also cultivated very user-friendly trade deals with its neighbors in southern Africa— especially Namibia, Zambia, Mozambique, Botswana, Lesotho and Swaziland. Since we have covered South Africa's considerable influence on the other nations of the Sub-Sahara in some detail in Chapter 3 and Chapter 7, we will revisit its impact here only as a brief recap. It is one of the Top 30 economies in the world, and remains #2 in Africa. It has the Sub-Sahara's largest user-friendly tariff system, and one of its most active platforms to attract foreign direct investment. Despite a shaky 2015, *FDI Magazine* still managed to rank South Africa "The #2 Best Future Market" on the African continent. And it remains far and away the nation of China's first best trading partner in the Sub-Sahara.

Exceeding even that of the United States, *China* is now Africa's number one trading partner—to all African nations—in terms of total capital investment. And once you take out the lucrative oil and commodity contracts in the North, it certainly emerges as number 1 in the Sub-Sahara. In fact, China's "No Strings" trade policies in the lower continent have been looked upon as the ultimate business model in the last 15 years—so much so that China requires a category all its own.

"NO STRINGS"—The China Connection

Well, let's get real (as they say). When it comes to FDI capital commitments in Africa, China certainly has. To no one's surprise, they are the number 1 "Go-to Nation" when it comes to African countries seeking investment capital.

On the surface China's "No Strings" policy of doing business in Africa would seem to be the ideal. Certainly the international economic juggernaut appears to have made all the right moves on the Continent especially in the last 15 years. Those are the facts. But what is the truth?

Not surprisingly, China's original fixation on African investment has been upon its natural resources, especially mining. But in the last five years in particular there has been a major paradigm shift to the services sector as China has seen the Sub-Sahara's rising tide of Afrillennials as the world's most prodigious new market for low cost Chinese products—especially in the area of electronics and telecommunications. Popping for a $9.5 billion investment in 2010 mostly in mining, China has increased its clout in the Sub-Sahara by ten times that amount to just over $100 billion by 2015. In 2016 alone, it was the number one source country in Africa by capital expenditure, investing $36 billion accounting for 39% of the continents total FDI investment. (In fact, China-based investments grew by 1262%.)

Much of China's influence in Africa has to do with its self-descriptive "no-strings" investment policy in building and creating homegrown African manufacturing in the Sub-Sahara. As of this writing, China has helped to develop entire industrial parks in Mauritius, and others are just undergoing completion in the Sub-Sahara's anchor nations—Nigeria, Kenya and South Africa, as well as Ghana. The original intent of these parks has been to shore up the infrastructure in those nations as well as encouraging Chinese firms to establish manufacturing industries in the parks, as they benefit from tax break holidays, favorable regulations and one-step access to major metropolitan markets through their "One Silk One Road," global network.

It comes as no surprise that the world's second largest consumer of petroleum and natural gas has gone into Africa with a considerable fuel addiction and need for imports. Originally, Angola was the leading supplier of oil to China, followed closely by Nigeria. Recently, however, new discoveries of oil and an immense (1 trillion cubic feet) field of natural gas in Mozambique have brought that nation into a high priority sphere among Chinese imports. And in 2016 China made $1.7 billion worth of infrastructure co-ventures on the East Coast of Tanzania, including the development of offshore exploration, refineries and delivery systems.

China's main strength and a source of unassailable leverage has been its willingness to go where no other FDI investors have gone before, and to commit itself not only to the nation's economy but also to its infrastructure. In the beginning, China built carefully and established relationships with Africa's most dependable governments and resource rich anchor nations. More recently, it has also been the first to venture into marginal nations such as Chad, Equatorial Guinea, Gabon, Congo-Brazzaville, and Sudan (now sending 60% of its rich oil reserves to the People's Republic of China).

Although China's original focus in time, energy and infrastructure has gone to the more reliable nations and FDI friendly governments, it is not where they have stopped. Such marginal nations as Zimbabwe, Somalia and Mali have also been awarded contracts. And everywhere the Chinese government (and its national corporations) have set down roots, they have contributed to the infrastructure as a part of "the deal." That infrastructure invariably includes electricity, water conservation, telecommunications and transportation.

The Sub-Sahara is notorious for not having any form of operable mass transit—trains, subways and buses—but China has been out to improve that as well. One of China's first introductions into Nigeria beyond the exportation of its petroleum products turned out to be a partnership between Chinese construction conglomerates and the Nigerian government to rebuild the rundown (colonial era) railway system between Lagos and the northern Nigerian city of Kano. More recently a major Chinese contractor set up a transportation agreement to repair and reconstruct the dilapidated but legendary Benguela Railway System with a network that runs from south coast of Zambia all the way up through the borders of the Democratic Republic of the Congo.

The extent to which China is committed to rebuilding Africa's underfunded mass transit may be most dramatically illustrated by its recent investment in light rail in Ethiopia, specifically in the nation's capital of Addis Ababa.

The system, which will expand next month to total 39 major stopping points across the city, is projected to carry 15,000 people per hour. A welcome addition to the capital's infrastructure, the rail project was built over a three-year period by a Chinese company after the Ethiopian government secured 85% of funding from the Export-Import Bank of China. And to the delight of everyone, it managed to outstrip a similar light rail project in Lagos, Nigeria that is still under construction. On the opening day, the citizens of Addis Ababa queued up around the block to be among the first, knowing that this new mass-transit system would be a permanent game changer in their lives.

In addition to construction project and rail systems, Chinese investors have also recognized the responsibility to provide education and training of locals for high skill jobs in the Sub-Sahara. So, in several countries from Sudan to South Africa, they have set up educational tech programs that have brought more than 75,000 homegrown Africans the job skills necessary to function in the new Sino driven industrial environment.

If China has exhibited one trait over the last decade and a half that sets it ahead of other nations, it has been its ability to play the "long game" where placing new businesses in Africa is concerned.

One of the reasons the Sub-Sahara in particular has been slow to develop FDI interest has been the unnecessary bureaucratic entanglements often hurled down in front of global investors. Some African nations have gotten the memo to loosen the leash on restricting foreign business, while others have not. As a result, the business climates from nation to nation are hugely divergent. In Rwanda, for example, it is possible to set up a business in two days. In Kenya, it can take 18 months. Cameroon takes 426 days and 33 procedures. Ghana, until recently took longer. In Angola, it takes a year and a month and about 41 procedures. But in Mauritius it's 96 hours.** Mauritius, along with South Africa and Botswana, is first among the best African nations to open a business. But almost every nation in the last five years has shown marked improvement.

In every case, with every nation, China has been patient. It has moved quickly into the more solid nations, secondarily into the resource rich nations, and ultimately into all nations (including and lately the "rogues"). And accompanying that long-term business horizon has been China's short term credit arrangements especially with newly reformed nations simply trying to get their bearings again in a very sophisticated, somewhat suspicious and largely reticent FDI participation pool.

** As a point of comparison, foreign registry for the United States takes 14 days and 16 procedures.

The thrust of China's avowed "No Strings" policy has been predicated upon a three-pronged approach to new African markets: *First,* non-intervention. (Never interfere with the policy of any government by trying to make it fit some moral paradigm.) *Second,* provide non-recourse loans for rebuilding infrastructure. *Third,* extend long-term credit—nation to nation but also from companies to individual African consumers. To be both accurate and candid, none of this had ever been tried before the Chinese came into the African mélange. They have formed a model that India, Malaysia and others, including the United States, are striving to emulate.

Today China is everywhere in Africa and many Chinese corporations and their products have become household names. Sinopec, China Mobile, Noble Group, China Bank and China Railway are now names in common usage found everywhere in the Sub-Sahara from Zambia to Chad. $106 billion in annual revenues and Chinese investment seems merely a starting point for the rosy future—one that on the surface seems almost Utopian in its potential for growth.

Then there is the China-Africa Conundrum (beneath the surface). Ideal scenarios only exist in fairy tales. And there has certainly been some blowback in the last 10 years when it comes to Chinese participation in the African markets. But not in the ways many might think.

First, the Chinese have lowered the bar so far on extensions of credit and loan parameters to African countries that both the World Bank and the EIN (Europe Independent Bank) have had to reconsider their guidelines for qualifying nations. Not surprisingly the commodity collapse of 2015 that saw oil and gas prices plummet to half their previous price per barrel value recently caused some serious credit retooling, especially for nations such as Nigeria, Angola, Mozambique and South Africa. But those economies will rally just as soon as the price of oil does.*** So the concerns are transitory and long-term optimism—for the heady investor at least— prevails. *A second offshoot of China credit* has been the fact that some nation states are less willing to be micromanaged by the World Bank and lender nations. So, they're not quite as ready to submit these to their constant oversight. *Third, China's intention* to become the Sub-Sahara's economic partner of first resort has had the desired effect. And now it beats the former first choice (the USA) by about 2 to 1 as a favored business relationship with long-term trust and "far less entanglements."

*** On the rebound as of this writing to nearly double its January 2016 lows.

Not to paint too rosy a picture, there has been some blowback on China's seeming unrestricted embrace. Although African Millennials truly flock to Chinese products and services, they are highly resistant to their cultural and political infusions. And there are barriers wherever Chinese communities spring up. There has been a Chinese diaspora especially to a handful of nations in the Sub-Sahara, and not always with a pleasant result. More than 1.5 million Chinese workers have moved to Southern and Eastern African nations (with about 350,000 in South Africa, 310,000 in Angola and 180,000 in Zambia and other resource rich nations). In virtually every case, the Chinese workers have displaced African laborers. They don't merge well at all in African societies and remain clannish to the point of being racist. Upheavals over the heavy influx of Chinese immigrants in places such as Zambia and South Africa have on more than one occasion been the cause of protests, riots and even violence.

In addition some Chinese construction and rebuilding of factories, utilities and transportation have proved to be structurally expedient and [well] "Chinese." They're shoddy at the core, evidently not built to last and have already started to break down in some areas.

Finally, the greatest criticism of the Chinese no-strings philosophy of breaking into African markets has been its occasional willingness to look the other way when it comes to kleptocracies, dictatorial regimes, rogue nations and political pariahs. Chinese President Xi Jingping—otherwise known for his anti-corruption campaign inside China as well as his sense of economic vision—has come under considerable criticism for his relationship with recently unseated Kleptocrat, Zimbabwe's Robert Mugabe and (arguably) the bloodiest dictator in the Sub-Sahara, Sudan's President Omar Al-Bashir.[†]

As it is, China resolutely remains Sudan's largest trading partner, and support from Beijing of the Al-Bashir regime remains unshaken. Zimbabwe's Mugabe, forced into retirement after 38 years, was rumored to have been using billions in Chinese developmental monies as his personal piggy bank, at least part of the reason he was overthrown by Emmerson Mnangagwa in what amounted to a bloodless coup.

At this point, we can make the argument of all moral relativists and merely observe that politics does indeed make strange bedfellows. On balance, China's investment in Africa has also been laced with a large dose of economic pragmatism. So the bottom line on China is that they have made their economic court-

---

[†] A former general in the Sudanese Army and dedicated Islamist, Bashir was indicted in 2014 by the International Crimes Commission (ICC) wing of the UN, but charges were dropped due to insufficient evidence.

Democracy. Africa. And Lipset's Law.

One of the myths of African development over the last 60 plus years has been based on an antique political notion laced with a touch of political naiveté. That is the misconception that somehow if all the nations in Africa were to merely adopt the model of "American Democracy" and keep to its principles of integrity of governance that all would be well, and each nation would prosper. Upon even a superficial examination, every nation in Africa calls itself "The Republic" of this or the "Democratic Republic" of that. In fact, there are only a handful of African countries that even come close on the Index of Economic Freedom. And only one nation (Mauritius) is even considered high enough on the index to be called a pure democracy.

Martin Lipset

The truth is (and the founding fathers of the United States knew this) that Democracy is a rather sophisticated political model of governance. And though it can in no way guarantee prosperity, it is in fact the best evidence of true capitalism at its ultimate expression. That's right, we just said that though democracy does not necessarily presage capitalism, capitalism—unaffected, uncorrupted capitalism—is an excellent pathway to democracy. We are convinced of it. And so was a political sociologist named Seymour Martin Lipset when he formulated something called Lipset's Law.

According to Lipset: "We find a significant and negative relationship between income and democracy: higher/lower incomes per capita hinder/trigger democratization..." Translation: One may try democracy, but for democracy to endure as a political model you need well-fed, well-housed, well-educated people. (In other words, starving, illiterate people do not make for an informed, committed citizenry.)

To validate his economic model, Lipset took several societies in Sub-Saharan Africa (SSA) portion of the sample where the relationship runs from political institutions – to suggest basically that democracy has a PPI economic cutoff point of roughly $6400 USD a year (of real) per capita income. Once a society reaches that point, its potential for permanent democratization becomes virtually indestructible. Anything below that Personal Prosperity Index level becomes shaky in inverse proportion to its distance from the $6400 median. So... democracy does have a dollar value. (And perhaps that's a good thing.)

ship of the Sub-Sahara work on every level. And in the end it is an excellent brand of economic symbiosis.

Summary

One simply cannot ignore the Elephant in the room. And that of course is the question: *How does one go about building an infallible national business model when doing business in Africa?* And the answer would have to be "All of the above."

It would be simplistic of us to try to superimpose a single economic game plan onto the most intricate world market and try to come up with a solution. For the best result we might recommend a hybrid, and it would go something like this:

> The integrity and economic intention of the 17 part plan of the Millennium Challenge Corporation; the savvy free democracy political model of a Mauritius; the rampant unapologetic entrepreneurialism of a newborn Nigeria; the rock solid resources (mining and financial) of a South Africa; the traditions, history and sense of self of an Egypt; the tech-savvy of a Millennial-driven Kenya; and the youthful dynamism and structural integrity of a Botswana.

Combine those with the solid infrastructure that comes with demanding FDI investors like the United States, and unconditional trust and optimism of that economic dragon called China and you would have the perfect investment model. In fact, you do have it; just not in the same country. And that is what makes the game of Africa one well worth playing.

CHAPTER 12

'The Gods of Dharma': Giving Back and Staying In

"Entrepreneurship is the cornerstone of African development and the key to local value creation in Africa. I am determined to ensure that Africa's next generation of entrepreneurs have the platform they need to turn their aspirations into sustainable businesses that will drive economic growth and job creation... for Africans."

— Tony O. Elemelu, Nigerian Billionaire

Nigerian billionaire Tony O. Elemelu is depictive of a new class of African mogul that we like to refer to as the "Gods of Dharma." Dharma is a Hindu, Buddhist, Jain, Sikh term that generally refers to "the path of righteousness," or more simply that of "doing good works." For our purposes here we point to a group of brilliant business entrepreneurs who recognize that their success is tied to the prosperity of others—their people, their nation, their African world. In that regard these visionaries have replaced the so-called political leaders of many African nations who have too often used their political power as a platform for exploitation and kleptocracy.

Many of these billionaire benefactors are not necessarily young in terms of their chronological age. Most have been perfecting their individual approach to becoming "Masters of the Universe" by realizing that they must look nowhere else but to themselves to be the channels and the mentors for the mass movement of Africa's Millennials toward realizing their potentials as well as the countries they live in—and that they are the last best hope of the new generations of young Africans to help forge the future. In so doing, these Titans of industry have created an entire new universe of opportunity through something now known as *Philanthrocapitalism.*

In a way Philanthrocapitalism is a tricky term, because, it is about how the real shakers and movers of the world apply their accumulated wealth, power and leverage to make a difference without "corrupting" the recipients with "free money" for its own sake. The concept, in a way was originated by Bill Gates and Warren Buffet with their very generous foundations that hold slush funds of billions of dollars. It has now been taken as a philosophy and embraced but with a slightly individualized approach—each one configured individually according to that particular billionaire's passionate focus.

In Africa, it is estimated that philanthrocapitalists "give away" about $7 billion a year in measurable funds. But the very implication of giving away (or charity) actually defies the subtext of what is really at stake, because what these visionary financiers, entrepreneurs and industrialists are doing is "investing" in the future. In doing so, they are applying the Laws of Manifestation—and the realization that what they put in now will come back to them a thousand fold. So virtually to the man (and woman), they have espoused causes they know will work. And like all truly brilliant entrepreneurs, they are very "hands-on" when it comes to following through on how it is done.

In all cases, these "creative capitalists" are the true heroes of a modern Africa. The good news is that there are hundreds of them. Unfortunately, we can only cover a few of them on these pages—some of the legends. By giving them the attention they deserve on these pages, we can also give you an insight into just how far this can go when you do it right…

Strive Masiyiwa— Zimbabwe/United Kingdom

Strive Masiyiwa probably deserves a category all his own because he is not only Zimbabwe's richest man but also one of the most generous humanitarians in the world. Through the funding and development of his Internet wireless telecom group Econet, Masiyiwa's personal net worth is estimated at anywhere from $640 Million *(Forbes)* to $1.4 billion USD *(Ventures Africa).* Strive is far less concerned over the actual amount of his fortune than he is about the degree to which his wealth may empower others. In the last 20 years through foundations he has set up, Masiyiwa has supported over 40,000 orphans with

IMAGE SOURCE: ECONETWIRELESS.COM

Strive Masiyiwa

educational programs and initiatives to see them all the way through secondary education. And his cause groups have been responsible for providing scholarships to another 100,000 students in Zimbabwe and other African nations. Recently, Strive took over from former UN Ambassador Kofi Annan to act as Chairman of AGRA, a funding group that has raised over $15 billion USD to help small African Farms and famers and provide equipment, information and infrastructure for independent agribusinesses.

Econet has partnerships and coventures in a dozen different countries, including United Kingdom, Australia, New Zealand, United Arab Emirates, China and the United States as well as Zimbabwe, Zambia, Botswana, Lesotho, Burundi and Rwanda. And it entails a dozen separate incarnations including Econet Wireless of South Africa, "2-Degrees" Wireless of New Zealand, and Liquid Telecom group in the UK.

It wasn't always easy going for Strive Masiyiwa. After returning to Zimbabwe and becoming its most enterprising businessmen, he almost faced bankruptcy trying to found Econet, due to the fact that the regime of President Robert Mugabe refused to license the new business for nearly five years. (A blockage, it was rumored, due to Masiyiwa's refusal to pay millions of dollars under the table to Mugabe's notorious "baksheesh" bureaucracy.)

After several appeals to the (then) independent Zimbabwe judiciary, Econet was eventually granted a license to operate and soon became one of that nation's largest industries, officially its second largest corporation by capitalization.

The experience didn't leave a very good taste in Masiyiwa's mouth, however, and after a few years the billionaire moved his residence and fortune out of the country—first to South Africa where he set up several businesses, and later to the United Kingdom where he now keeps his headquarters.

Despite his expatriate status, Strive's heart and mind are always in Africa where he constantly devotes his time to empowering others. Actively involved in the IRC (International Rescue Committee) helping refugees all over the world, as well as the African Union to fight HIV, Ebola and other diseases in the Sub-Sahara, Masiyiwa also recently co-founded the Carbon War Room (with Virgin's Richard Branson) to combat the effects of global warming.

It seems Strive Masiyiwa is one of those rare individuals who is constantly finding ways to make this world a better place—ways and means that pay dividends in the process. In doing so, he defines the New Millennialist in a very capital sense.

Tony O. Elemelu—Nigeria

Tony O. Elemelu

Tony O. Elemelu is a different kind of benefactor in that this Nigerian billionaire is a man who loves to see his investments in others help create new entrepreneurs. So it is only fitting that he is given credit as the originator of what has come to be known as *Africapitalism.*

This portmanteau term is self-defining in that it signifies an acknowledgement that the best chance for growth, progress and empowerment of the African economy will come through economic transformation of value-added private sector businesses. "Tony O," as he is called by many associates, acknowledges that at least some of his business philosophy comes from his courses of study at Harvard Business School. And the 60 year-old entrepreneur tips his hat to the CSV—Creating Shared Value—theory of business building taught him by famed economist Michael Porter.

In 2010, Tony Elumelu founded Heirs Holdings, an African investment company that has amassed several holdings in financial services, power generation, oil and gas, agribusiness, real estate and hospitality (hotels and resorts). He is also the former CEO of UBA (United Bank of Africa) Group, one of the largest banks in Nigeria. And his Transcontinental Corporation Nigeria (Transcorp) is Nigeria's largest listed conglomerate.

In 2011, Tony O established The Tony Elumelu Foundation, an Africa-based and Africa-funded philanthropic organization dedicated to developing young entrepreneurs and small businesses all across the Continent. Not just adding his name to another "charitable foundation," Tony Elumelu believes that Africa's business future will come from empowering what he believes is an Armada of smart young entrepreneurs who have the vision, the energy and the dedication—but need only the tools and the situational opportunity—to "shape the destiny of a Continent." In so doing he is determined to see that these young business people get the opportunity to do just that. And he has taken several steps to see it through.

Recently he set up The Tony Elumelu Entrepreneurship Programme (as a part of the *Africapitalism Institute*), a $100 million pilot program to fund and develop 10,000 new African businesses in the next 10 years, add 1 million new jobs and $10 billion in revenue spreading across several nations in the Sub-Sahara.

The Elumelu Nigeria Empowerment Fund is a non-profit Tony set up recently to help repair and rebuild entire communities in his Nigerian homeland that have been ravaged by environmental hazards, natural disasters and economic exploitation. And in each case, the goal is to rebuild and empower these communities to become productive, educated and ultimately self-sustaining parts of the national economy.

In 2012, Tony O Elumelu gave $6.4 million USD in economic and humanitarian relief to Nigerian flood victims. In the same year, he was recognized by *Forbes Magazine* as one of the "25 Most Powerful People in Africa." And he is one of the sitting Chairs of the World Economic Forum (WCF) that recently met in Kigali, Rwanda.

Although a patriotic Nigerian, Tony O. Elumelu is anything but a xenophobe and has expanded Heirs Group and Transcorp interests all across the Sub-Sahara, including Kenya, Tanzania, Ethiopia, Liberia, Zambia and Rwanda.

Believing that all boats rise with the tide, Tony O Elumelu's philosophy is very pragmatic. "I believe that businesses acting as businesses (not as charitable donors) are the most powerful tools for addressing the issues we now face."

Mobeste Ibrahim— United Kingdom [Sudan]

Sudanese-born Mobeste Ibrahim has, from the beginning, been caught in something of a dilemma. After all, what do you do, when you are a highly regarded, international billionaire with impeccable business ethics who comes from a country where the nation's President is on the ICC hit list as an international war criminal?*

In "Mo" Ibrahim's case, you do what he did in 2007 and establish the "Ibrahim Institute of African Governance" (IIAG), a non-profit organization that ranks African governments on 4 points of progress and integrity: 1) Safety & Rule of Law; 2) Participation & Human Rights;

Mobeste Ibrahim

3) Sustainable Economic Opportunity & Business Ethics; 4) Human Development & Quality of Life. Using 100 different guidelines set by 30 different international and African institutions, Ibrahim's IIAG has set the bar high for African countries. And now some canny governments are scrambling to make it to the top of the list.

The Founder and CEO of international telecom giant, Celtel, Ibrahim has been dubbed the most powerful black man in the UK as well as the "Bill Gates of Africa" for his philanthropic efforts on the Continent over the last 10 years.

A self-made mogul whose net worth is estimated at $3.4 billion USD, Ibrahim has unique roots in that he is one of the few CEO's who also holds a PhD in Electri-

---

* *ICC* is an acronym for the International Criminal Court, a UN affiliate based in The Hague.

cal Engineering. Originally a standout with British Telecom and later at Cellnet, Mo became known for optimizing platforms that worked across several electronic applications. After founding MSI Communications, which later became Celtel, Ibrahim took up permanent residence in the United Kingdom rather than return to war torn Sudan but maintained strong ties to Africa, especially focusing on FDI engagement in the Sub-Sahara and his establishment of the Mo Ibrahim Foundation and what has now become the Mo Ibrahim Prize ($5 million) for *Achievement in African Leadership*.

Outspoken about integrity in business as being key to integrity in governance, Ibrahim is noted for once having observed that, "For every crooked government official, you have 20 crooked businessmen who are influencing them." One of Ibrahim's primary crusades is for "transparency" in business and identifiable companies with responsible leadership.

According to Ibrahim: "Corruption distorts markets by not allowing the best and most competitive companies to win contracts or have their projects and developments approved. Making beneficial ownership transparency a global norm…can increase competitiveness in national markets, and make sure that there is a level playing field where the same rules apply to all companies in all jurisdictions.

"Transparency is tantamount to doing good business. Beneficial ownership helps companies know who they are doing business with and can reduce the costs of due diligence provided information is more easily available. Knowing who you are investing in or trading with can better inform investment decisions and reduce the risk of misallocated capital."

Mobeste Ibrahim is the first African-based businessman to have signed the Giving Pledge (founded by Bill Gates and Warren Buffet) to contribute half his wealth after his death, much of it earmarked to go to groups in Africa. Mo summarizes his reasons for doing so: "I made money…I wanted to give it back to Africa but I wanted to give it back in a meaningful way. So I really want to do something that deals with the root of the problem of hunger, of disease, and of the ills we have in our society."

Folorunsho Alakija—Nigeria

Nigerian power broker, Folorunsho Alakija enjoys a unique position in global financial circles in that she is not only the second richest woman in Africa but also the second richest black woman in the world (after Oprah).

Nor does she have a problem flexing her distaff money muscles since she has recently expanded her $7.6 billion oil empire into buying up real estate in nations all over the world, not the least of which was an estimated $200 million worth of new acquisitions in the very tight real estate of the United Kingdom.

With an estimated personal net worth just under $2.2 billion, Flo can be counted truly as a self-made mogul. Starting out as an executive secretary in 1974 for Sijuade Enterprises and (later) for First National Bank (of Chicago), she founded her own tailoring company Supreme Stitches and her Rose of Sharon Foundation (that soon became a household name in the Sub-Sahara). By the early 1990s, she acquired some OPL (operating petroleum licenses) in the Agami Field off

Folorunsho Alakija

the shore of Lagos and struck oil—in what can only be described as a "major find," the first of many to follow.

Lifting this rather odd combination of what amounts to an oil, fashion and real estate empire into world prominence, Folorunsho Alakija has risen to be acknowledged by both *Forbes* and *Bloomberg* as one of the 100 most powerful women in the world.

Folorunsho likes to point to her life as an "open book" and has little problem sharing her career as a role model for other women. "I have told as much of my life as I could to encourage people: to inspire others to get to where they should be, where they want to be, because everyone could use some help along the way."

So, it should come as a surprise to no one that Flo's philanthropic endeavors have also been focused on providing resources specifically for African women. Mindful of that objective, her Rose of Sharon Foundation concentrates principally on funding widows, orphans and single women in helping them start businesses by providing them with scholarships for higher education and business grants (where none were available before). She also heads up the FASS (Folorunsho Alakija Scholarship Society) that provides higher education to hundreds of underprivileged children. Flo recently took on the role as a benefactor for the National Heritage Council and Endowment for the Arts in Lagos and is "Chief Matron" of AYE (Africa's Young Entrepreneurs), a program to fund and mentor startup African businesses primarily in Nigeria and West Africa.

Nathan Kirsh—Swaziland

Nathan Kirsh (85) might easily be credited these days as being the man who saved his adopted nation of Swaziland. That is a categorical statement, and (one might argue) a hyperbole. But ask any Swazi and you'll be told it is merely accurate.

Nathan Kirsh

There is little doubt that Kirsh, a native South African whose total holdings are estimated at $4.4 billion, is indisputably the richest man in that tiny enclave of Southern Africa. And it is a fact, easily verified, that he is also its most magnanimous humanitarian.

At least he's trying to be—without much help from the United States and the Obama Administration who have withheld funds from the AGOA (African Growth and Opportunity Act) due to what they view as worker violations. Kirsh has seen to it that these caveats are being dealt with, but so far the US (very reminiscent of the Jimmy Carter years) still has its knickers in a twist and has chosen to delay a review.[**] As recently as 2015, Kirsh, a South African who has adopted Swaziland as his new home, wasn't wasting time, and was actively shuttling to build new business for Swaziland through the UK, Australia and other parts of the world.

The bulk of Nathan Kirsh's current fortune comes from Jetro Holdings. Jetro is a food commodity conglomerate that operates Jetro Cash and Carry stores and Restaurant Depots in the New York City area, supplying wholesale goods to small stores, bodegas and restaurants through all the NYC burrows.

In fact, Kirsh earned his first billion by monopolizing the small goods market in New York City. And according to *Forbes Magazine,* his philanthropic efforts are concentrated mainly on Swaziland, where—between 2012 and 2014—he provided approximately 10,000 people with starter capital for small businesses. According to Kirsh's own group research seven out of ten recipients are women with a success rate for his program sitting at a bullish 72%. He is also actively involved in infusing Swazi schools with funds and tech support to make it the first nation in Africa to boast 100% guaranteed computer literacy for all graduates.

In addition, Nathan is credited for having created 8200 new small businesses in Swaziland and a number of jobs in the textile industry that supports more than 14,000 people. His Kirsh Holding Group, a real estate development company, has joint holdings 50/50 with the Swazi government.

However controversial, Kirsh's contributions to Swaziland may appear to outsiders, their benefits inside that tiny nation's borders are decidedly positive. Much due to his efforts, Swaziland's ratings on several fronts are on the uptick. Technically a Con-

---

** It is not that the US dictates policy for African countries. But membership in the AGOA is the African version of an A+ rating with the Better Business Bureau or "The Good Housekeeping Seal of Approval." It legitimizes and ultimately opens one up to funding—something for a small country like Swaziland that is like plasma.

stitutional Monarchy, Swaziland is one of three "kingdoms" remaining in Africa. And despite some bumps in the road with the government, if it continues to thrive at all in the future, much of it will be due to the philanthropy of its Number 1 Citizen—a nice Jewish boy from the suburbs of Johannesburg.

Mohamed Mansour—Egypt

IMAGE SOURCE: AFRIQUETIMES.COM

Mohamed Mansour

Mohamed Mansour is the second richest man in Egypt with an estimated $4.1 billion fortune from his investment company the Mansour Group. Currently the Mansour group owns Egypt's largest grocery store Metro and Egypt's McDonald's franchises, along with other regional businesses. Recently Mohamed Mansour founded the Lead Foundation, a nonprofit that has provided over 1.3 million loans to small businesses many of which focus upon empowering underprivileged women in Egypt and Northern Africa. Mohamed also chairs the Monsour Foundation for Development—a non-profit focused on fostering the progress and growth of a modern Egyptian society by eliminating illiteracy, poverty, disease and cultural bias.

Mohamed (along with brothers Yaseen and Youssef) are more or less the Egyptian version of the Bass Brothers. With monies derived from their General Motors franchises in Egypt, and Caterpillar franchises in Russia and six other African nations, the Monsour brothers have extensive holdings in real estate and numerous US industries. All are philanthropically committed to numerous charities. But it is Mohamed who carries the conscience of Egypt with him—and it was his willingness to ride out the ravages of the Arab spring (of 2011) and the replacement of the Moursi regime that has paid dividends.

Recent evidence indicates the fact that Mohamed Monsour definitely believes in capitalism with a conscience. In 2015, he cut loose his considerable holdings in Philip Morris Corporation, which it is estimated would cost him an additional $900 million in profits in the coming two years.

Ashish Thakkar—Uganda/ Dubai

Ashish Thakkar **is commonly described as "Africa's youngest billionaire."** Technically, he's not. (His estimated net worth is somewhere north of $425 million.) But his impact on Africa, purely in terms of synergy, has amounted to billions of dol-

Ashish Thakkar

lars and rising. And his career is quite remarkable by any system of measurement, especially considering the fact that this 36-year-old entrepreneur put together his broad-spectrum business empire from scratch.

Starting out with a small computer shop that he opened up after leaving school in Uganda at age 15, he locked onto a series of brilliant business innovations that just seemed to tap perfectly into the mindset of the average "Afrilennial" in the Sub-Sahara. Very much like the parable of *The Purloined Letter*, it was a very basic need that no one saw: *Credit!* Africa's U-25 market needed someone who believed in them enough to extend them a line of credit, and not enough banks and retailers wanted to take the chance. Ashish Thakkar was willing to "make the leap of faith by extending credit to those who needed it." And the rewards for this "good karma" were increased exponentially.

Born in the UK of Indian extraction, Ashish Thakkar has since built the Mara Group, a business conglomerate with vast holdings in technology, hospitality, eCommerce and (most recently) banking. As Mara Group's founder and CEO, Ashish has seen it grow into a pan-African businesses operating in Sub-Sahara and many other parts of the world as well. At present, the company has over 8,000 employees working in 19 African countries and 21 nations across the globe.

Starting with the Mara Group but by no means letting that be his "end game," Ashish Thakkar was the one global investor willing to "roll the dice" by aligning his fate with Barclay Capital's controversial ex CEO Bob Diamond in 2013 to joint venture on an investment fund focused on Africa. Appropriately named Atlas Mara, the Thakkar-Diamond financial group used some good business chemistry and some shared insights into making solid financial inroads into the psyche of global markets. Along the way, they managed to raise $325 million through a share flotation to capitalize the company. Since that time, Diamond-Thakkar and company have become

> *"The Indian Tiger and the Chinese Dragon have had their days, and it's now the African Lion's turn."*
>
> — Ashish Thakkar, CEO/Mara Group

principal investors in setting up new banks in African nations recently vacated by Barclays. By filling the void left by queasy European banks, the courageous capitalization Atlas Mara offers has reaped dividends.

In 2014, Ashish Thakkar also established the Mara Foundation, a non-profit enterprise that encourages and supports young entrepreneurs in Africa. And he works with governments all across the Sub-Sahara—from Kenya to Cameroon—anywhere people are willing to give voice (and franchise) to young Afrilennial businessmen. In 2014, together with the Ghanaian President John Dramani Mahama and Ashish launched Mara Mentor, an African multi-lingual online portal and mobile app for youth mentorship and entrepreneurship.

"We have a very young demographic," He recently told the US-Africa Business Forum (covered on CNN). "85% of our populations are under the age of 35. We have an extremely entrepreneurial society and culture. Still, entrepreneurship is not in the education system…yet. It's something, frankly, that I am extremely passionate about, because the answer to unemployment is not foreign direct investment or large scale manufacturing plants, etc. It's going to be nurturing *small and medium enterprises—SME's*. So, it's great to see that there is a real entrepreneurial vibe coming into the system, and innovation is totally embedded into that."

Praised for his sense of trends, this Dubai-based entrepreneur won the MTV Base Leadership Award at the 2014 MTV Africa Music Awards. And in 2012, the Mara Group was named by the World Economic Forum as one of the dynamic high-growth companies.

As adventurous as he is optimistic, Ashish Thakkar has a bucket list that is, by any measurement, daring. Beyond "thinking globally and acting locally," Ashish is going galactic—evidenced by the fact that recently he was the first African to sign up for Richard Branson's Virgin GALACTIC space travel ventures. So when people tell Thakkar, "The sky is the limit," he can assure them it's not.

Summary

In this chapter, we have actually covered some of the true giants among African business and industry—the moguls, the entrepreneurs, the whales, The Gods of Dharma. And we've done it for a simple reason: because their reach is wide and deep, and they know the inroads. They also exemplify that elusive concept called Aréte—a Greek word that simply means "excellence." More than that, the Athenians of the 5th Century BC used the term, *Aréte,* to define the life of a man who had acquired a level of wisdom and prosperity that flowed over into everything and everyone in his realm of experience; so much so that his very existence was a force for good.

These individuals, and dozens of others like them in Africa are the difference makers. They are the Aréte for that continent and the role models for others to follow.

Still the question arises, what about the small businessperson and the SME (Small and Medium-Sized Entrepreneur)? How do we empower them? What are the secrets? Is there a way to navigate the maze of African enterprise?

In the next chapter—"Africa's Millennial Millionaires"— we will be taking an intimate look on how some of the Continent's most creative young business minds are coming to grips with their marketplace and learning at light-speed how to master the game.

CHAPTER 13

U-35 Masters of Momentum: Africa's Millennial Millionaires

If one theme is consistent throughout this book it is this: Africa is Youth. And youth will drive the Global Marketplace...all the way through this Millennium and beyond.

It brings the power of numbers. It is the Life Force of the planet. And it will not be denied. Africa's advantage—its untapped advantage at this point—is that it is preponderantly the youngest place in the known universe. This should come as no surprise to anyone reading this, because we've been bombarding you relentlessly for 12 Chapters on this very topic. What we do want to emphasize here is that this is not just cheerleading; nor is it subjective.

- **Currently, of the current world population of 7.3 billion people,** 1.2 billion (16%) live in Africa while the vast majority of 4.4 billion (64%) are in Asia. Currently, this gap will be chipped away in this century.*

- **The rub for us lies in the fact that the projected population in 2050 will be 9.7 billion people.** This denotes a slowed global growth rate of 2.4 billion, while 1.3 billion is projected to be coming from Africa. In other words, while the rest of the world is virtually "downsizing" in the next 35 years, Africa's population will more than double. If this rate projection proves accurate, the

---

* **Most projections are UN forecasts.** The United Nation's forecasts are based on what is called the medium projection variant, which assumes a decline of fertility for countries where large families are prevalent, and an increase in those countries where the average is less than two children per woman.

continent will account for 39% of world population by 2100, while Asia's will fall to 44%.

- **What's more, by 2050 the populations in 28 African countries are projected to double.** And over the next 35 years, half of the world's total growth will be concentrated in nine countries, five of them in Africa: *Nigeria, Democratic Republic of the Congo, Ethiopia, Tanzania and Uganda.* (The others are India, Pakistan, Indonesia and the United States.)

- **In the decade between 2010-2015—at 98 births per 1,000 women aged between 15 and 19—Africa has had the highest adolescent fertility rate in the world.** And since the infant mortality rate is down at inverse proportions, this upward trend brings with it some significant health and social consequences.

- **On average, 64 in every 100 Africans are under 25 years of age—making it the runaway youngest population of any continent.** This implies a phenomenal manpower advantage in the next four decades because workers will outstrip the number of dependents. At the same time, this could bring tremendous challenges to find worthwhile employment, especially among undereducated unskilled laborers.

- **Globally, life expectancy has risen by three years since 2000, and is now 70 years.** This was greatly helped by Africa, where life expectancy this millennium has grown between the years 2010-2015 (measured by a jump of six years from 54 to 60.4 years of age).

You have just read a ream of numbers run by you in quantum progressions, seemingly headed toward a conclusion that can be easily drawn.

Certainly projections—especially categorical ones—can go off target by the time any cycle is complete. And even though the trends appear solid, they are often subject to the cosmic shifts of climate, wars, political twists of fortune and economic downturns.

Even so, even if the metrics are only right by half, Africa still remains the most rapidly advancing youth market in the world. And that can be a blessing. Or it can be a curse. It will all depend upon good governance, a rapid expansion of proper health, education and social services for Africa's Gen Y and Gen Z who will need all that and more if they are to develop to their full potential in the decades to come.

Much of this will be dependent upon viable Foreign Direct Investment as well as homegrown business and industry in the next 20 years in particular.

We have already pointed to the mentoring and programs for encouraging young African entrepreneurs established by billionaire philanthrocapitalists like Tony O. Elemelu with The Tony Elumelu Foundation, the Africa-funded philanthropic organization specifically set up to develop young entrepreneurs and small businesses across Africa. We also noted the work of (U-35 wizard) Ashish Thakkar and the Mara Foundation that empowers young entrepreneurs especially in East and Southern Africa.

Another African small business benefactor is **Jean-Claude Bastos de Morais,** a Swiss-Angolan. In 2003, when 30 years of civil conflict finally ended and peace came at last to Angola, Bastos de Morais returned to that war torn nation and launched Quantum Global Group, an international financial advisory, asset management and real estate consulting firm.

*Jean-Claude
Bastos de Morais*

After he established Banco Kwanza, Angola's first investment bank in 2008, Jean-Claude set up African Innovation Foundation (AIF), a Swiss-based organization that promotes innovation and sustainable development for Africa. The African Innovation Foundation mobilizes innovators across the continent to release their untapped potential to make a difference in the ways Africans live, work, and learn. AIF also annually awards the *Innovation Prize for Africa (IPA),* an annual fund that provides $150,000 to young companies that contribute toward developing new products, increasing efficiency or saving cost in Africa.

In addition to these magnanimous philanthrocapitalists, we are also bearing witness to the emergence of groups now in business specifically to tap into new Millennial-run companies striving to make a difference, especially in the Sub-Sahara.

One such synergizing influence is Africa's Young Entrepreneurs (AYE), a Nigeria based company with an extensive Internet presence and a long list of new clients. Africa's Young Entrepreneurs are committed to empowering young entrepreneurs across Africa by creating platforms that facilitate intra-trade on the continent. One of AYE's prime directives is to motivate and empower the next generation of outstanding African entrepreneurs—the ones they believe, "Will shape the economies and political landscapes of their home countries."

At the moment, AYE specializes in creating platforms and business networks that facilitate intra-trade on the continent. And they go about it in a number of ways:

Working inside AYE is AYEEN, a think tank devoted specifically to developing young entrepreneurs inside the nation of Nigeria, and AYESA, a yearly conference held in Abidjan to teach people how to create new businesses, and to teach Millennial businesses how to network with other like-minded entrepreneurs all across Central and Southern Africa.

There are many groups with good intentions, but AYE is following through with complete programs for African nations throughout the Sub-Sahara, including Ethiopia, Ghana, South Africa, Kenya and Nigeria, just to name a few. We refer you to their website here: http://ayeonline.org. It is an Internet surfer safari well worth the taking.

Ultimately, the measurable by-product of the synergy created by all these energetic groups and individuals is an entire new generation of "Red Hot" U-35 entrepreneurs and business innovators who are not only springing up all over the Sub-Sahara but also cashing in on the fruits of their labors in ways that encourage, inspire and challenge others.

RED HOT U-35 ENTREPRENEURS – THE FUTURE

Simbarashe Mhuriro

Zimbabwe, Founder of Oxygen Africa Limited

Thirty-one-year-old Simbarashe Mhuriro brought Oxygen Africa a long way in a short time. Founded in 2009 as an investment advisory company to help facilitate foreign investors in Zimbabwe, Oxygen rose to meet the need early on and soon became the focus of a merger. In 2013, Mhuriro's young company partnered with Swiss-based Meeco Group, a renewable energy company, to establish Oursun Energy Zimbabwe. Oursun was a joint venture Independent Power Producer that specializes in the development, building, owning, and operating of utility-scale solar photovoltaic (PV) energy projects in Zimbabwe. The partnership ended last year, partly due to the inability to create a network for photovoltaics that could function with consistency. However, Oxygen Africa has raised $7 million and is currently developing two 5 MW grid-connected solar plants in Zimbabwe.

As it is presently structured, Oxygen Africa plans to focus on providing renewable energy sources for the agriculture, manufacture, telecom and tourism especially as it applies to off-the-grid regions in Zimbabwe and neighboring countries where energy storage is scarcely available but always in demand.

Ntombenhle Khathwane

Swaziland/South Africa, Founder of Afrobotanics

Everyone involved on a global basis knows that personal care can be a labyrinth—even more so, the fine art of hair care, which amounts to 9% of a global market of $400 billion. When you get into the hair care needs of Sub-Sahara Africa, you are looking at a niche market inside a niche market that still amounts to about $160 million USD. So the pie, though smaller, is still quite enough for a few new enterprising marketers. This fact was clearly not lost on Swazi-born entrepreneur Ntombenhle Khathwane. At 32, Ntombenhle is the founder

of AfroBotanics, a Johannesburg-based manufacturer and marketer of hair care products using African botanical oils and other natural products noted for restoring and repairing damaged hair.

AFROB🍂TANICS

When Ntombenhle was growing up, her mother owned a series of boutiques and hair salons. So her affinity for hair and the care and feeding of it has always come naturally. At the same time, she saw a huge gap between actual customer need and the products that were available in Southern Africa at that time, most of which were trying to market products utterly unsuited to the needs of African women. After detailed research in places such as the United States, she established relationships with several Southern African contract manufacturers in 2011 and started developing sensitive pH balanced formulations as well as the packaging and design for her new product line.

Formally established in 2010, AfroBotanics has an advantage over other hair care manufacturers in the Sub-Sahara in that it has sidestepped the inattentive "big-blanket" approach to personal care that condemns so many brands out of the gate. As such it takes great pains to educate the consumer on the natural ingredients in its Black Pearl and other premium formulations so that people can make their product choices with a sense of confidence in Afrobotanics' product integrity—that what they are buying is both healthy and highly personalized just for them.

Vanessa Zommi

Cameroon, Founder of Emerald Moringa Tea

Vanessa Zommi is a classic case of a young Afrilennial who was not willing to accept the hand that life had dealt her. So when her mother was diagnosed with Type II diabetes, Zommi, 21, set out to find alternative treatments and wholesome foods that would keep her mother both healthy and stable. Presently about 15% of the Buea population where Vanessa grew up suffers from diabetes, and the cases are rising at an alarming rate.

Determined to find solutions that would help her mother and others, Vanessa came upon the legend of the rejuvenating *Moringa oleifera* tree that grew in her home region. What she discovered was that the leaves harvested from the moringa and processed into a tea could reduce blood sugar levels and provide a balancing, restorative food source that was perfect

for diabetics. A short time later, Vanessa partnered with local moringa farmers who supplied her with the leaves, enabling her to process the leaves into moringa tea—a "finished crop" that she put into tea bags. Emerald Moringa, the company she founded, now sells this tea across Cameroon.

According to research from Zommi's group, Moringa Emerald Tea boosts the body's energy while lowering the sugar level in the human system. And though this kind of data probably wouldn't fly with the draconian oversight of organizations such as the FDA (in the US), in Cameroon, Vanessa Zommi and company sell this as a healthy beverage in over 40 outlets. So Vanessa and her company are expanding the franchise by making a positive difference in people's lives, putting out a healthy product that actually tastes good, and gaining some marvelous momentum in the meantime.

Eugene Mbugua

Kenya, Founder of Young Rich TV

There is a new cottage industry blossoming in Kenya. And its strategy is simple if a bit ironic: It involves becoming a millionaire by producing a TV show about young African Millionaires!

It is called "Young Rich." And the show's producer, Eugene Mbugua, is the founder of one of Kenya's most successful television production companies. His company, Young Rich Television Limited, produces two of Kenya's most popular TV programs— 'Young Rich' a weekly show that profiles Kenya's successful Millennial entrepreneurs (now in its ninth full season), and 'Get In The Kitchen' (in year four) an extremely popular cooking show out of Nairobi.

Already media darlings for years, both shows have enjoyed long runs and command viewership in the millions. Part of that success has attracted sponsorship from several blue-chip companies in Kenya as well as Tanzania and other neighboring countries in East Africa. Mbugua is also in the publishing businesses and owns *My*

Yearbook Limited, a company that produces yearbooks and publications for companies, schools and governments. Pointing to Mbugua's ability to diversify is the fact that the real-estate company he owns is now developing a 188-unit youth hostel to provide housing for students of Kenya's Egerton University.

Rachel Sibande

Malawi, Co-Founder and CEO of mHub

The first tech incubator in Malawi, mHub, has never been short of confidence—or optimism. In its way the company reflects the energy of its CEO Rachel Sibande who believes there is enough entrepreneurial potential in the country to turn it into a force to be reckoned with in the region.

Launched in 2013 by Sibande and co-founders Austin Madinga and Angel Chirwa, mHub is comprised of a core group of IT enthusiasts that specializes in working with high-tech startups with a special focus on building young technology entrepreneurs through training, skills development and mentorship. The mHub approach is to function as a kind of collective *internet group think* that helps new businesses work from the "inside-out," where they share knowledge and market insights, finally transferring them into an ICT and broad-based entrepreneurship.

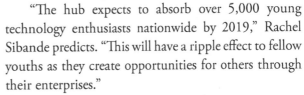

"The hub expects to absorb over 5,000 young technology enthusiasts nationwide by 2019," Rachel Sibande predicts. "This will have a ripple effect to fellow youths as they create opportunities for others through their enterprises."

As it is presently set up, mHub connects young striving (and occasionally struggling) Internet entrepreneurs with seasoned industry icons to develop new skillsets and effectively network in their respective areas of expertise.

Up to now, tech hubs in Southern Africa have led a fragile existence, and survival is not guaranteed. But thus far mHub has had solid financial backing and a good business model that is seeing it successfully through to the next level. Time will tell, and determination is the key. At the moment, mHub appears to have both on its side.

Kelvin Nyame, Rashad Seini and Kofi Amuasi

Ghana, Co-founders of MeQasa

Kelvin Nyame,
CEO and co-founder of
MeQasa

MeQasa.com founded by a trio of U-35 whiz kids has rapidly become one of Ghana's leading online real estate classified businesses. Established in 2013 by Ghanaian entrepreneurs, Kelvin Nyame, Rashad Seini and Kofi Amuasi, who are all graduates of the tech entrepreneurship training program at the Meltwater Entrepreneurial School of Technology (MEST) based in Accra, Ghana. MeQasa provides a free service that helps brokers, landlords and other real estate industry professionals to conduct business efficiently online, while simplifying the search experience for prospective tenants and buyers.

Recently, MeQasa.com secured a $500,000 investment from Frontier Digital Ventures—a global VC firm headquartered in Kuala Lumpur, Malaysia that prides itself in successful cash infusions to aggressive young companies that can also provide a solid business model.

Frontier Digital Ventures' portfolio involves companies in five key frontier regions including Central America, Middle East & North Africa, East Africa, West Africa and South Asia. MeQasa plans to use the investment to expand the band of its sales and marketing outreach, as well as accelerate access to its mobile and Internet services.

Although effective launched in Ghana, MeQasa sees every new market across the Sub-Sahara—especially in neighboring nations such as Nigeria and Cote d'Ivoire— as an opportunity for expansion and a place to lock in their easy use and very effective Internet, P2P real-estate network.

Nelisiwe Masango

South Africa, Bear Run Investments Director

Bear Run Investments Director Nelisiwe Masango is 23 years old. One occasionally needs reminding because this superstar entrepreneur is already running three fully functional businesses. Her energy and maturity prove at the outset that one's chronological age is merely a number, and that maturity and business acumen like hers requires a different kind of arithmetic.

"Neli" is from Boksburg, South Africa, 30 kilometres east of Johannesburg, something for which she doesn't take a great deal of pride, although she (as much as anyone) is doing a great deal to put it on the map.

At this point, Neli is noted for being something of a crusader—crusades that often entail rescuing other young entrepreneurs from deceitful business practices, while at the same time empowering them to learn how to build companies of their own.

"I started Bear Run Investments after witnessing numerous people get caught in the web of deceitful pyramid scheme owners and 'get rich quick' companies,"

Neli remembers. And by establishing Bear Run investment, she felt she could help educate others learn about the proper channels of investing and, at the same time, introduce them to fully regulated investment companies that played by the rules. That way young companies and Millennial investors could benefit from the fairness of a level playing field."

Originally Nelisiwe Masango wanted to be a brain surgeon—and certainly had the academic credentials to do so—but felt she would be limited as a doctor because, "I only have two hands to assist one person at a time."

For her, money and the legitimate power to attain it could help free so many people in so many ways. So after a freshman year working toward a BA in Entrepreneurial Management in 2011, Masango got a job trading on the floor of the JSE (Johannesburg Stock Exchange) where she soon came to learn how the investment world generally operated.

After being a trader for two years, Neli came up with the marketing model for Bear Run in 2013 and gave herself time to learn and grow the business. "Starting my company with no money has taught me a lot. It has taught me how to network with the right people, and it has taught me the value of money and how to manage it."

Now, Masango has expanded her enterprise and has established two more businesses—a recruitment/headhunter firm, Gentle Hands Agency and FeFine, an acronym for "Females with Finances."

Running three companies at 25 may take some doing, but part of the Millennial edge is the belief that, if you have the desire, all goals will be reached. That is Nelisiwe Masango's philosophy in a nutshell.

Summary

If anything, Afrillennials are quick learners. In the beginning, it is simply a matter of survival. In the end—and through proper networks, mentors and sensible anticipation of market needs—it is an opportunity to be seized, met and mastered. And at present they are doing just that.

Even the most conservative appraiser of markets in the Sub-Sahara observes, and very accurately, that the surge of new U-35 commercial enterprises is impressive but not a surprise. SME's and new mega-companies run by African Millennials are growing at a faster rate than anywhere else in the world—including the US, the UK and South America.

Whether they are able to continue to do so in the future will rely upon three things: *1) Sponsorship, 2) Mentorship, and 3) A Government that cares.* Well, in Africa, they have the first two…and that may just prove to be enough.

Silver Linings Playbook:
Good Things in Bad Places

I t wouldn't be an accurate portrait of Africa if we didn't discuss it, warts and all. It is important to focus on the challenges that exist because there are many, and at times they seem insurmountable. And yet that is where the illusion is at its most dangerous. Because, if there's one thing I have learned about Africa it is that adversity tempers the steel.

Pick up any magazine, surf to any news channel, catch any viral broadcast on social media or (if you're really caught in old paradigms) read about it in the morning press. Peruse at any headline, catch any soundbite or newsflash from an international trouble spot. It won't take long to find some very bad news about some nation in Africa somewhere—corruption, terrorism, civil war, atrocities by ISIS or some other radical jihadist terror groups determined to bring down governments that were not Sharia compliant, territorial disputes, secessions such as South Sudan, Eritrea and of course (perennial agitations from Biafra and Western Sahara—all these just for starters).

Yes, there are still some nasty truths in Africa. They still have slavery in Mauritania (about 300,000 by most estimates, almost all black). In the North of Mali the Muslim dominated government placed a ban on playing music under penalty of imprisonment and amputation. In Somalia, Al Shabaab has placed a fatwa on all cell phone business apps. Sudanese President Omar al-Bashir is Number 1 on the ICC's War Crimes List for human rights atrocities. And in Nigeria, President Muhammadu Buhari has spent his first two years in office trying to track down $45 billion in missing funds from the nation's treasury. And since late 2016, he has had to ferret out (Boko Haram) moles in his own government. That's the bad news, and it travels fast.

And yes! Things could be better. So in order to show you how we are handling our challenges—all of them—let's deal with the basics first.

The basic challenges in Africa are, and always have been, the Big Three—*Hunger, Illiteracy and Disease (HID)*—all of which combine to form the big *"H"*: *Hardship*. And the first thing we have to take into consideration when addressing them is the realization that they are all interactive, each one overlapping into the other in a kind of sinister domino effect that, on the surface, seems geometrically irresistible.

Hunger is by all the etiology of lifestyle triggered by *Hardship* (a more broad-spectrum expression of poverty). And the offshoot of *Illiteracy* (Ignorance) comes from lack of education often due to ill health and mal-nutrition and the simple inability of getting children to school. When you have hunger (or famine) linked to poverty, you very often create the seedbed for *Disease;* or at least a far greater susceptibility to so many strains of it. (And given Africa's balmy tropical and sub-tropical climates as natural growth media for mosquitoes, fungi and bacteria, diseases tend to fester simply by close proximity to Nature.)

Institutions such as the World Hunger Project attribute hunger to such tangible connectors as poverty and disease but also to a lack of women's rights (especially in education), pernicious diseases and basic infrastructure failures such as sanitation and clean water. What they are now discovering as well is the surprising advent of such modern phenomena as urbanization, where entire farming communities move to big African cities longing for improvements in quality of life only to hit the invisible wall of unemployment (as much as 40% in some countries), sanitation issues and urban squalor. No question, each of these things has a triggering effect on the other in ways that accelerate to a where all hit in a Perfect Storm of spontaneous convergence.

The things that don't get reported often enough are the concerted efforts that so many nations, cause groups, international agencies and foreign investors are making collectively to deal with them, many of them, immediately. The challenges, as they always have been, come down to a single question: How in the world do they manage?

Our answer for this is to rely on something we call COAT: *Community Outreach, Activation and Technology.* This is not a gimmick acronym as much as it is a viable course of action—although we admit that sometimes our initiatives do not always take place in the same order. The main thing to understand at the outset is that in every case, to some degree, we apply our COAT principals to cover the HID.

So… Challenge, Meet the Solution!

Hunger. Let's get the nasty facts out of the way. About 845 million people in the world go hungry every day. Of those, about one third, or 280 million, are in the

African Sub-Sahara (ranking it just a bit behind Asia as the world's worst). In terms of percentage of population, seven of the ten nations in the world that are the most malnourished are in Africa: Burundi, Chad, Ethiopia, Eritrea, Madagascar, Sudan and Zambia. These are the poster children for African hunger, and all the clichés prevail. And there are some anomalies here because some of these countries such as Ethiopia and Madagascar in particular are very rich in natural resources, grow-crops and abundant indigenous flora (and in the case of Madagascar, some of the most varied in the world). So, it is often the governments that are culpable for failing to address the needs of the people.

The same issues prevail in other nations such as Nigeria, Gabon, Angola and Mozambique that are resource rich, have relatively high GDP (false PPI ratings) and otherwise have no excuse for ignoring the basic needs of feeding their own people.

There is no question that hunger is a complicated social issue in Africa and that lack of education, unemployment and diseases that are concomitant with poverty all have their influences. The simple fact nonetheless remains that—depending upon the area—61% to 80% of all jobs in Africa are agricultural, as in small and subsistence farms. So, if we address the issue at the level of livelihood, we will be able to mitigate much of the problem simply by having each country apply the technology necessary to address the food production issues at the source.

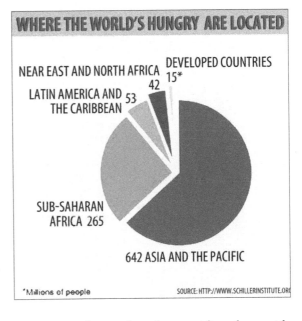

What isn't being examined often enough are the means by which some nations such as Ghana, Rwanda, Botswana, Uganda and Kenya are not only empowering farmers but also providing them with the technology, the access to basics and the benefits of virtual farm-to-market techniques that have traditionally been missing. This is particularly true, as we have covered in our other chapters devoted to the accomplishments of specific nations. Uganda's burgeoning Organic Farms (encouraged by Health Ministry subsidy and support), Ethiopia's pioneering farms such as Luna Farms, and Kenya's remarkable spillover e-technologies such as M-Farm and iCow have not only empowered local

SME farms in their respective nations but also carried on—through Internet and smart phone apps—to neighboring nations and virtually tens of thousands of agribusinesses throughout the Sub-Sahara. In addition we have the work of cultural heroes such as EGHL CEO James Mwangi and his work to empower small and medium sized farms with credit, industry networking and access to new growing technologies and inroads to international associations such as AGRA.* There is also the groundbreaking work of a group called *The Comprehensive Africa Agriculture Development Program (CAADP)* is now in its tenth year.

Since its inception in 2006, this AU-NEPAD agriculture program has been work-ing to bring a "stakeholder" model to its agricultural network in a way that empowers growers, farmers and food industry autonomy to those who have never experienced it before.**

According to its own mission statement CAADP has been working for the last 10 plus years to increase across-the-board investment in agriculture, and foster entre-preneurship in agribusinesses and agrifood value chains. Understanding the synergy of creating such a chain reaction, CAADP proudly points to the fact that it has, over the last decade, increased investments in agriculture, eliminated many "strip mine" farms, cut down on predatory farm-to-market practices and helped increase overall productivity in a number of target nations.

Treating Africa's farms as diversified ecosystems, CAADP has tried to capitalize on the relatively low population density of farmland in the Sub-Sahara, rising global food demand and the positive trends for new sources of development funding.

Over the last decade, where countries have increased investments in agriculture as per CAADP targets, every nation operating inside the guidelines has seen reduc-tions in hunger and poverty, as well as significant increases in productivity. As of 2016 CAADP partnering nations have included Ghana, Togo, Zambia, Burundi, Burkina Faso, Mali, Niger, Congo, Senegal, Ethiopia and Malawi.

At present, CAADP has put in place a set of objectives that includes its Continen-tal vision for the next fifty years: *Agenda 2063*. Given the fact that Africa is projected to have a population of 2.5 billion people by 2050, the majority of whom will be

---

* *AGRA. Alliance for a Green Revolution in Africa* remains controversial in that, though funded largely by the Bill and Melinda Gates foundation, it has strong ties to Monsanto and Gargill, the largest producers of GMO farming programs in the world. Still, in a world where hunger is still a survival issue, food programs that increase output by as much as 800% may have to be considered, at least on an *ad hoc* basis.

** NEPAD. New Partnership for Africa's Development. The 2001 merger of two groups in Africa devoted to the eradication of poverty and the empowerment of African economies to grow and develop through cooperation and unity of purpose—to integrate Africa into the world community.

women and youth under 16 years of age. This prediction alone summarizes the scale of our agricultural challenges: to feed Africans and to create wealth for them, and to conserve resources for future generations.

Along the way, it has been setting in place a strong platform for action: 1) to give more emphasis to farming as a business by raising the profile of farming as a profession, and by helping SME farms with credit and technology; 2) to understand that the principal investors in African farms are the farmers themselves (nearly $100 billion every year in their farms, despite an almost scandalous lack of credit facilities for the vast majority; and 3) work into the mural of agribusiness FDI based cooperatives and partnerships that are proving very helpful in providing upstream (inputs) and downstream (processing) of African agriculture, including infrastructure and large-scale land-based investment.

Over the years, the CAADP has established a 6 Priority Wish List for truly effective farm production. *Priority One:* Increasing agricultural production sustainable agricultural intensification. This includes the use of "smart" subsidy policies by the nations themselves, encouraging the adoption of innovations and securing access to resources for women and young people in particular. *Priority Two:* Support will be offered to family farms that make optimal use of small acreage farms. *Priority Three:* Synergize the structure and functioning of markets based on minimizing market failures such as monopolies, credit crashes, crop failures and production slumps. *Priority Four:* Enhance interaction with public infrastructure, access to energy and water. *Priority Five:* Secure standardized information on balanced pricing, international market distortions and price volatility. *Priority Six:* Provide better organized collective bargaining to improve Africa's access to developed and emerging countries, including sane tariff policies and standards to provide a level playing field in all markets.

CAADP stresses the fact that there is a need for each nation to advance its role as mentor and subsidizer of R&D and infrastructure. Their purpose for doing this is to provide—for the first time in most instances—respectable food quality, nutritional standards and special market sensitivity to small (subsistence) farms that would normally not be integrated into the market. Even though the task is daunting, CAADP is also dedicated to getting thousands of small farms to the next level of SME potential as a part of "the rising tide that lifts all boats" where future farm markets are concerned.

Illiteracy. Life is simple. "Knowledge is power." That quote comes from Francis Bacon. And today in Africa it has become the key progression point for any society that wants to grow and improve. Numerous times in this book, we have profiled countries and made mention of literacy rates as an absolute index of their evolution as a nation. In recognizing its impact on poverty, health, active citizenship and empowerment, the

ENDURINGLY FERTILE FARMLAND

"What a waste!" is not always a negative term. Especially if you are following the compost traditions of women on farms in the nations of Ghana and Liberia, kitchen waste mixed with ash and other carbon is mixed into nutritionally depleted soil, transforming them (sooner rather than later) into some of the richest "Black Earth" anywhere in the Sub-Sahara.

It has not only proved a timeless technique but also a true teaching tool to modern agronomists who have only recently figured out the fact that this "quantum soup" of organic waste has very positive long range implications when it comes to replenishing the local farmland. Apparently this African terra preta, "dark earth," stores as much as 300% more organic carbon than other soils. So it not only contributes to better production with fewer plowing cycles, it might also help counteract the carbonization of local environments.

The most encouraging aspect of these findings by US Soil scientists is that these successful techniques were achieved, not in neighboring nations. Rather they were nations separated by several other nation states in West Africa. So...conclusion! These techniques may be applied locally anywhere in the world—especially in overpopulated soil starved nations of Asia—and the applications work in small gardens or large industrial farms...much to the chagrin of chemical companies and the delight of environmentalists everywhere who see it as micro-tool against the ravages of climate change.

COURTESY OF BILL ZIMMERMAN, USAID FARMER-TO-FARMER VOLUNTEER

Workers preparing for in situ trench composting.

overlaps in impact are impossible to ignore. So in a way it all starts here as an absolute iron law: "Illiteracy blocks opportunity."

It is often hard to explain illiteracy and the ignorance that goes with it to someone in a society where one is bombarded with information virtually out of the womb. In roughly one-third of the rest of the world, people grow up with no regular access to media. As a child or a young adult, you pick up a book and can't read the words, visit a new city and can't decipher the street signs, receive packaged foods and medicines but can't make out the labels and don't have a clue about working a computer or refining an electronic app. With increased urbanization, Africa's cities are now filled with the youthful dispossessed—poor children, many homeless or orphaned, who cannot afford to go to school. Many are affected by diseases from malaria to HIV and don't know how to ask for help.

One would assume that learning to read and write is a fundamental right, and it is in practically every African nation. And yet even today, 38 % of African adults are illiterate. And two-thirds of those are women. Granted the growth of literacy, especially in the Sub-Sahara has improved exponentially in the last 25 years, even though the numbers often appear skewed.

For example, in 1990 the adult literacy rate in all of Africa was 53%. In 2015 it was estimated to be 64%. By contrast, in 1990 there were 133 million illiterate adults in Africa's Sub-Sahara, and yet in 2015 the estimate is 181 million. (On the surface, this would appear to be an atrocious lapse toward illiteracy, were it not for the fact that the 1990 population of Africa was 680 million. In 2015 it was 1.2 billion people—nearly double. The emphasis here is pointed. And that is the definition of an adult is anyone over 21 years of age. And anyone studying this document knows by now that roughly 50% of all African nations are under 21, and most have half their populations under 18.

This is one area where the UN involvement in certain regions of the world works very well in the manifestation of UNESCO. The United Nations Educational, Scientific and Cultural Organization is a specialized UN agency put in place to promote

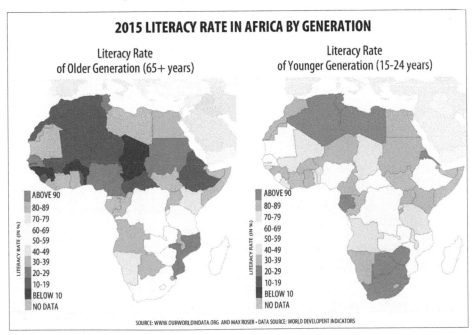

SOURCE: WWW.OURWORLDINDATA.ORG AND MAX ROSER • DATA SOURCE: WORLD DEVELOPENT INDICATORS

international collaboration through educational, scientific, and cultural reforms in order to increase universal respect for justice, the rule of law, and human rights outlined in the UN Charter. Following its global agenda, UNESCO has over 190 member states and field offices all over the world. And it pursues its objectives through five major programs: *education, natural sciences, social sciences, culture and communications.*

UNESCO's regional office headquartered in Senegal's capital city of Dakar covers countries that are among the twenty nations that rank lowest in the Human Development Index—all of them 50% or lower, and many of them in the Sub-Sahara. Burkina Faso, Gambia, Guinea-Bissau, Mali, Niger and Senegal—have literacy rates below 50% with literacy among women averaging as much as 20 points lower.

For many disadvantaged young people and adults, non-formal education has become one of the main routes to learning. Non-formal education reaches people in their own context and ideally in their own local language. By offering solution packages to key national power brokers and building capacity through them, the organization aims to make non-formal education an important part of its literacy programs. By offering more sources for advocacy and incorporating the use of national languages, countries like Burkina Faso, Mali, Niger, and Senegal have made great strides toward expanding literacy.

UNESCO also does a pretty decent job of working with governments by developing partnerships in the private sector through the use of *ICT—Information Communication and Technology.* Absolutely, virtual schooling—whether formal or informal—is making all the difference. And education by electronic apps has gone viral in places like Kenya, Tanzania, Rwanda, and even Ethiopia and Sudan.

The ALP Answer! Another way in which Africa's youth are getting double doses of literacy have come with something called the *Africa Library Project (ALP).* ALP works with everyone they can—from the Peace Corps to UNESCO to local community organizers and every school they can—anything to get more books to regions of Africa that would otherwise not have them.

For decades, the biggest barrier to increasing literacy has been the lack of books, especially in rural areas. Africa is the only continent where more than half of parents are not able to help their children with homework due to illiteracy, so the influence of local libraries and reading centers become more important than ever.

As synchronicity would have it, books—physical, bound books—in developed nations such as the United States have in many ways become the collateral damage of modern technology. Because e-Books are taking over the modern marketplace libraries are getting bombarded by castoff volumes of everything from western fiction to entire encyclopedia's and reference books. So they're just not accepting books the way they used to. These days in the United States there is literally no market for them anywhere and hundreds of thousands of books are entirely too often dumped off or recycled as scrap.

Beginning with book drives in the US, the Africa Library project has since its inception in 2006 shipped more than 1.8 million books to establish over 1,770 libraries in participating nations in Africa. Zimbabwe, Zambia, Cameroon, Lesotho, Nigeria, Botswana, Swaziland, Malawi, Ghana, South Africa and Sierra Leone—all these nations and more are subscribers now committed to the ALP model. And participation in this non-profit library network is expanding throughout the Sub-Sahara.

Thus far, the improvements are measurable and encouraging. Many of ALP's partner countries have shown improved literacy rates and, as a by-product of this kind of community outreach, have managed to encourage government investment in education. Botswana, for example, increased its adult literacy rate from 69% in 1991 to 87% in 2008, and invests 19% of its government spending in education (as opposed to 13% in the US). Lesotho invests 13% of its GDP in education (compared to 5% in the US).

Yes, these instances of educational subsidy are very rare in the Sub-Sahara, when in fact they shouldn't be. And we admit to making comparisons in terms of percentage to the United States, not to denigrate US expenditures on education (although there are critics who will also pick up that argument). But it does raise the issue that for most African nations to improve the productivity of their nations, they are going to have to make 100% literacy levels a national priority. And that will mean spending a larger percentage of their government budgets relative to GDP to do it. (A small price to pay when you think about it.)

Global e-Schools. Abidjan, Cote d'Ivoire. In June 2016, African Development Bank and the UN educational organization UNESCO hosted a conference in Cote d'Ivoire for something called the Global e-Schools and Communications Initiative (GESCI).

Three years after its inaugural convention, the pan-African Conference opened this session by highlighting the progress made by countries such as Kenya—especially in the area of (EE) Electronic Education, and the benefits that have followed. Following the Kenyan Model and using technology from companies such as Eneza Education (from iHub), countries across East Africa are actively pushing to integrate more technology into classrooms across the continent with full curricula and complete classroom required courses and a full selection of "electives."

"Five years ago, the government announced that they were going to give laptops to kids," Jerome Morrissey, GESCI's Chief Executive Officer remembers. "Everybody started to laugh, saying that this is ridiculous, that we should be buying books. But what has happened is that it has stimulated inter-ministerial action and now, practically all the primary schools have got electricity in anticipation."

As we previously mentioned, Africa's population is expected to double by 2050, so it is bound to face a shortage of teachers and formal access to physical classrooms, especially in rural areas. So this forum in particular aims to show that these technologies not only help but also throw open entire new electronic educational landscapes that never existed before.

Cote d'Ivoire entrepreneur Thierry N'Doufou, CEO of the company behind the first African-made educational tablet, observed that his product, Qelasy, is now available in six countries and is already partnering with NGOs, government bodies and telecommunication companies to develop educational content. Thus far, other tablet-based education programs have been launched in Kenya, South Africa, Zambia and Cote d'Ivoire. And more are predicted to follow. "The fact that there are many forums of this kind organized lately that reveal an intention throughout the continent on how to turn pilot programs into full-scale developments."

Despite rapid growth just since 2013 and hundreds of thousands of users, it is estimated that only 8% of households in Africa's Sub-Sahara possess a tablet or a computer. That number is predicted to triple in the next two years. But the Literacy Gap among young Afrillennials remains wide, and progress is still measured.

Sill, in Africa's Sub-Sahara, youth literacy rates (ages 15-24) have increased over the past 25 years, which leads to a projected improvement by about 200% over previous decades. However, youth literacy rates in the Sub-Sahara are roughly 71%, just a notch behind the continent of Asia as growing the slowest of any region, and yet it has taken quantum leaps ahead of the pace just 10 years ago. So with the Millennials (the "Afrillennials") there is both hope and significant progress.

Education for Women: Still yet to be resolved is the huge disparity between literacy for women and men. While 69% of all African men can read, less than half of the women (48.5%) do. So much of this disregard for women's literacy has to do with centuries of social (often tribal) custom that still carries through to this day.

At present there is a huge cultural bias in this area, and it is a fact that among African Millennials about 12% of all women have had a child by the age of 16. Literacy then, especially in a language a woman understands, ought to make a difference in her life and consequently in the life of her family.

As a simple rule of thumb, African women who receive primary and secondary levels of education are more inclined to integrate the following "civilized" patterns into their lifestyle choices: 1) They will use health clinics and hospitals and return to the clinic if their children's health does not improve; 2) About 88% of the time, they will start families at a later age and have fewer, healthier children; 3) They are far more

CAMFED: Educating African Women

CAMFED—Campaign for Female Education—is an international non-profit organization that is taking on class and gender inequality by supporting girls to go to school and succeed, and empowering young women to step up as leaders of change. In many nations in Africa, school-age girls are the first to be excluded from primary and secondary education. They are the first to drop out, or be pulled out of school by their families, the first to be failed by the system. And they're often forced to work or marry where they face the perils of early pregnancy and HIV/AIDS.

In sub-Saharan Africa, 28 million girls are out of school. Poverty is the greatest barrier to accessing an education. So overcoming this barrier by investing in girls and women is a proven way to improve the health and wealth of a whole nation. Education for all African women has been described as the "silver bullet" in terms of what it can achieve. Women with even a secondary education 1) will earn 25% more on average in their lifetime, 2) will save 90% of their earnings for their families, and 3) be 3 X less likely to become HIV Positive. Based out to address child and maternal mortality, raise families out of poverty,

accelerate economic development, and help communities deal with climate change CAMFED has been structured to address every significant issue that Afrilennial women face today.

Since its founding in 1993, Camfed's innovative education programs in Zimbabwe, Zambia, Ghana, Gabon, Tanzania and Malawi have directly supported over 1,419,000 students to attend primary and secondary school, and over 3.5 million children have benefitted from improved learning environments created by the Camfed system.

inclined to have better personal health and nutrition; 4) They will bring up families that enjoy improved housing, better clothing, higher income, and regular access to water and sanitation; 5) About 18% of them will be able to become employed and contribute directly to the family income.

All are pretty strong endorsements for educating women. So the question invariably arises: Where does a woman in the Sub-Sahara go to encounter such elusive opportunities? Apparently, it depends upon the nation in which they live.

There is little question that in countries where literacy is higher and the gender gap is narrower, cultural and social and economic progress begins to take quantum

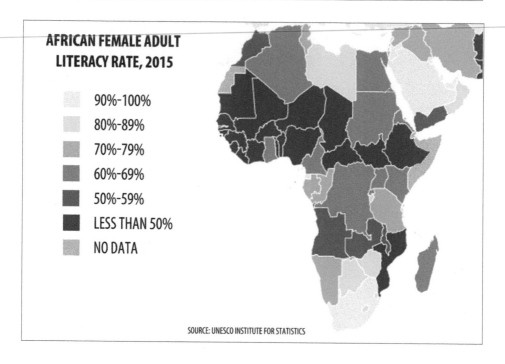

AFRICAN FEMALE ADULT LITERACY RATE, 2015

90%-100%
80%-89%
70%-79%
60%-69%
50%-59%
LESS THAN 50%
NO DATA

SOURCE: UNESCO INSTITUTE FOR STATISTICS

leaps. Botswana, South Africa, Rwanda, Mauritius, The Seychelles, Namibia, Burundi, Swaziland and Lesotho—all these nations have three things in common. First they all enjoy literacy rates in the 70% to 95% range. Second, they have educational parity among men and women (within 2% points). Third, without exception, they have made greater economic and sociological strides than nations where literacy is low and educational disparity between genders is both deep and broad.

So there are times when statistics are hard taskmasters. They are also the best teachers for those willing to learn. As is often the case with African leadership, learning a lesson is one thing, having the integrity of purpose to put them into action is entirely another.

Disease. Good to get this out of the way up front. All the horror stories you've heard about Africa being something of a disease factory are pretty much true. About six of the world's ten deadliest diseases can be found in the Sub-Sahara more than any other place in the world. And most of it is directly due to climate, poverty, a lack of information/education and inadequate national health programs.

It is not so much that these challenges don't exist in other parts of the world. It's that the health challenges themselves all exist in the same place at the same time in what amounts to a perfect storm of disease, pollution, pestilence and plague. That should come as no surprise since the world press manages to jump on every incidence of it. What they so often do not cover is just how much is being done in African nations to overcome it in some absolutely brilliant and innovative ways. And one of the reasons so much progress is being made rests with the fact that Africa is on the very front line where so much of the world's "circumstantial illness" takes place. So let's get some the nasty business out of the way, and cover some of the villains.

Malaria is the perennial global pandemic that strikes about 500 million people a year, more than 300 million in the Sub-Sahara. It comes from the mosquito, whose bite and rebite pattern of behavior makes it the most dangerous creature on earth, killing about 3 million human beings a year.

The second major mosquito borne disease is *dengue fever,* which attacks about 50 million people a year in Africa alone and kills another half million.

Another creature borne diseases is *trypanosomiasis* or *sleeping sickness.* Spread by the infamous tsetse fly in many African countries, it breaks out in about 450,000 cases a year and can cause permanent neurological damage and even death.

River blindness, or *onchocerciasis* is a disease that is almost exclusive to Africa. Hitting about 18 million people a year, it is borne by a parasitic worm that can enter the human body and live there for years.

Then we have pollution born diseases like *cholera* (from contaminated water) and *diarrhea* that occur among the more than 350,000 people a year, the majority of whom are undernourished and living in squalor.

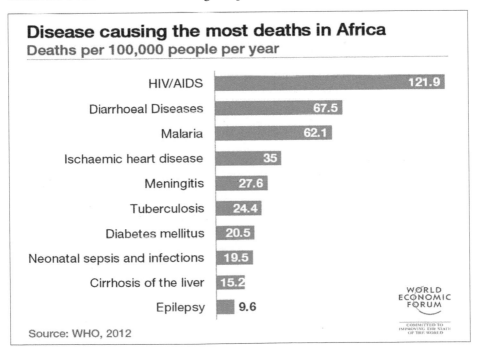

Disease causing the most deaths in Africa
Deaths per 100,000 people per year

Disease	Deaths per 100,000
HIV/AIDS	121.9
Diarrhoeal Diseases	67.5
Malaria	62.1
Ischaemic heart disease	35
Meningitis	27.6
Tuberculosis	24.4
Diabetes mellitus	20.5
Neonatal sepsis and infections	19.5
Cirrhosis of the liver	15.2
Epilepsy	9.6

WORLD
ECONOMIC
FORUM
COMMITTED TO
IMPROVING THE STATE
OF THE WORLD

Source: WHO, 2012

Tuberculosis and *HIV/AIDS* round out the major African ailments at about 25 million cases. And seeing all these numbers tends to make one wonder whether or not anyone in Africa is ever well at all.

Now for the Good News: What we have to be both aware of and grateful for are the one two health punch of *WHO* and the *CDC* both as global monitors and first responders to any major health crisis that may strike anywhere at any time on planet earth.

WHO (World Health Organization) is headquartered in Geneva, Switzerland and acts as the United Nation's health management body. Founded in 1948 it has 7000 health professionals in six offices who spend 98% of their working days monitoring, anticipating and preventing diseases while promoting sound health practices around the world. WHO focuses, by necessity, on world trouble spots and spends a great deal of its time rushing information, assistance and proactive, prophylactic medical treatment to any trouble spot that might pop up anywhere in the world.

In just one forty day period in 2016 alone, WHO arranged for 2 million people to be vaccinated against Yellow Fever in the Democratic Republic of the Congo, monitored and forewarned Nigeria of more than 300 cases of Lassa Fever that had cropped up in the northeastern quadrant of the country, and set up a system of safe blood transfusions for more than 100,000 patients in South Sudan. WHO officially announced the final lockdown of Ebola in Nigeria, and just finished a program in Thailand, Moldavia and Sri Lanka to eliminate altogether the mother-to-child transmission of HIV and infantile (or congenital) syphilis.

The *Center for Disease Control,* better known simply as the *CDC,* is entirely based in the United States and claims jurisdiction over diseases that may directly affect the USA mainland, its states, territories or citizens—including any travel in and out. Officially, the CDC's prime directive is, "to protect public health and safety through the control and prevention of disease, injury, and disability. That includes applying national attention on developing and applying disease control and prevention especially of infectious pathogens, food borne disease, environmental health, work safety and health, health promotion, injury prevention and educational activities designed to improve the health of US Citizens anywhere in the world. So by the time you get through that rather broad description, you end up with an umbrella that covers the same areas in the world as WHO, but just happens to be extremely well funded, and with a staff of twice as many (15,000) "contractors" and the ability to move in any trouble spot on a moment's notice.

Working with crack medical teams from splendid non-profit medical groups such as "Doctors Without Borders," the CDC has been remarkably resourceful and unselfish in helping to treat and shut down a number of global pandemics, and other critical issues surrounding war, natural disasters such as earthquake and flood and migratory catastrophe and punitive diaspora.

What's more, CDC has the best computer control and monitoring system in the world, and can pick up a plague area in a matter of a day or two, isolate it and make appropriate adjustments to monitor its spread, take appropriate measures to shut it down and prevent future occasions. The CDC, unlike WHO, is limited in that it may only intervene when invited by the nation or nations in question, and/or take measures against its spread to the United States and North America.

The drawback to both of these splendid and well-intended health agencies is the fact that they have a lot of world to cover. They are very often forced to make their critical judgments electronically and from a perspective that is simply too far removed from the source. As a result (as we reported on the Ebola fiasco) they are driven to make evaluations that are inaccurate and can result either in overkill or misapplications of resources that are occasionally even comical.

What the CDC and WHO have been able to do, perhaps through mere proximity, is to provide appropriate role models for others to follow on a more concentrated regional basis...as has now been taking place recently in Africa.

Welcome to Africa's own version of the CDC. The flashing dots above the control panel got his attention; and it's a good thing that they did. When Ethiopian Health Minister Kesete Admasu was touring the U.S. Centers for Disease Control and Prevention in Atlanta in 2012, he couldn't help but notice that the lights on the main computer screen were blinking over a satellite image of Eastern Africa, and when Admasu asked what they represented, he was informed that it had to do with an outbreak of 4,000 cases of Hepatitis E in South Sudan, a country that shares a border with his own home country.

Wondering why he had to come halfway around the world to know what was going on in his own backyard, Admasu found himself arriving at this conviction. "We need a CDC of our own in Africa."

The following summer, at a meeting of the African Union in Nigeria, Admasu stressed the importance of taking this significant step in health autonomy to the leaders of the AU's other 54 countries. Finally in the spring of 2015, when the biggest Ebola outbreak in history had killed 10,000 people, the majority of African states and the U.S. agreed to combine their energies and respective expertise to create an agency that would respond to outbreaks, sync communications between member states and improve public health preparedness.

Launching in January 2017, the first phase of the new agency—CDC Africa— has been able to start up a surveillance-and-response unit headquartered in the Ethiopian capital of Addis Ababa that includes an emergency operations center closely simulating the one Admasu walked through on his visit to CDC headquarters in Atlanta, Georgia. Phase Two will establish five regional collaborating centers across the continent.

Despite an optimistic and well-intended beginning, others are not convinced the new operation will have enough money or expertise to make a difference.

Muhammad Ali Pate, former Minister of State for Health in Nigeria, remains as one of the initiative's most vocal critics: "I want to be optimistic but this will not work if the structure and capacity is weak like other health agencies," he was quoted as saying after evaluating the organization's game plan.

Pate's main concern is the fact that WHO and the CDC, despite access to all the advanced health technology in the world—botched the read on the E-Bola epidemic in 2015—under-responding in some areas and overreacting in many others.

Many African health officials see several roadblocks to the African CDC's success. First there is the outdated sense of territorial imperative where the health of individual nations is concerned. Then there is an initial shortage of staff. Within the African Sub-Sahara, for example, there exists an inability to hire and retain experienced epidemiologists and insufficient funding. As a point of progress, a staff of 11 people and a budget of $6.9 million were allocated for the period July 2015 to December 2016. More realistic estimates have set a figure of $60 million and a staff of 300 to run what soon could become a robust agency.

Then again, naysayers always seem to speak the loudest. And this is an initiative that is long overdue. In the words of US President John F. Kennedy: "Some people see what exists and ask why? I look upon what is possible and ask why not?"

For anyone who understands that progress takes courage, technology and a stout heart, the African CDC is an idea whose time has come. Additional funds are already being allocated to fund the second phase of the project, and officials at the US CDC and African Union say more staff are being recruited, including a director.

Private Enterprise and Technology to the Rescue: Voxiva Mobile Health Messaging. It's a given that 90% of all health, wellness and medical progress lies in early detection, education and prevention.

Since 2001 Voxiva became one of the first health and technology companies in the world to invent interactive mobile health services that would help people in developing nations, marginalized regions and remote parts of the world to have instant access to electronic medical diagnosis, health counseling and prevention.

By 2014 Voxiva had deployed mobile health services in 17 countries in Africa, Asia, Europe, and North and South America. Specializing in helping public health systems deploy tools to fight disease, Voxiva's versatile tech tool and Care4life treatment portfolio offers evidence-based health guidelines, behavior modification techniques for prevention, prophylactic medical advice, pre-natal and maternal health counseling, breaking addictive health hazard patterns such as smoking cessation and drug use and new state-of-the-art tools in diabetes self-management.

For subscribers, personalized health information can be sent via text messaging, mobile web and mobile applications. Starting out with test markets in Peru, Voxiva's disease surveillance system was able to document over 100,000 health events that led to the detection of 18 disease outbreaks in a 30-month period.

And the last few years, Voxiva's Rwanda detection model has turned out to be the first and longest-standing national health information system in Africa, managing records for 100,000 people receiving HIV/AIDS treatment.

It's no secret that Africa has about 27.5 million of the world's 33 million cases of HIV/AIDS, making it the most serious global pandemic in the world.

Although traditionally Rwanda is not the most critical of African nations, its infection rate of 3.5% of a population of 11 million inhabitants is still unacceptably high. In response, the Kigali government started expanding anti-retroviral (ARV) care and treatment for people living with HIV/AIDS, so that by 2014 as many as 120,000 adults and children were receiving treatment. Through Voxiva's system, the Rwanda Health Ministry was able to set up something called TRACnet, an information solution designed to collect, store, retrieve, and disseminate critical program, drug, and patient details related to HIV/AIDS care and treatment. Through TRACnet the Rwanda Health Ministry has been able to scale up HIV/AIDS tracking and detection and quickly provide clinical services in remote areas both to detect, anticipate and treat the disease.

With a bilingual English and French telephone and web interface, TRACnet employs a practical and sustainable approach to using information technology. By leveraging existing infrastructure—including mobile telephone networks, connected and standalone computers, and underlying paper record systems—TRACnet has been deployed nationwide to connect every health facility in the nation as well as posts in some neighboring countries to provide ARV treatment and related services.

TRACnet provides a central repository of HIV/AIDS program information and delivers real time information for decision-making. As such, it allows decision-makers and supervisors to quickly analyze and respond to program information and is now being adopted in neighboring nations such as Tanzania, Zambia, Burundi and Uganda.

A pioneer in interactive mobile health and wellness programs, Voxvia announced that by 2014 their services had delivered more than 100 million health messages to consumers by text message. Voxiva's Care4life portfolio of programs promote maternal & child health (Text4baby & Text4kids), adult health & wellness (Txt4health),

smoking cessation (Text2quit), and diabetes self-management (Care4life Diabetes). Working with several leading health organizations to develop content for its programs, Voxiva uses guidelines from WHO, the CDC, Doctors without Borders and other international health groups. And all its services are designed to help users take appropriate preventative health actions to stay healthy, more effectively manage chronic illness, and improve the quality metrics by which the health care industry is measured. Along the way, Voxiva intends to make them available to nations and health ministries on all continents.

Matters of the Heart—The "Cameroon" Cardio Pad. In the geometric progressions of medical technology, mobile apps to monitor one's heart and body functions from a cell phone and tablet are nothing new. But this new 10 inch touch screen monitor conceived and developed by Cameroon entrepreneur Arthur Zing is a quantum leap in detection technology because it perfectly fits the health profile and demographic of the average African patient. That's because it gives patients with heart problems a medical diagnosis within minutes that could dramatically improve healthcare for rural residents far from hospitals.

A recipient of the Royal Academy of Engineering's Africa Prize (for innovation and design) the Cardio Pad was originally inspired by Arthur Zing's own experience growing up in rural Cameroon where he witnessed his own uncle succumbing to cardiovascular complications because the technology was simply not in place to help him. After graduating from the University of Yaoundé with a degree in computer science Zing decided to devote the next year to learning everything he could about medical electronics from the Internet until he had amassed enough research to start designing his tablet.

Arthur Zang's award winning Cardio Pad is the first device of its kind specifically designed for rural patients. It functions by means of Bluetooth-connected electrodes, and it gives accurate feedback in a matter of minutes. It sends a digitized electrocardiogram (ECG or EKG) to a national healthcare center for a cardiologist to evaluate and return a diagnosis to the patient. The whole process takes less than 20 minutes and the doctor and patient never have to interact.

The Cardio Pad comes with a complete diagnostic kit any layman can use, including instructions, cables, electrodes, and the tablet itself. The Cardio Pad is now being used in villages in Gabon, Nepal, and India and will be expanding from Cameroon to other ECOWAS nations in the Sub-Sahara.

Summary

It is no secret. Africa's challenges have no place to HIDe. Hunger, Illiteracy and Disease on the Continent are omnipresent, pervasive and seemingly indelible. They are also being addressed in a slow but relentless fashion, government-by-government, piece-by-piece, individual achievement by individual achievement until the issues are resolved.

There is a COAT that will cover this if one will but choose to look, work with others and find the solutions. Many governments are choosing to do so. And as so often is the case, they are being inspired and often shamed into good works by well organized non-profits and individual entrepreneurs of every stripe—Afrillennials and old pros, billionaires and startups who are determined to see their respective worlds overreach to their potential.

I discover this and bear witness to it, because I believe with a whole heart that the human spirit yearns for resolution, for goodness and for progress. That it is what Abraham Lincoln referred to as the Divine Spark, and that is what will guide us to the next level, and a very strong finish indeed.

CHAPTER 15

Africa Winning Economies — AWE: A New Africa Union?

There is a term called "cautious optimism." And it applies to the continent of Africa more than any other place in the world. A great deal of that has to do with the dynamics that are now providing an entirely new subtext, especially for the future of the Sub-Sahara.

The main consideration has everything to do with in which direction the arrow of progress is pointed. And though the fluctuations from year to year may seem manic in the expression of their details, the overall direction is decidedly North.

Every year—year-in, year-out—major studies of Africa's progress are conducted by every financial collective from the International Monetary Fund (IMF) to *Forbes Magazine*, and from charting schema from *The Economist* all the way through major financial gauges such as Price Waterhouse Cooper (PwC) and Ernst and Young (EY). Then there are evaluations from the UN, The World Bank, The Millennium Challenge Fund, The Index of Economic Opportunity, The Transparency Index, the Legatum Prosperity Index and a dozen other interested bodies. Every one of the continent's 54 nations is a target of considerable scrutiny; and no one escapes notice. These studies, ratings and projection models are made of every nation on every continent, but none are seemingly as hotly focused as these. And the reason is simple: *economic potential.*

We have been emphasizing that potential in every imaginable way for the last 260-plus pages, and have even told you what we believe will be the best places to connect and do business. And yet even as we do, the ground shifts beneath our feet. The game changes literally with the latest release from the Internet. And today's despot is tomorrow's economic turnaround in the making. So the information coming out of this or any other manual for entrepreneurs is only as accurate as tomorrow's headlines.

Nothing is etched in stone. That is the blessing as well as the curse. And yet the constants remain.

If there are three terms that would describe the business climate in Africa it would be these: *1) volatile; 2) unlimited; 3) constantly in flux.* These are not necessarily bad descriptions as much as they are accurate.

Africa's volatility also includes explosive growth in population among Afrillennials who now comprise 68% of the population under 30 (as opposed to 30% in South America and 22% in North America). They in turn have triggered a "blow up" of digital technology in the Sub-Sahara—one that is seeing tens of millions of young adults from Gambia to Tanzania using their apps to seek new access to civilization, beginning with their start in life through education. Using their apps and (often voice activated) list of prompts on smart phones and electronic tablets, they are making use of all levels of eSchooling, eConference think tanks, mastering the art of smart-phone farming, conducting daily financial transactions, and enjoying access to eGovernments on a daily basis.

It is the Afrillennials who are driving Africa's $32.5 billion in fashion and $12.5 billion in film, arts and entertainment. 27% have their own apartments. 22% are buying cars. It is that same 68% who are driving the Exodus from rural farms to Africa's major metropolitan areas in what amounts to the most massive urbanization in world history; and it's all happening in geometric progressions.

We have emphasized this *ad infinitum* (perhaps *ad nauseam*) in this book. But if some of you reading this document have gotten the message, many nation-states in the Sub-Sahara have not. Or worse: they have but are choosing not to act upon it. And many are doing so at their own peril.

All this upward mobility puts a strain on infrastructure. And some African nations have been ready for it while others have not. Morocco, Egypt and Tunisia have addressed all issues of basic human needs such as power, water, sanitation, transportation and education as bastions of modernization. But they reside in the Mediterranean North with more direct access to Europe.

The Sub-Sahara is a different issue. The geographic reality of vast land mass and cultural disparity have always had a say—much of it having to do with national governments using these false barriers as excuses for doing nothing. But Youth is Life. "Life" will find a way. And so the game has changed. Nowadays the demographic momentum that youth has set in motion forces an equal and opposite compensation at all the social pressure points—demanding that basic needs be met all across the board.

Nations such as Ethiopia, Kenya, Tanzania, Uganda and Mozambique—previously content to let their youth lay waste on rural farms or remote tribal enclaves—are now forced to cope with a young, vibrant, upwardly mobile, nascent middle class intent on finding jobs and having life on their own terms. Nations like Mauritius, South Africa, Ghana and Botswana have been well prepared with properly established urban amenities, sufficient power grids, good roads and sanitation. Rwanda has had the biggest turnaround of any nation in the world, and Benin proved to be the surprise of 2016. All have advanced remarkably, and yet there is still so much more that needs to be done.

A third group such as Nigeria and Angola, totally unprepared for the quantum leaps their young populations have taken, now perch on the verge of collapse due to failure to adjust to the times. Nigeria—the economic engine of the Sub-Sahara—at least has the compensation of massive rises in population combined with geometrically progressing industries, phenomenal diversification and exponential urban sprawl to explain its growing pains. Angola on the other hand—the filthy rich mono-economic kleptocracy that it is—has nothing to justify its failure, other than government corruption at every level combined with blatant indifference to its own people.

Smaller satellite nations of the western Sub-Sahara such as Chad and Sierra Leone have the scars of war and revolution from which to recover. Then there are the core casualty nations such as Zimbabwe, Libya, Sudan and the Democratic Republic of the Congo that remain the poster children for corruption and dysfunction at every level (some of them perennially perching on the edge of darkness).

And yet even in 2016, not a great year due to commodity crises across the board and the tanking price of oil, many investment indicators are willing to look past the pessimism of the IMF and the World Bank and make positive mid-term to long term projections of their own. These projections were justified somewhat in the first half of 2017, due to a slight uptick in overall commodity prices and the seeming willingness of Nigeria, Angola and Mozambique to shore up their infrastructure just enough to meet new market demands.

A 21st Century African Business Agenda

In May 2017, an *Africa Business Agenda* survey released by Price Waterhouse Cooper (PwC) continued to press home the fact that Africa is, and will continue to be, a vital growth opportunity for Foreign Direct Investment. And much of that investment is being dictated by what has been accurately described as an exponential *Digital Revolution,* triggering as its by-product a surprisingly resilient market in the Sub-Sahara.

According to the agenda initiatives like the SMART Africa Alliance, in collaboration with global technology, many tech brands have for the last 15 years been cultivating a fully functioning tech-savvy generation in the Sub-Sahara—one that will transform a number of industries as well as the countries they serve.

In that regard, Standard & Poor's has developed its own unique "Skills for Africa Program" (SAP). The SAP initiative is offering students in the Sub-Sahara free to low-cost access to education as well as initiating a special program directed at helping SME companies and startups find new ways not only to establish themselves but also find new inroads into their chosen target markets.

SAP is also setting up special programs to empower Africa's youth for this super-tech century by teaching digital literacy and what many consider to be the most important new application of this millennia: coding and IT development and training. In an initiative that is growing exponentially, SAP has been conducting seminars for field reps to train 150,000 youth in 30 countries for Africa Code Week in October 2016. And as recently as August of 2015, 89,000 Millennials and Gen Z between the ages of 8 and 24 years were being taught all the intricacies of new tech coding.

Similar to the iHub and Eneza models but with an added "hook," the Skills for Africa Programs has also set up a new educational network that uses a hybrid approach to teaching that combines both classroom and e-learning. The unique self-study e-learning environment allows students to study as needed without requiring 24-hour Internet access; a key factor in many of the locations in question. More important, SAP has also maintained a level of sensitivity to both Francophone and Anglophone nations by offering training kits in English, French and Portuguese (for Angola and Mozambique). Beginning with a 54 station partner-based association throughout Africa in 2013, that network has more than doubled in the last three years.

Clearly *technology* and the *Afrillennial youth movement* are two legs on the platform of the African opportunity. In fact, Africa (at 64% under 30) is the youngest continent in the world. And only South America has a population that approaches it (at 41%). Asia, with the exception of India and Indonesia, is an aging economy. So is Europe. And even North America (at roughly 1 in 3 under 34 years of age) comes nowhere near the Afrillennial curve.

There is no question that digital technology and telecommunications—the Internet and its virtual world—form the glue that holds the substructure of the Sub-Sahara together. As well as education, virtual farming, banking and online retail opportunities as well as government access, it is the gateway to anticipating every B2B and B2P market to market need—all through implementing customer relationship management systems, interpreting the complex and evolving needs of customers through data and analytics, and improving communication and engagement by means of social media both out of major vehicles such as Facebook to regional African super-networks such as Safari.com and funafrique.com

All these platforms and more form the wave of the future. And yet all this technology still comes at a hefty cost. And at the moment that cost is exorbitant to a degree that borders on extortion. We touched on this earlier, but it bears repeating that in some nations such as Kenya, Nigeria and even South Africa, where the full-spectrum of services are readily available, the average tech-savvy user is paying 1990s *a la carte* prices for smart phone and internet subscriptions that often amount to 35% of their annual income. And yet users are willing to incur the cost because it often means the difference between gaining income, education, and connection to the world or being banished back to a life of disenfranchisement.

Eventually competition should drive down the costs, but for now these "services" are expensive. And yet even in view of the challenges, they also bring inroads for new products and new networks that the users can afford. Such persistent progress has actually managed to override the current global economic crisis caused by the EU meltdown—a trickledown effect that always seems to flow downhill to the more fragile markets of the world.

In spite of all that, after more than a decade of urbanization, African marketers and manufacturers are using technologies to challenge business models and disrupt competitors in markets.

No question, Africa is still vulnerable to its fair share of external economic shocks, including a decline in commodity prices fuelled by the economic slowdown in China. It is also feeling the ripple effect from the collapse in value of the emerging market currencies against the US-dollar and the recent UK *Brexit* from the EU. Add to this the chaos of the Trump Era that has shattered America's politics and damaged its international brand, and we are all bearing witness to a run of economic instability that has turned global arbitrage into a crapshoot.

Granted, Africa is still nowhere near the top of the economic food chain as a driving force in world markets. And yet, reverting to the Law of Pure Potential, it is only a matter of time. Having the vision to look beyond all the red flags waved over the global morass of the summer and fall of 2016, and the political uncertainty of the spring of 2017, smart FDI companies and CEOs believe that Africa is due for a massive paradigm shift upward even in the next 15 months—one that will drive it to new growth spikes inside the next three years. And one of the catalysts for growth has proved to be something of an intangible when examined in terms of simple commoditization. That is something called *Shared Responsibility.*

Everything that it implies, Shared Responsibility is a new disruptive African business model in that it has formed a new kind of bond that bypasses governments and goes through international finance and FDI corporations directly to their counterpart "players" in the Sahara and Sub-Sahara. Using digital and Internet technology, these savvy investors are leveraging international groups and economic associations to set up the next successful business models all through the continent.

Most African governments, even the corrupt ones, have been willing to adopt something of a *laissez faire* approach where developing their home-grown businesses is concerned. So, if they don't act directly as facilitators, they have either privatized government ownership of major industries, or at the very least have loosened the reins on foreign business coming to the Sub-Sahara to set up shop.

A True African Union: AWE Membership has its Privileges

OK, let's get something out of the way up front. Because anyone reading this proposal is going to think, "Oh great! All we need is another council, committee, trade organization or economic union in Africa, when none of the ones we already have work all that well to begin with." But indulge me on this for the next few pages while I endeavor to make my point.

Recently Ernst and Young, generally conservative in its international financial evaluations, was very willing to put out its now famous *Africa Attractiveness Index* (AAI) and list 20 top nations as great places to do business despite recent downturns in the global economy that have seemingly hit Africa the hardest.

The list itself is not dissimilar to so many other international business metrics used to determine desirability of African nations. And like others of their kind, they provide a 5 Point Guideline includes *1) Governance, 2) Diversity, 3) Infrastructure, 4) Business enablement* and *5) Human development.*

No need to put the whip to this horse any further except to note that, as these five criteria continue to be established, the same 20 or 25 nations in Africa always show up on the list. Give or take some possible imminent shifts in governance, the AAI list for 2016, ranked the 20 "Hot Markets" according to the previously mentioned five point guideline, ranking the nations as follows: 1) South Africa; 2) Morocco; 3) Egypt; 4) Kenya; 5) Mauritius; 6) Ghana; 7) Botswana; 8) Tunisia; 9) Rwanda; 10) Cote d'Ivoire (Ivory Coast); 11) Senegal; 12) Tanzania; 13) Uganda: 14) Ethiopia; 15) Nigeria; 16) Algeria; 17) Zambia; 18) Namibia; 19) Benin; 20) Mozambique.

If the list looks familiar, it is because you have seen practically every one of these nations in other chapters in this doctrine and for pretty much the same reasons: They are the one's who have gotten their acts together—at least in most of the metrics that matter. They've met all the criteria from most of the international indexes. And they are the drivers of the African economy.

Most of them belong to, or are at the core of about two-dozen different economic and trade unions in Africa. Through the WTO, ECOWAS, COMESA, AYE, OECD or KINGS—there exists a veritable alphabet soup of associations willing to facilitate new international business throughout the African continent, some far more efficient at it than others.

Many of them have come into being primarily due to shared economic and geo-political goals, while others have been set up on a regional basis to head off possible crossover disputes over shared resources, bodies of water and national borders. Still others such as the Francophone nations (Cameroon, Chad, Gabon, Algeria, Senegal and others) are tied together by language and (more or less) a common currency to form the loosely constructed *Afrique Francopohonie*. And other self-directed groups such as KINGS nations (Kenya, Nigeria, Ghana and South Africa) have a special connection in the fact that they are primarily Francophone in colonial legacy and number themselves among the most consistently buoyant economies in Africa. (The single exception is Ivory Coast [Cote d'Ivoire], which still has Francophonic roots.)

All of them function under the aegis of the 54 member-nation African Union, an association originally spun out of the (toothless) OAU and primarily set in place to stabilize Africa, offering something of a solid point of reference, arbitration and communication. With Morocco rejoining in 2017, all 54 nations are once again members of the African Union (AU). Given socio-economic and political diversity of its member nations, the intent of the original African Union was to establish a set of guidelines that helped to make it a kind of mini United Nations. Some of its originally stated goals and objectives are basic and consistent with this kind of charter:

- To achieve greater solidarity between the African countries and Africans.

- To defend the sovereignty, territorial integrity and independence of its Member States.

- To accelerate the political and social-economic integration of the continent.

- To promote and defend African common positions on issues of interest to the continent and its peoples.

- To encourage international cooperation, taking due account of the Charter of the United Nations and the Charter of the Declaration of Human Rights.

- To promote peace, security and stability on the continent.

- To promote democratic principles and institutions, popular participation and good governance...and so forth.

We resort to that somewhat pejorative term, "and so forth," because the list of initiatives is long and comprised mainly of spinoffs of the same concepts expressed in the original ten or so. And if the AU has been good for one thing it has been that it has at least provided all its member nations someplace to go to shine the light on Africa's problems, challenges and disputes. From that rare point of departure, they have at least taken some initial steps toward resolution. Unfortunately, the primary representatives of member nations are the presidents, prime ministers or heads of governments themselves. And so the AU often reduces down to a kind of "good old boys club" at

NEW FROM THE AU: A 54 Nation Passport

Well... it took bouncing Africa's richest man to get the ball rolling on this. And when influential people flex their muscles in the right way, only good things can come of it. So, in March 2016, when Nigeria's mega-billionaire Philanthrocapitalist Aliko Dangote got turned away at South African immigration for forgetting one of his of 8 passports (while his American  business associates breezed right through) it caused something of a stir in global business circles, and leaders inside the African Union saw this as an opportunity to modernize.

Up until recently—especially due to vast differences in governance, border disputes and concerns over radical jihad terrorist groups—African nations have less trust for each other than they have for Europeans or North Americans coming to the continent. So, in fact, nearly 60% of African nations require special travel visas for entry from other African nations, while only 42% require visas from other foreign nationals.

Now that is about to change. Recently, African Union set in motion an AU Passport for free travel between its 54 member nations without requiring a Visa. Currently set up as an e-Passport between consenting countries, it will eliminate a great deal of entangling paperwork that many African nations require of one another. Having launched in August 2016, this e-Visa program is still only available on a limited basis, mainly to political functionaries.

And frequent travelers will still have to be vetted and qualified with background checks. Skeptics believe the experiment will fail—that there are just too many issues to overcome. Still, the AU passport will be in effect for some and, if the test works, eventually available to all. And for the first time in a long time the AU has come up with something that just might serve every member nation in a very positive way.

the top of the political food chain who are doing little or nothing to shake up their own (or each other's) hold on power.

With that kind of troubling wink-and-a-nod network, the AU has done virtually nothing to stop civil wars, end corruption, or roll back human rights abuses in nations like Libya, Chad, Sudan, Somalia, Mali, Zimbabwe, Eritrea, Djibouti, the Democratic Republic of the Congo or half a dozen other consistently miasmic regions of the continent.

Much like the UN, after which it has modeled itself, the AU has primarily been a forum for expression and debate. In very real terms it has done very little indeed to promote economic growth and progress. Those are left to the core economic coalitions such as COMESA (Common Market for Eastern and Southern Africa) that we mentioned earlier. Some of them are good as far as they go. But few of them go far enough.

And they might even do well to create a separate core economic union of their own along the model of the European Union.

Or should they?

The European Economic Union (EEU later shortened to EU) was originally formed out of nations bound together by four points of mutual concern: Common political commitment to democracy, a high human rights record and shared cultural commitment; 2) a standardized set of laws for all member nations; 3) mutual economic interests, including solid financial underpinnings, free trade and special nations relationships; 4) a common currency —the Euro—presumably based upon solid financial reserves, and 5) free travel between nations, and multicultural opportunities for citizenship, lowered border restrictions and (essentially) a common access passport.

The premise for amalgamating and developing the European Union was to create an improved "quality of life" for all member states, concentrated economic power, and a dedication to high standards of globalization. It was originally established with the shared belief that all boats would be lifted with the tide. And its ultimate objective was to make this union of European nations the most powerful globalized economic force in the world. In terms of pure economics over the last 40 years it has succeeded. And if it had just stuck to that simplified objective it would have succeeded without complications.

The complications have come with crossover standards for government policy without sensitivity to local issues, immigration and (perceived or real) threats to national autonomy of its member nations—one that caused the "Brexit" of the United Kingdom and is yet again promising to shake the entire coalition to its foundations. The departure of this core economic power from the EU has thus far proved to be earthshaking in terms of global economic markets. And yet, even though the immediate fallout and repercussions have been economic, the underlying causes for the UK's withdrawal and the EU's shaky status have everything to do with the fact that the European Union (an *Economic Union* of nations) lost sight of its original purpose for forming in the first place and started trying to muscle all its member nations into a "one size fit all" philosophy of governance.

So, let Africa learn from Europe's mistakes and keep our eyes on the prize—economic stability, growth partnership and investment, and mutual benefit. And the proposal before us is to form and establish a coalition of African Winning Economies (AWE). This membership is not for everyone. Applying nations have to qualify. They have to achieve certain levels of accomplishment based on the five criteria.**

And they have to uphold the high standards set for true economic progress in Africa. If participating nations kept the integrity of purpose for this kind of coalition that would be something of which we could all be in AWE.

Starting with 10 of the nations originally noted, AWE could provide a list of criteria and shared benefits that would work for everyone. Among the initial nations to steer the destiny of AWE, this book has already pretty well defined the core nations. By all criteria of measurement, Botswana, Ghana, Mauritius, Morocco and Tunisia would be automatic selections for the Core. By sheer force of economic influence and what amounts to 56% of Africa's total GDP, South Africa, Nigeria, Kenya, Egypt and Algeria would round out the 10 Core Nations of AWE. We also acknowledge that, by sheer force of political and global economic influence, the last five would supersede the first five were it not for the fact that each of them has serious issues of leadership at the very top. Nevertheless, purely in terms of government structure and global economic leverage, the fundamentals are undeniably sound.

One of the strengths of AWE lies in the fact that it is at heart a meritocracy. So the bonds are all ones, not of geography or spheres of influence, but of high standards. And, since four of AWE's ten founding nations are in North Africa and six are in the Sub-Sahara, the organization immediately cuts through that very physical "Great Wall of Africa" called the Sahara Desert and goes more to essential issues of economic viability and positive approaches to credible FDI commitment and financial stability.

Having qualified the 10 Core Nations that form AWE, we would then look to a list of 10 Candidate nations, any three of which would be submitted for admission pending certain improvements in the five criteria for a three-year qualification period. They would join by contributing to the participation pool for funds directly pointed at helping them elevate their most critical core issues—infrastructure, educa-

---

** *Criteria vary depending upon the grading institution. But this five point guideline contains the most salient points of a sound economy:* 1) Governance, 2) Diversity, 3) Infrastructure, 4) Business enablement and 5) Human development.

tion, power grids, water and sanitation, social services and/or business facility—to lift them to AWE's standards for acceptance. Once inside, they would be able to benefit from an AWE *favored nation status* for international travel and visas, trade and tariffs, and even its own credit-based virtual money (like a Bitcoin) used only for special trade inside the AWE umbrella.

The first nation to be admitted would be Rwanda, based upon the merit of its political and economic epiphany just since 2013. The next nations up for admission would logically be Ethiopia, Cote d'Ivoire, Cameroon, Senegal, Uganda, Namibia, Zambia, Namibia and Tanzania—all of which are verging on a breakthrough in all the areas of focus. (Of course they wouldn't all come at once. They would still have to qualify. And if they did the benefits would well be worth the price of admission.)

The secret sauce in all of this would be the fact that the organization itself would not be run by any government agencies or political hacks but by the Africaplitalists themselves—agents of billionaires and successful entrepreneurs from the private sector. These bold African billionaires have already done more through their private foundations and business-building funds to promote prosperity in their own countries than any of the nations themselves. So why not indeed take the next step? Because these are the people who actually know how things work. Not as farfetched as it may seem, it is already an uncomfortable truth that international corporations have more political leverage than most nations. Seven of the twenty top GDPs in the world are corporations, so why not the good guy capitalists? Africa is full of them.

Part of the greatest challenge of African progress has been due to the fact that, even today, 25 of Africa's 54 nations are being governed by current or former generals, military leaders who have survived a great conflict and managed to seize and hold power since that time. Chad, Sudan, South Sudan, Somalia, Mali, Malawi, Mauritania, Djibouti, Eritrea and Democratic Republic of The Congo—all these and many more are almost always the economic casualties of military consequence. And all these nations manage to appear on all international "hit lists" as criminally corrupt or inheriting legacies of malfeasance.

Africa now has its own "ruling class"—the Philanthrocapitalists. (We say that, not ashamedly, but proudly…and certainly not because they look upon themselves as such.) Most have worked their way up from nothing. Almost all have a vision for Africa's future that is now looking beyond the flawed governments they serve and to future generations. And if this treatise is a plea for the virtues of capitalism, we plead guilty as charged.

So, we now come to the final conclusion: When Africa Arrives (and it will) it will be because of this: *the relentless disruption of doing "business as usual," and the rise of innovation."* And for that, what we are going to need is a little shock and AWE!

Summary: The Search for "Wakanda"

At the risk of overstating the case, we're going to have to say that "the cat is out of the bag" where Africa is concerned. As a new quantum point of reference, it has taken form in a hot new Hollywood Film appropriately titled *Black Panther* that has just leapt into the billion dollar club of top 20 all time box office grossers. Adapted from the original Marvel comic book series, *Black Panther,* it features a superhero, T'Challa, hereditary king of Wakanda, a space age meritocracy that has been "hiding in plain sight" for about half a millennium. Saved from the taint of the European Colonialism that came thundering down with the African Scramble, Wakanda is actually an all black home nation with superb technology, a high standard of living, and a mineral called "vibranium" that can do everything from launching rockets to curing cancer.

What this delightful if wishful mythology has tapped into is the undiscovered continent of the new African Spirit. And it does heat up the hypothetical scenario that sticks with us all to this moment: "What would have happened to an Africa left to its own devices, unassisted by the colonial plunder disguised as "civilization?"

Proponents of racial stereotyping would continue to insist that little or no progress would have been made had Europe not interceded to convert and civilize those savages of the Sub-Sahara. They would also argue with equal fervor that some African nations have degraded since the departure of their colonial overlords (Zimbabwe [Rhodesia] and the Democratic Republic of the Congo being held up as classic examples of beautiful nations destroyed by rampant kleptocracy).

And yet to answer all this we have refutation in legion, and a generation of Afrilennials—immersed in new technology—setting the bar higher every single day.

Of course, there isn't a Wakanda yet. But the end game may be nearer than you think, a masterpiece of civilization just beneath the surface. What we do know for certain is that there are "pieces" of the puzzle rapidly fitting into place. And Africapitalism, combined with sensible global optimism, may hold the treasure map to that fantastic kingdom in the sky.

CHAPTER 16

Hot Markets: Cool Contacts

I t is something of a rarity in business publishing these days, but this is a closing chapter that you can actually put to use. Let's face it. Why should we bring you this far and then leave you with nothing more than a wrap up chapter, and a pep rally and little else to show for it?

For true professionals all success is built around a good business model—one with a solid foundation and a long-term sense of purpose. That means gathering credible data in the beginning and putting it into a format anyone can use, reference and build.

In the final analysis, any guide for savvy entrepreneurs should be about effective networking and knowing the next moves to make in any market. Usually, that is best served by legitimate inside information. (And let's face it, all good business transactions work from leverage.)

So, this is where I would like to help you benefit from some benchmarks that my associates and I have managed to put together. And we have done it by using several international business metrics—known criteria from credible sources—that anyone can understand and everyone can put to use.

✓ National Rankings in Africa (based on the Heritage Foundation Index of Economic Freedom and the Transparency Index).

✓ The Legatum Prosperity Index – Based on 12 Criteria, including the following: economy; entrepreneurship and opportunity; governance, health, education, safety and security, personal freedom, and social capital. Some of these criteria may overlap or seem to duplicate. But they also serve a purpose—to cross-reference. And more often than not, nations that score high with one rating system, score high across the board.

✔ There are however a few anomalies such as "Government Stability" and FDI Friendly Environments that we have begun to recognize change almost from month to month.

✔ For our measurements of Government Stability, we have used a 9 Stanine 1-9 rating system – 9 in this case being the most stable.*

✔ Our criteria for environments friendly to Foreign Direct Investment (FDI) are based on recent (in-year) shifts in government policy, are reflective of the summary opinions of international corporations, the IMF, the World Bank, and other financial opinion makers. As such, it is an imprecise but well-considered conclusion. And we will use simple language such as "Good. Excellent. Fair. Poor. And Superior — with added gradients from one state to another. We will also note areas where movement is taking place in one direction or the other.

✔ As for the rest, our contact and recommendations come with permission and an understanding that we will be expanding the lists on this living document as we progress over the weeks and months. Cheers!

---

* Stanine ratings have the least possibility of error due to number clarity, with emphasis on the norm. The US Air Force first put this system into effective use as capability tests in the 1960s.

HOT MARKETS — COOL CONTACTS

BOTSWANA

Ranking: 2

Legatum Prosperity Index Ranking:* 54

Global Economic Freedom Ranking:**
#30

Bullish New Fields of Business, Manufacturing and Marketing: Cattle, Diamonds, Copper, Nickel, Potash, Investment.

Government stability (Stanine rating): 8

FDI Business Friendly Rating: Good to Excellent.

Areas of Opportunity: B2B, Technology and Telecommunications, Banking and Finance, Eco-tourism, Startups.

Best Cities: Gaborone, Francistown

Government Agency Contacts: Ministry of Foreign Affairs and International Cooperation (MoFAIC) on the government portal.

Ministry of Finance and Development Planning, P.O. Box 008, Gaborone, Tel: (+267) 350-100

CAMEROON

Ranking: 27

Legatum Prosperity Index Rating: 127

Global Freedom Ranking: #130

Bullish New Fields of Business, Manufacturing and Marketing: Cotton, Cocoa, Coffee, Crude Oil, Broad Spectrum Agriculture, Banking and Finance, B2B Financial Technology.

Government stability: 4

FDI Business Friendly ranking: Inconsistent but improving

Areas of Opportunity: —

Best Cities: Yaounde, Douala

Government Agency Contacts: Ministere de l'Economie et des Finances (Ministry of Economy, Planning and Regional Development)

Additional Contacts: International Chamber of Commerce, Rue Pasteur, P.O Box. 4011, Douala, Cameroon, Tel: +(237) 42-6855

Ministry of Industrial and Commercial Development, Yaounde, Cameroon, Tel: +(237) 22-25-12

COTE D'IVOIRE

Ranking: 10

Legatum Prosperity Index Rating: 123

Global Economic Freedom Ranking: #92

Bullish New Fields of Business, Manufacturing and Marketing: Financial services, tourism, Real-Estate Development, Retail and Fashion.

Government stability: 6

FDI Business Friendly Rating: Good to Excellent

Areas of Opportunity: B2B, SBE Startups, Startups, telecommunications,

Best Cities: Abidjan

---

* The Legatum Prosperity Index is an annual ranking developed by the Legatum Institute, a division of the private investment firm Legatum. The ranking is based on a variety of factors including wealth, economic growth, education, health, personal well-being, and quality of life.

** The Index of Economic Freedom is an annual index and ranking created by The Heritage Foundation and The Wall Street Journal in 1995 to measure the degree of economic freedom in the world's nations.

Government Agency Contact: Ministry of Trade, Minister Youssouf Soumahoro, Boulevard de la Cathédral, Abidjan, Immeuble CCIA 26ème BPV 143

ETHIOPIA

Ranking: 37
Legatum Prosperity Index Rating: 132
Global Economic Freedom Ranking: #148
Bullish New Fields of Business, Manufacturing and Marketing: Agriculture, Agribusiness, Finished Food Products, Technology and telecommunications, Real-Estate Development, Retail and Fashion.
Government stability: 3
FDI Business Friendly Rating: Good to Excellent.
Areas of Opportunity: Telecommunications, Virtual Business Technology, Exports, Infrastructure and Construction, Travel and Transportation.
Best Cities: Addis Ababa
Government Agency Contacts: Tanya.cole@trade.gov, Ministry of Finance and Economic Development, infopr@mofed.gov.et, P.O. Box: 1037 or 1905,
Tel: 251-11-1552400 /251-11-1226698,
Fax: 251-11-1551355 /251-11-1553814
Additional Contacts: Ministry of Trade and Industry, P. O. Box 2559, Addis Ababa
Tel: +(251) 1 510033
Ethiopian Investment Authority, P. O. Box 2313, Addis Ababa, Tel: +(251) 1 510033

GABON

Ranking: 15
Legatum Prosperity Index Rating: 120

Global Economic Freedom Ranking: #105
Bullish New Fields of Business, Manufacturing and Marketing: Petroleum, Natural Gas, Agriculture, Mining.
Government Stability: 8
FDI Business Friendly Rating: Excellent.
Areas of Opportunity: Infrastructure, Education, Technology, Construction, Retail Diversification.
Best Cities: Libreville
Government Agency Contacts: Investing in Gabon: http://en.legabon.org/investing-in-gabon/actors-andpartnersforumafrica.com/lang/content_fr/downloads/Gabon_Investor_Zone_Brochure.pdf

GHANA

Ranking: 5
Legatum Prosperity Index Ranking: 87
Global Economic Freedom Ranking: #110
Bullish New Fields of Business, Manufacturing and Marketing: Petroleum, Natural Gas, Gold, Diamonds, Technology, Real Estate and Development, Construction.
Government stability: 9
FDI Business Friendly Rating: Rapidly Privatizing. Most Improved.
Areas of Opportunity: Education, Infrastructure, Banking and Finance.
Best Cities: Accra, Kumasi
Government Agency Contacts: paul.taylor@trade.gov, http://www.ghanaweb.com/GhanaHomePage/business/

Information Services Department, P.O. Box 745, Accra, Ghana, Tel: +233 0 302 228054, Fax: +233 0 302 228089, Email: info.isd@isd.gov.gh
Additional Contacts: Ghana National Chamber Of Commerce, 65, Kojo Thompson Road, P. O. Box 2325, Accra,
Iel: + (233) 21 662427,
Email: gncc@ncs.com.gh
Ghana Investment Promotion Center, P.O. Box M193, Accra, Tel: +(233) 21 66 5125 – 9, gipc@ghana.com

KENYA

Ranking:19
Legatum Prosperity Index Rating: 97
Global Economic Freedom Ranking: #115
Bullish New Fields of Business, Manufacturing and Marketing: Oil and Natural Gas, Technology, Telecommunications, Tourism, Virtual Banking and Finance, Mobile Money.
Government stability: 4
FDI Business Friendly Rating: Fair. Gradual Improvement.
Areas of Opportunity: Internet, Tech Innovation, Intellectual Property, Virtual Education, Virtual Business, SME Startups and Development.
Best Cities: Nairobi, Mombasa, Nakuru
Government Agency Contacts: Ministry of Finance and Planning, Treasury Building, Harambee Avenue, P.O. Box 30007, Nairobi. Tel: +(254) 2 338111, francis.peters@trade.gov, http://www.investmentkenya.com/doing-business
Head Office: Kenya Railways Headquarters, Block D, 4th Floor Workshop Road, off Haile

Selasie Avenue, P.O. Box 55704-00200, City Square Nairobi, Kenya.
Pilot Lines: +254 (730) 104-200 ||+254 (730) 104-210
Email: info@investmentkenya.com

MAURITIUS

Ranking: 1
Legatum Prosperity Index Rating: 30
Global Economic Freedom Ranking: #14
Bullish New Fields of Business, Manufacturing and Marketing: Technology, Telecommunications, Information Technology, Banking, Financial Services, "Offshore Enterprises," Fishing,
Government stability: 9
FDI Business Friendly ranking: Excellent to Superior.
Areas of Opportunity: Business building, International Banking, Aviation Development and Finance, Shipping And Ship Management, Corporate Establishment And Licensing, International Data Processing, International finance. Offshore Funds Management.
Best Cities: Port Louis
Government Agency Contacts: 10th Floor, One Cathedral Square Building 16, Jules Koenig Street Port Louis 11328 Republic of Mauritius. Email: contact@investmauritius.com
Website: www.investmauritius.com T: +230 203 3800, Fax: + 230 210 8560
Additional Contacts: Mauritius Offshore Business Activities Authority — MOBAA, Tel: +(230) 210 7000

Ranking: 8

Legatum Prosperity Index Rating: 101

Global Economic Freedom Rating: #85

Bullish New Fields of Business, Manufacturing and Marketing: Vibrant Tourism, Manufacturing, Aeronautics, Tech Manufacturing, Telecommunications, Electronics, Retail.

Government stability: 9

FDI Business Friendly Rating– Good.

Areas of Opportunity: Banking And Finance, Electronic Banking, Virtual Currency, Petroleum and Natural Gas (Western Sahara).

Best Cities: Casablanca, Marrakesh, Tangier

Government Agency Contact: Minister of Finance and Economics (M. Mohammed Boussaid) http://www.finances.gov.ma/depf/

MOZAMBIQUE

Ranking: 31

Legatum Prosperity Index Rating: 122

Global Economic Freedom Index: 139

Bullish New Fields of Business, Manufacturing and Marketing: Petroleum, natural gas, aluminum, banking and finance, foreign exchange.

Government Stability: 4

FDI Business Friendly Ranking: Fair to Good.

Areas of Opportunity: Commercial real estate, shopping malls, building complexes, multiple unit housing, reverse diaspora

Best Cities: Maputo

Government Agency Contacts: jane.kitson@trade.gov

Minister: Adriano Meleiane
Vice Minister: Amelia Nakhare

Endereço: Praça da Marinha Popular
Maputo Caixa postal: C.P. 272,
Telefone: 258-21-315000/4, 82300516 Fax: 258-21-306261, 420137

Additional Contacts: Mozambique Chamber of Congress.
Tel: +(258) 1491970

TMIC — Trade and Market Information Center, 1008 25th September Ave., 4th Floor
PO Box 4487, Maputo
Tel: +(258) 1 424242

NAMIBIA

Ranking: 8

Legatum Prosperity Ranking: 111

Global Economic Freedom Index: 81

Bullish New Fields of Business: Diamonds, copper, silver, lead, uranium

Government Stability: 5

FDI Business Friendly Rating: Good to Excellent.

Areas of Opportunity: Tourism, technology, banking and finance.

Best Cities: Windhoek

Government Agency Contacts: Ministry of Trade and Industry Permanent Secretary Brendan Simbwaye Square, Goethe Street Private Bag 13340, Windhoek
Telephone: +264-61-283-7332
Fax: +264-61-220227
Website: http://www.mti.gov.na

NIGERIA

Ranking: 20

Legatum Prosperity Ranking: 135

Global Economic Freedom Index: #116

Bullish New Fields of Business, manufacturing and marketing: oil and natural gas, electronics, technology, telecommunications, entertainment, fashion, concrete and construction, banking and finance.

Government Stability: 3

FDI Business Friendly Rating: Fair to Good.

Areas of Opportunity: Telecommunications, banking and finance, film, music, SME business building, startups, infrastructure, shipping, international trade.

Best Cities: Lagos, Kano, Abuja

Government Agency Contacts:
brian.mccleary@trade.gov
Ministry of Economic Development, Plot 1181, Aguiyi Ironsi Street, Maitama District, P.M.B. 381, Garki Abuja
Tel: +234(09) 2904 882, +234 (0)704 634 6232
+234 (0) 809 223 3488, +234 (0)803 617 2020
Email: infodesk@nipc.gov.ng
osicinfodesk@nipc.gov.ng

RWANDA

Ranking: 4

Legatum Prosperity Index Rating: 88

Global Economic Freedom Rating: #71

Bullish New Fields of Business, Manufacturing and Marketing: modern technology, communications, Internet and smart-phone marketing and virtual banking apps, business building

Government Stability: 8

FDI Business Friendly Rating: Fair to Good. Improving.

Areas of Opportunity: Internet, eco-tourism, startups, retail and real estate.

Best Cities: Kigali

Government Agency Contacts: Ministry of Finance and Economic Planning, Claver Gatete Ministry of Finance and Economic Planning, P.O BOX 158, Kigali-Rwanda, Telephone: +250-252-575-756 Fax: +250-252-577-581, Email: mfin@minecofin.gov.rw

Chamber of Commerce and Industry, B.P. 319, Kigali, Rwanda, Tel: +(250) 83538 / 83541

SENEGAL

Ranking: 18

Legatum Prosperity Index Rating: 106

Global Economic Freedom Ranking: #111

Bullish New Fields of Business, Manufacturing and Marketing: Natural oils and bituminous production, gold reserves, cement production, fishing, and tourism.

Government Stability: 5

FDI Business Friendly ranking: Fair to Good.

Areas of Opportunity: Tourism, startups, renewable energy (solar), medical technology, and education.

Best Cities: Dakar

Government Agency Contacts:
http://www.commerce.gouv.sn/

Email: contact@ambasenegal-us.org Website: http://www.ambasenegal-us.org/

Additional Contacts: Chamber of Commerce and Industry, 1 Palace of Independence, BP 118 Dakar, Tel: +(221) 823 71 89

Center for External Trade, Tel: +(221) 820 04 54

SOUTH AFRICA

Ranking: 7
Legatum Prosperity Index Rating: 48
Global Economic Freedom Rating: #80
Bullish New Fields of Business, Manufacturing and Marketing: Oil and Natural Gas, Electronics, Technology, Telecommunications, Entertainment, Fashion, Banking and Finance.
Government Stability: 3
FDI Business Friendly Rating: Good.
Areas of Opportunity: Tourism, startups, renewable energy, retail, fashion, publishing, real estate, development and construction, SME startups.
Best Cities: Cape Town, Johannesburg, Durban
Government Agency Contact:
donald.nay@trade.gov
Sandile Tyini, Economic Minister
Email : STyini@thedti.gov.za
Telephones: 202-274-7973/7975/7977
Direct: 202-445-0268
Additional Contacts: South African Chamber of Business (SACOB), Tel: +(27)-11-358-9729

TANZANIA

Ranking: 17
Legatum Prosperity Index Rating: 109
Global Economic Freedom Rating: #110
Bullish New Fields of Business, Manufacturing and Marketing: Oil and natural gas, electronics, tourism, technology, national parks, virtual banking, virtual education, mobile money,

Government Stability: 4
FDI Business Friendly Rating: Good.
Areas of Opportunity: Virtual education, telecommunications, urbanization, education, infrastructure.
Best Cities: Dar es Salaam, Arusha
Government Agency Contacts:
RJ.Donovan@trade.gov, Permanent Secretary, Ministry of Finance and Planning, 1 Madaraka Street, 11468 Dar es salaam, P.O. Box 9111, Dar es Salaam, Phone: +255 222-111-174-6.

UGANDA

Ranking: 13
Legatum Prosperity Index Rating: 116
Global Economic Freedom Rating: #102
Bullish New Fields of Business, Manufacturing and Marketing: Value-added manufacturing, commercial fishing, agro-processing facilities, tobacco, and coffee.
Government Stability: 7
FDI Business Friendly Rating: Fair. Improving.
Areas of Opportunity: Organic farming, finished food products manufacturing and marketing, virtual education, mobile money, phenomenal youth dynamic (Afrillennials 50% under 15.)
Best Cities: Kampala
Government Agency Contacts:
Hon. Matia Kasaijja/ Minister of Finance and Economic Planning,
Tel: +256414707100
Fax : +256414230163
Website: http://www.finance.go.ug/index.php?option=com_content&view=article&id=8&Itemid=21

Additional Contacts: Uganda Development Corporation Limited
PO Box 7042
Kampala, Tel: +(256) 41 234381/3,
Telex: +(256) 41) 61069
UGADEV, Uganda National Chamber of Commerce and Industry
Plot 17/19 Jinja Road, P
.O. Box 3809, Kampala

ZAMBIA

Ranking:16
Legatum Prosperity Index Rating: 108
Global Economic Freedom Ranking:
#106
Bullish New Fields of Business, Manufacturing and Marketing: Copper, aluminum, mining, agriculture, building and development.
Government Stability: 6
Areas of Opportunity: Infrastructure, Virtual Education, Youth Development (Afrillennials), Import-Export, SME startups, and urbanization.
Best Cities: Lusaka, Kitwe, Chipata.
Government Agency Contacts: New Government Complex, 9th & 10th Floor, Nasser Road, Lusaka, Zambia Lusaka
Tel: +260 211 228 301/9
http://www.zambia.gov.zm/index.php/ministries-all-government-ministries/123-ministry-of-commerce-trade-and-industry
Additional Contacts: Zambia Investment Center, PO Box 34580, Lusaka,
Tel: +(260) 1 252990

Ministry of Commerce Trade and Industry, PO Box 31968/34373, Lusaka, Tel: +(260) 1 228301

SUMMARY

As we mentioned in the beginning, we write on shifting sands. So the list we have just completed will be undergoing changes, from time to time. More nations, ratings and contacts will be added as we are legitimately able to provide you with credible sources. As this is a business book, there has to be a bottom line. And the bottom line is this: In the world of the 21st century entrepreneur it is all about the Network. What we are bringing to the table is an up-game interconnective. It is by no means a finish. It is a start and, we hope, a good one. To be continued…

In Appreciation…

To my late parents; it's impossible to thank you adequately for everything you've done, from loving me unconditionally to raising me in a stable household where you instilled traditional values and taught your children to celebrate and embrace life. I could not have asked for better parents or role models. And to my siblings: Steve, Joe, Biola, Agnes and Francis—thanks for all of the wonderful memories of growing up, and for your continued support and encouragement. For all of my loved ones who have gone on to a better life, especially Grand Pa Adekanmbi, who taught me principles of entrepreneurship, you are always close in my heart. A special thank you to a good mate, Olumide, for showing me that anything is possible with faith, hard work and determination. For all of my wonderful friends old and new-thanks for always being there for me!

And to my co-author, Robert, my constant champion throughout the writing process, thank you for the late-night Skype sessions! Finally, this dedication would not be complete without a very special thank you to the readers, who dream of becoming financially independent and building a happy, successful, and rewarding business on the continent of Africa. It is my hope and dream that this book might be that first step.

The authors would also like to thank all the people, companies, groups and philanthrocapitalists who made the writing of this book worthwhile. They include the Index of Economic Freedom, the Brookings Institution, *CNBC Africa,* Ernst and Young, *Forbes Magazine, The Borgen Project, This Is Africa (The Financial Times),* Price Waterhouse Cooper, *The Africa Report,* Michael Osu, The Millennium Challenge Corporation, *Quartz Africa* and other great research resources, as well as Fideli Publishing and all the content rich nations of Africa who have made researching and writing this book a constant inspiration.

GLOSSARY OF TERMS
(ACRONYMS)

AAI: Africa Attractiveness Index

AFC: Africa Finance Corporation

AFRICOM: US Africa Command

AFSA: Agro-ecology Fund for food Sovereignty in Africa

AGOA: African Growth and Opportunity Act

AIF: African Innovation Foundation

AU: African Union

AWE: Africa Winning Economies

AYE: Africa's Young Entrepreneurs

BRICS (Nations): Brazil, Russia, India, China, South Africa

CAADP: Comprehensive Africa Agriculture Development Programme

CAMFED: Campaign for Female Education (in Africa)

CBN: Central Bank of Nigeria

CDC: Center for Disease Control

CEMAC: Economic and Monetary Union of Central Africa

COMESA: Common Market for Eastern and Southern Africa

EU: European Union (also EEU/ European Economic Union)

EAC: East African Community

ECOWAS: Economic Community of West African States

EIB: Europe Independent Bank

FAO: Food and Agriculture Organization

FDI: Foreign Direct Investment

FEWS: Famine Early Warning System

GDDS: General Data Dissemination System (Data Bank for the UN and IMF)

GDP: Gross Domestic Product

GESCI: Global e-Schools and Communications Initiative

GIEWS: Global Information and Early Warning System

ICC: International Criminal Court

ICJ: International Court of Justice

IEA: International Energy Agency

IFC: International Funding Corporation

IIAG: Ibrahim Institute of African Growth

IMF: International Monetary Fund

LC: Letters of Credit

KINGS: Kenya, Ivory Coast, Nigeria, Ghana & South Africa

MPA: Maritime Protection Authority

NEPAD: New Partnership for Africa's Development

NNPC: Nigeria National Petroleum Corporation

NOGAMU: Natural Organic Agricultural Movement of Uganda

OECD: Organization for Economic Cooperation and Development

RISEN: Rwanda, Ivory Coast, Senegal, Ethiopia, & Nigeria

SACU: Southern Africa Customs Union

SADC: Southern African Development Community

SARS: South African Revenue Service

SDDS: Special Data Dissemination Standards (for the IMF and World Bank)

SEF: Somali Economic Forum

SME: Small to Medium-Size Enterprise

SPDR: Standard & Poors Depositary Receipts ("Spider")

SSA: Sub-Sahara Africa

STICKS: Stability, Technology, Infrastructure, Credit, Kinetic resource, Strategic alliances.

SUN: Stand Up for Nigeria

UNHCR: United Nations High Commissioner on Refugees

UNDP: United Nations Development Program

UNED: United Nations Economic Development

WHO: World Health Organization

Index

S

Bibliography

2016 Index of Economic Freedom. "Rankings for Algeria Botswana, Cameroon, Cote d' Ivoire, Egypt, Ethiopia, Ghana, Gabon, Kenya, Mauritius, Liberia, Madagascar, Morocco, Mozambique, Namibia, Nigeria, Rwanda, Senegal, Somalia, South Africa, Tanzania, Tunisia, Uganda, Zambia, Democratic Republic of Congo, et al." *Heritage Foundation/Wall Street Journal.* New York, NY. 2016. http://www.heritage.org/index/ranking

Adegoke, Yemisi and Paul Adelpoju, "Plastic or not? Over 100 bags of fake rice seized I Nigeria," CNN Marketplace, Africa. 2016. http://edition.cnn.com/2016/12/23/africa/nigeria-fake-plastic-rice/

Aling'o, Peter and Hawa Noor. "Signs of Violence Ahead of Kenya's 2017 Elections," *All Africa.* June, 2017. http://allafrica.com/stories/201606180004.html

Analyze Africa 2017 Investment Report. "Africa Regional Trends." *The Financial Times.* London, UK. 2017. http://forms.fdiintelligence.com/africainvestmentreport/files/Africa_Investment_Report-2017.pdf

Baher, Kamal and Fareed Mahdy, "Africa Launches Largest Trading Block With 620 Million Consumers." IPS. *Interpress Service Agency.* New York, NY. 2016.

Bates, Robert H. "Income and Democracy: Lipset's Law Inverted." *Weatherford Center for International Affairs.* Harvard University. Boston, MA. 2012 http://wcfia.harvard.edu/publications/income-and-democracy-lipset's-law-inverted

BBC News. "Kenya's Raila Odinga Inaugurates Himself as President," London, UK. January 30, 2018. http://www.bbc.com/news/world-africa-42870292

Berman, Jonathan, *Success in Africa.* Bibliomotion, Inc. Brookline, MA. 2013.

The Berlin Conference: The General Act of Feb. 26, 1885. Federation of the Free States of Africa. (FFSA). http://www.africafederation.net/Berlin_1885.htm

Brock, Joe, "RPT-Africa's big cities offer investors hope in hard times," *Reuters.* February, 2016. http://www.reuters.com/article/africa-cities-idUSL8N15T0BI

Burgis, Tom, *The Looting Machine.* Public Affairs Books. New York, NY. 2012

Chambon, Frédéric, *Digital Lab Africa.* DISCOP Africa. Abidjan, Cote d'Ivoire. 2015.

Chiloanne, Thabang. Nedbank-NBF Networking Forum, ACGN Report. 2016. http://www.afcgn.org/

CNBC Africa. "Ethiopia's Parliament ratifies a state of emergency imposed after its Prime Minister resigns," Reuters, New York, NY, March 2, 2018. https://www.cnbcafrica.com/news/east-africa/2018/03/02/ethiopias-parliament-ratifies-state-emergency-imposed-prime-minister-resigns/?utm_source=C

CNBC Africa Reporter, "Becoming a successful African entrepreneur." CNBC, New York, NY. June, 2016. http://www.cnbcafrica.com/news/east-africa/2016/06/02/becoMming-a-successful-african-entrepreneur/?utm_source=Africa.com+TOP10&utm_campaign=2e1f86e910#

Douglas, Kate. "Bob Diamond snatching up African banks despite the sector's dismal outlook." *How We Made it in AFRICA.* DHL. Cape Town, South Africa. January, 2016. http://www.howwemadeitinafrica.com/bob-diamond-snatching-up-african-banks-despite-the-sectors-dismal-outlook/53158/

Editorial Staff. "Top 10 African Countries with the Biggest Economies. See their contrasting GDP." *Answers Africa.* Lagos, Nigeria. August 20, 2015. http://answersafrica.com/largest-economies-africa.html

Esposito, Mark and Terrence Tse. "How Africa offers opportunities beyond land, labour and commodities," THE CONVERSATION [US Pilot]. Lagos, Nigeria. January, 2016. https://theconversation.com/how-africa-offers-opportunities-beyond-land-labour-and-commodities-53390

Fast Company Staff, "Top 10 Most Innovative Companies in Africa." Fast Company. 2014. http://www.fastcompany.com/3026686/most-innovative-companies-2014/the-top-10-most-innovative-companies-in-africa

Features. "Counter-terrorism: Morocco Helps France Dismantle Terror Cell in St-Denis," *The North Africa Post.* Rabat, Morocco. November, 2015.

French, Howard W. *China's Second Continent.* First Vision Books. New York, NY. 2015.

Griswald, Patrick J. "That was then, this is (surprisingly) now." WAN (Why Africa Now). Dar es Salaam, Tanzania. February 2016.

http://whyafricanow.com/2016/02/24/that-was-then-and-this-is-surprisingly-now/

Gilpin, Lindsey, "The world's unlikely leader in mobile payments: Kenya," *The Tech Republic*. March, 2014.
http://www.techrepublic.com/article/the-worlds-unlikely-leader-in-mobile-payments-kenya/

Gohosh, Palash. "Portuguese Mozambique, A Story of Reverse Migration." *IBT/ International Business Times*. New York, NY. 2/21/12. http://www.ibtimes.com/portuguese-mozambique-story-reverse-migration-214108

Hendy, Iheoma. "China to Invest $60 Billion in Nigeria." *Buzz Nigeria*. Lagos, Nigeria. 2015. http://buzznigeria.com/international-relations-china-to-invest-60bn-in-nigeria/

Higgins, Abigail, "Venture Capital in Kenya Awaiting Liftoff." *The Africa Report*. Nairobi, Kenya. June 2016. http://www.theafricareport.com/East-Horn-Africa/venture-capital-waiting-for-lift-off.html

Hochschild, Adam, *King Leopold's Ghost*. Houghton Mifflin. Boston, MA. 1998.

Idriss, Musah, " Ghanaian millionaire quits Microsoft to build university that Educates young Africans," *Rising Africa*. March 31, 2015. http://www.risingafrica.org/success-stories/business/ghanaian-millionaire-quits-microsoft-to-build-university-that-educates-young-africans/

Kazeem, Yami, "Ghana is betting on telemedicine to help plug gaps in its rural healthcare system," *Quartz Africa*. Accra, Ghana. June 7, 2016.

Kuo, Lily, "A Heart Monitoring Tablet in Cameroon Produces EKGs in 20 Minutes." *Quartz Africa*. Nairobi, Kenya. June, 2016.
http://qz.com/700434/a-heart-monitoring-tablet-in-cameroon-produces-ekgs-in-20-minutes/?utm_source=Africa.com+TOP10&utm_campaign=4fc36d7dd2-Daily_News_June_086_8_2016&utm_medium=email&utm_term=0_4b5b352bca-4fc36d7dd2-29079105

Kuo, Lily, "Kenya, home to the world's fastest runners, will soon produce high-performance running shoes," *Quartz Africa*. Nairobi, Kenya. May, 2016.
http://qz.com/692874/kenya-home-to-the-worlds-fastest-runners-will-soon-produce-high-performance-running-shoes/?utm_source=Africa.com+TOP10&utm_campaign=7600cc4644-Daily_News_May_275_27_2016&utm_medium=email&utm_term=0_4b5b352bca-7600cc4644-29079105

Li, Hangwei and Jacqueline Muna Musiitwa, "Despite Slowdown, China's Migrants Rooted In Africa." *This is Africa. (The Financial Times).* London, UK 2016. http://www.thisisafricaonline.com/ftauthor/view/Hangwei+Li+%26+Jacqueline+Muna+Musiitwa

Machel, Graca, "Five Women Giving Africa's Entrepreneurs a Helping Hand," Africa.com. 2015. http://www.africa.com/5-women-giving-africas-entrepreneurs-helping-hand/

Matasile, Trust. "Money Is Nigeria's Main Problem: First's Babatunde Fowler." *CNBC Africa.* February, 2016. http://www.cnbcafrica.com/news/western-africa/2016/02/12/nigeria-oil-revenue-babatunde-fowler/

Mantashe, Gwede (Secretary General, African National Congress). "ANC has full confidence in SA President Zuma and Finance Minister Gordhan," *CNBC Africa.* Cape Town. March, 2016.

Mbaku, John Mukum, "Foresight Africa 2017: Election Spotlight on Kenya," *Brookings,* Monday January 30, 2017. https://www.brookings.edu/blog/africa-in-focus/2017/01/30foresight-africa-2017-election-spotlight-on-kenya/

Mbanjwa, Nozipho. "The New Biz Kids on the Block," *Forbes Woman Africa,* CNBC Africa. Special Report. New York, NY, March 2017.

Meredith, Martin, *The Fortunes of Africa.* Public Affairs books. New York, NY. 2014

Mikiva, Karen, "10 Most Common Africa Deadly Diseases," AFK Insider. Nairobi, Kenya. March 23, 2016. http://afkinsider.com/46218/common-deadly-african-diseases/

Milta, Aviwe, "Red Flag Indicators African Banks Must Look Out For," GMT. *CNBC Africa.* February, 2016. http://www.cnbcafrica.com/news/southern-africa/2016/02/15/red-flag-indicators-african-banks-must-look-out-for/

Moyo, Dambisa. *Dead Aid,* Farrar, Straus & Giroux. New York, NY. 2009

Mousavizadeh, Alexandra & the Prosperity Index Team. "The Africa Prosperity Report ± 2016," Legatum Prosperity Index. London, UK. https://lif.blob.core.windows.net/lif/docs/default-source/publications/2016-africa-prosperity-report-pdf.pdf?sfvrsn=2

Muhammad, Omar. "Africas Economic Slowdown is Not Deterring Investors," *Quartz Africa.* February, 2016. http://qz.com/624596/africas-economic-slowdown-is-not-deterring-investors/

Muhammadou, " Ghanaian millionaire quits Microsoft to build university that Educates young Africans,"AFRIKAtech, October. 2015. http://www.afrikatech.com /2015/10/23/ghanaian-millionaire-quits-microsoft-to-build-university-that-educates-young-africans/

Mutiso, Lilian, "Top 10 Women in Africa's Manufacturing Industry," *AFK Insider.* Nairobi, Kenya. February, 2016. http://afkinsider.com/119651/top-10-women-in-african-manufacturing-industry/3/

Mwiti, Lee, "Africa and its visa pains —where even billionaire Dangote-type big fish have nightmares," Mail & Guardian Africa. Manchester, UK. March, 2016. http://mgafrica.com/article/2016-03-27-africa-and-its-visa-regime-headachewhere-even-dangote-sized-big-fish-have-nightmares

Nsehe, Mfonobong, "The African Billionaires 2016," *Forbes Magazine.* New York, NY. March, 2016.

Nsehe, Mfonobong, "The Black Knight of Africa: How Robert Gumede is Expanding his Legacy Across the Continent ," *Forbes Magazine.* New York, NY. July 1, 2016. http://www.forbes.com/sites/mfonobongnsehe/2016/07/01/the-black-knight-of-africa-how-robert-gumede-is-expanding-his-legacy-across-the-continent/2/#7d0f02ca2983

Oredola, Temi. *JTO Fashion Blog.* Lagos, Nigeria. 2016.

Olopade, Dayo. *The Bright Continent,* Mariner Books/Houghton, Mifflin, Harcourt. Boston, MA. 2014

Onyulo, Tonny. "More Phones, Few Banks, and Years of Instability are Transforming Somalia Into a Cashless Society." *QUARTZ Africa.* February, 2016. http://qz.com/625258/more-phones-few-banks-and-years-of-instability-are-transforming-somalia-to-a-cashless-society/

Okpalike, Chika J. B. Gabriel, and Kanayo Louis Nwadialor, "Contributions of Christian Missionaries in building the Nigerian Nation," Academic Journal of Interdisciplinary Studies, MCSER Publishing, Rome-Italy. Volume 4 No. 2. July 2015.

Our Impact. *Millennium Challenge Corporation.* (United States of America.) 2016. https://www.mcc.gov/our-impact

Patrick A., "The African Union Passport Set to Launch This Month," *Answers Africa.* Lagos, Nigeria. July 2, 2016. http://answersafrica.com/african-union-passport-launch-month.html

Prahalad, C.K. *The Fortune at the Bottom of the Pyramid,* Wharton School Publishing. Upper Saddle River, NJ. 2006.

Pegg, David. "25 Facts About Africa." LIST 25. *Science and Technology.* 2014. http://list25.com/25-interesting-facts-africa/2/

Reader, John. *AFRICA/Biography of a Continent.* Vintage Books (Random House). New York, NY 1997.

Reuters. "RPT-Africa's big cities offer investors hope in hard times," *CNBC Africa.* New York. NY. February, 2016.

Robach, Amy, "GMA on Safari: Experience Africa. 'Garden of Eden in Tanzania in 360 Degree View'," ABC Good Morning America. New York, NY. February 2016. http://abcnews.go.com/Lifestyle/gma-safari-experience-africas-garden-eden-tanzania-live/story?id=37040995

Robinson, Josh. "Africa's Top 20 Fastest Growing Economies." *Bloomberg Markets.* New York. NY. 2015.

Renaissance Capital. "The Big Four Challenges Facing Nigerian Banks," *CNBC Africa.* New York. NY. December, 2015.

Rodney, Walter. *How Europe Underdeveloped Africa,* Black Classic Press. Baltimore, MD. 2011.

Shepherd, Wade, "Beijing to the World: 'Don't Call The Belt and Road Initiative, OBOR,'" *Forbes.* New York, August 1, 2017. https://www.forbes.com/sites/wadeshepard/2017/08/01beijing-to-the-world-please-stop-saying-obor/#2cddd52017d4

Soyinka, Wole. *Of Africa.* Yale University Press. New Haven, CT. 2012.

Spooner, Samantha. "Africa's cities can be tough; but there are ways to make them happy places for all." Mail & Guardian Africa. Manchester, UK. February, 2016. http://mgafrica.com/author/samantha-spooner

Staff Blog. "Africa's Philanthropic Billionaires." *The Borgen Project.* Seattle, WA. 2013.

Staff Article. "Barclay's Reviews Africa Strategy." *The Herald.* Johannesburg, SA. 2015. http://www.herald.co.zw/barclays-reviews-africa-strategy/

Staff. "DISCOP Africa launches Digital Lab Africa." *Bizcommunity Africa.* Abidjan, Cote d'Ivoire, 2016. http://www.bizcommunity.com/Article/54/66/145841.html

Staff. *International Literacy Day 2015.* (United Nations Educational Scientific and Cultural Organization). UNESCO. Africa Office. Dakar, Senegal. 2016.

Staff. "Know Why These 10 African Businesses Received Funding." *Africa Business Jumpstart.* London, UK. 2016. http://africajumpstart.com/2016/01/06/know-why-these-10-african-businesses-received-funding/

Staff. "Nigeria will stop fuel importation by 2019 – Kachikwu," *Vanguard,* May 22, 2017. http://www.vanguardngr.com/2017/02/nigeria-will-stop-fuel-importation-2019-ka-chikwu/

Staff. "Secret Aid Worker: How can we fight inequality if we live as privileged ex-pats?" *The Guardian*. Manchester, UK. December, 2015.
http://www.theguardian.com/global-development-professionals-network/2015/dec/29/secret-aid-worker-how-can-we-fight-inequality-if-we-live-as-privileged-expats

Staff Writer. "Seven Untapped Business Opportunities in Sub-Saharan Africa." DHL. Nairobi, Kenya. February, 2016. http://www.howwemadeitinafrica.com/seven-untapped-business-opportunities-in-sub-saharan-africa/53510/

Staff Writer. "Toyota's Expansion in Africa." *How We Made it in AFRICA*. DHL. Cape Town, South Africa. January, 2016.
http://www.howwemadeitinafrica.com/toyota-expansion-in-africa/53190/

Stevenson, Tom. "Egypt begins sell-off of state owned companies," *This Is Africa,* The Financial Times, London, UK. 2017.
http://www.thisisafricaonline.com/News/Egypt-begins-sell-off-of-state-owned-companies?utm_campaign=TIA+enews+July+2nd+issue&utm_source=emailCampaign&utm_medium=email&utm_content=

Thakkar, Ashish J. *The Lion Awakes,* St. Martins Press. New York, NY. 2015.

"The Africa Business Agenda 2016." Price Waterhouse Cooper. (153 CEOs from 18 Countries). Cape Town. 2016.
http://www.pwc.co.za/en/publications/africa-business-agenda.html

The Citizen. "Nigeria Signs $80 Billion Oil Infrastructure Deal with China." *All Africa*. Lagos, Nigeria. 2016.
http://allafrica.com/view/group/main/main/id/00044434.html

Staff. "These fashion movers and shakers will inspire wardrobe envy." *African Voices*. CNN STYLE. Atlanta, GA. May. 2016.

Timekeeper. "The sad road from Kyoto to Durban." *The Economist*. London, UK. December 3, 2011. http://www.economist.com/node/21541028

Toure, Mamadou. D-Think Tank. Africa 2.0. Johannesburg, Republic of South Africa. 2010. http://www.africa2point0.org/index.php?lang=en

Watson, Kirsta, "How a 700-year-old farming technique could help end hunger and climate change." *Global Citizen*. New York, NY. June 23, 2016.

Vekelsberg, Viktor, "Technological Hunger and an Abundance of Resources, (BRICS on the Heels of Africa)" *BRICS Business Magazine*. M. Mediacrat. Publishing. Brand Development. Moscow, Russia. 2015. http://bricsmagazine.com/en/articles/brics-on-the-heels-of-africa

Volkov, Vladimir. "25 Faces of the New Africa." *BRICS Business Magazine.* M. Mediacrat. Publishing. Brand Development. Moscow, Russia. 2016. http://bricsmagazine.com/en/articles/25-faces-of-the-new-africa

Very, Christine, "Top 10 Misconceptions About Africa," *LISTVERSE.* London, UK. December 2011. http://listverse.com/2011/12/15/top-10-misconceptions-about-africa/

Yasmin, Seema. "Africa Starts Its Own Disease Control Agency." *Scientific American.* New York, NY. June, 2016.

Xalima. "Africa has a real chance to follow in the footsteps of Asia." *Xalima.com.* Canada. Paris. Senegal. 2011. http://xalimasn.com/africa-rising-after-decades-of-slow-growth-africa-has-a-real-chance-to-follow-in-the-footsteps-of-asia/

About the Authors

Mark Byron is a successful startup entrepreneur and investment director in the complicated world of finance who has mastered a unique ability to leverage current market trends and meld them into emerging markets. As Co-Founder of Barton-Heyman, Ltd. A company with business partnership in the U.K. and Sub-Sahara Africa of London and Lagos, Nigeria, Mark heads a group of experienced professionals who have come together to form a financial vanguard in African markets. For that reason he has developed a unique strategy and laid it all out in his groundbreaking book, *AFRICA ARRIVES/ A Savvy Entrepreneur's Guide to the World's Hottest Market* as an exceptional guide for both experienced entrepreneurs and savvy investors looking for leverage in new markets. In it, you'll learn how to navigate the intricate currents of the 54 nations in what every financial expert has predicted will be the world's hottest market for the next 50 years. If you are looking to Africa to invest, start up a new business, co-venture or make connections. Africa Arrives is a great place to start.

Robert Joseph Ahola is an author, playwright, producer and director who lives in Malibu, California. As CEO of Galahad Films, Robert has authored 14 published and/or produced plays, including *Pavlov's Cats, Judas Agonistes, The Ghost and Josh Gibson,* and *NARCISSUS: The Last Days of Lord Byron.* An environmental activist and world traveler, Robert is the author of twenty-two published books including *The Silent Healer, The Return of the Hummingbird Wizard,* and *I, Dragon. Africa Arrives,* co-authored with Mark Byron, is his tenth work of non-fiction.